Race, Ethnicity, and Multiculturalism

MISSOURI SYMPOSIUM ON RESEARCH AND EDUCATIONAL POLICY
VOLUME I
GARLAND REFERENCE LIBRARY OF SOCIAL SCIENCE
VOLUME 1029

Race, Ethnicity, and Multiculturalism
Policy and Practice

Edited by
Peter M. Hall

Garland Publishing, Inc.
New York and London
1997

Library of Congress Cataloging-in-Publication Data

Race, ethnicity, and multiculturalism : policy and practice / edited by Peter M. Hall.
      p.   cm. — (Missouri Symposium on Research and Educational
Policy ; v. 1) (Garland reference library of social science ; v. 1029)
      Emerged from the first Missouri Symposium on Research and Educa-
tional Policy held Mar. 24–26, 1994.
      Includes bibliographical references and indexes.
      ISBN 0-8153-2011-6 (hc. : alk. paper). — ISBN 0-8153-2442-1
(pbk. : alk. paper)
      1. Minorities—Education—United States—Congresses. 2. Afro-Ameri-
cans—Education—Congresses. 3. Multicultural education—United States—
Congresses. 4. Multiculturalism—United States—Congresses. 5. Education
and state—United States—Congresses.   I. Hall, Peter M. II. Missouri Symposium on Research and Educational Policy (1st : 1994) III. Series.
IV. Series : Missouri Symposium on Research and Educational Policy. Missouri Symposium on Research and Educational Policy ; v. 1.
      LC3731.R24   1997
      371.97'00973—dc20   96–40991
                                                                              CIP

Cover photograph by Tony Donovan, The Ivoryton Studio.
Paperback cover design by Robert Vankeirsbilck.

Printed on acid-free, 250-year-life paper
Manufactured in the United States of America

Series Preface

One of the abiding mysteries of American education concerns the uneasy relation between research, policy, and practices in our schools. On the one hand, Americans honor research, spend a good deal on research in the physical and biological sciences, think that research evidence *should* be used in social planning, and strongly encourage research in our classrooms and schools. On the other, appallingly little is now spent on educational research, the vast bulk of policy planning for education proceeds without benefit of research, and the actual practices of our classrooms and schools are often unknown or are at odds with (or harmed by) educational "reforms" touted by ideologues and politicians.

But despite all aridity, some talented researchers *do* manage to cobble together resources needed for insightful studies of American education, and then a second problem arises. Reports of the knowledge evolved in those studies normally appear in sources designed for peers: papers delivered at professional meetings, journal articles, technical reports, and (occasionally) books designed to be read by others in the research community. Unfortunately, such reports are *not* designed for educators, citizens, or political leaders interested in education, and so far our country has *not* evolved effective, national means for disseminating knowledge from educational research to users such as these. In addition, our country is massive, it generates a truly staggering amount of information, and even accessible reports of research knowledge concerned with education tend to get lost amidst the huge oversupply of competing messages.

Responding to this need, several years ago we made a proposal to our campus, the University of Missouri-Columbia, to sponsor a series of regular symposia on research and educational policy. Each symposium was to be held on our campus, focus on a topic of vital interest to educators and policymakers, bring researchers and potential users of educational research knowledge together, feature original contributions by major scholars who had conducted significant studies of the topic chosen, and generate a major volume of original research papers. Having established support for this proposal from administrators at our campus, we then asked whether Garland Publishing would produce the volumes that were generated from these symposia and received a warm welcome from Senior Editor, Marie Ellen Larcada.

Through this series, then, we hope to expand the influence of the Missouri Symposia beyond our campus, not only to provide sources of useful knowledge for educators and others vitally involved with American education, but also to stimulate further research and potential leadership from the research community on crucial educational issues. As of this writing, two volumes representing Missouri Symposia have now been completed, the first concerned with *Race, Ethnicity, and Multiculturalism,* the second focused on *Gender, Equity, and Schooling.* Both, indeed, take on crucial topics in education, both publish original papers that represent extensions of contributions that were first presented here on the Missouri campus, and both provide access to original and highly significant research contributions.

We hope that these two initial volumes will stimulate broad interest and will help to begin bridging the gulf between researchers and the education community. They will shortly be followed by others.

Bruce J. Biddle
Barbara J. Bank
Harris Cooper
Peter M. Hall

Columbia, MO

Contents

Figures and Tables   vii

Preface   ix

Chapter 1.   Race, Ethnicity, and Schooling in   3
America: An Introduction
Peter M. Hall

Chapter 2.   Education in a Multicultural Society   41
Bart Landry

Chapter 3.   Familial Predictors of Educational   63
Attainment: Regional and Racial
Variations
Aaron Thompson
Reid Luhman

Chapter 4.   Teachers as Social Scientists: Learning   89
about Culture from Household
Research
Luis C. Moll
Norma González

Chapter 5.   Tracking Untracking: The Conse-   115
quences of Placing Low-Track Students
in High-Track Classes
Hugh Mehan

Chapter 6.   Changing the Discourse in Schools   151
Eugene Eubanks
Ralph Parish
Dianne Smith

Chapter 7.   Making Multicultural Education Policy:
              The Transformation of Intentions   169
              Margaret Placier
              Peter M. Hall
              Barbara Jo Davis

Chapter 8.   The Integration of Restructuring   203
              and Multicultural Education as a Policy
              for Equity and Diversity
              Peter M. Hall

Author Index   219

Subject Index   227

Contributors   233

Figures and Tables

Figure 2.1   Legal Immigrants Admitted to
the U.S. by Region: 1820-1890   43

2.2   Legal Immigrants Admitted to
the U. S. by Region: 1890-1920   44

2.3   Legal Immigrants Admitted to
the U.S. by Region: 1971-1980   46

2.4   U. S. Racial and Ethnic Composition:
1990   47

2.5   Projected U. S. Racial and Ethnic
Composition: 2050   48

3.1   Northern African American Educational Attainment by Mother's
Educational Attainment   81

3.2   Northern European American Educational Attainment by Mother's
Educational Attainment   82

5.1   The College Enrollment of AVID
Students   122

5.2   The Enrollment of AVID, SDCD,
and U. S. Students in Four-Year
Colleges   124

	5.3	The Enrollment of African American Students in Four-Year Colleges	126
	5.4	The Enrollment of Latino Students in Four-Year Colleges	128
	5.5	AVID Parents' Income and Students' College Enrollment	130
	5.6	AVID Parents' Education and Students' College Enrollment	132
Table	3.1	Multiple Regression of Family History Variables with Education by Race	76
	3.2	Means, Standard Deviations, and Multiple Regression Analysis for the South Region	78
	3.3	Means, Standard Deviations, and Multiple Regression Analysis for the North Region	79

Preface

The first Missouri Symposium on Research and Educational Policy was held March 24-26, 1994 on the topic of Race, Ethnicity, and Multiculturalism. The purposes of the symposium are to provide interdisciplinary perspectives and assessment of current knowledge to stimulate discussion of current problems and suggestions for changes to generate improvement in educational conditions, processes, and outcomes. Each year the symposium will have a different theme chosen from such areas as the relationship between social issues and educational institutions; the educational consequence of disciplinary paradigms and research programs, and the implementation of educational change and reform.

The first symposium was organized to provide a systematic examination of the theme by addressing in order the broad societal and cultural context in America, the relationship of family and community to schooling, the role of the teacher in relation to community and households, schooling and classroom practices, schoolwide culture, structure and governance, and multiculturalism. Four of the chapters in the volume (Landry, Moll and González, Mehan, and Eubanks et al.) are revisions of presentations at the symposium. Two other chapters (Thompson and Luhman and Placier et al.) are additions to complete the original symposium agenda. The first and last chapters by the editor provide an orientation to the issues and a review of the literature and a drawing together and extension of policy ideas and implications found in chapters by other authors.

Readers will notice that the key terms of race and ethnicity, the labels for particular categories, and the equivalent or comparable general designations are used differently in the chapters that follow. No attempt was made to standardize their usage. This was intentional because there exists variation in the discourse of both academia and the general society about these terms. This reflects both the fact that this language changes over time and is frequently contested at any point in time. To demand consistency would distort the conversations and exchanges currently taking place.

The symposium would not have taken place without the generous material support from the following: the Danforth Foundation and the University of Missouri-Columbia; specifically, the Center for Research in Social Behavior, the Graduate School, College of Arts and Science, College of Education, Department of Psychology, and the Department of Sociology.

In addition, the organizers acknowledge the extremely able and valuable assistance of Billye Adams, Kathy Craighead, Pat Shanks, Joe Deering, Jack Glazier, Bruce Henson, Patrick McGinty, Nancy Myers, Mary Jo Neitz, Kevin Payne, Margaret Placier, and Daniel Thompson.

Finally, this volume benefitted greatly from the support and professional skills of Marie Ellen Larcada and Phyllis Korper of Garland Publishing.

Race, Ethnicity, and Multiculturalism

CHAPTER 1

Race, Ethnicity, and Schooling in America: An Introduction

Peter M. Hall

RACE AND ETHNICITY AS CONTESTED SOCIO-POLITICAL MEANINGS

This volume explores the relationship between education and race and ethnicity with particular emphasis on black Americans. In this chapter I present some basic data about educational attainment and performance and introduce some factors that shape the processes and outcomes of the relationship. The relationship, however, does not occur in a vacuum. It is first necessary to discuss the meanings of race and ethnicity: their establishment, maintenance, alteration and consequences. These meanings and consequences must also be grounded in the historical, structural, and cultural context of American society.

During World War II, *An American Dilemma: The Negro Problem and American Democracy* (1944) by Swedish social scientist Gunnar Myrdal was published. That book maintained that restrictions on blacks contradicted our public values. Resolution of "the Negro problem" could occur by aligning our behaviors and laws with the national ideals so that blacks could enter the social, economic, and political mainstream. Over the next 20 years, numerous steps were taken to achieve that equality and justice. In 1954 the U.S. Supreme Court declared *de jure* school segregation unconstitutional and directed its dismantling "with all deliberate speed." In the early 1960s, many young black and white college students, along with local oppressed citizens, challenged other forms of segregation in the South. In 1964 and 1965 civil rights legislation outlawed discrimination in American institutions. For many Americans, the words and sounds of Martin Luther King's

"I have a dream," Bob Dylan's "Blowin' in the Wind," and Lyndon Johnson's echo of the movement anthem "We Shall Overcome" define the moment as one of great optimism.

Yet in 1994 some blacks met in Detroit to formulate a campaign to win reparations for unjust treatment and unmet promises over several centuries. A veteran black journalist remarked that "in the 1960s we (black and white) thought we could get beyond the problems of race. Now we've gone the other way" (*New York Times*, July 18, 1995). A prominent black intellectual (Gates, 1994) wrote a memoir expressing nostalgia for the warm community of his (segregated) youth. In 1995, school segregation still exists, and the U.S. Supreme Court is limiting desegregation programs. Finally, the 1994 Congressional elections produced a majority for conservative Republicans who have moved to limit and roll back programs that benefit the poor, minorities, and immigrants, all accompanied by a rhetoric of individual responsibility and a color-blind society.

Race frames and forms a great divide in this country. Cornel West, a philosopher, titled a collection of essays *Race Matters*, using a double entendre to emphasize the breadth and depth of the issue (West, 1993). Andrew Hacker, a political scientist, underlines that point in his title *Two Nations: Black and White, Separate, Hostile, Unequal* (Hacker, 1992). Robert Blauner (1989) observes there are two different perspectives on race. Blacks tend to assert its centrality in our history and everyday life while whites tend to perceive it as peripheral and nonessential. This divide also occurs in a society increasingly populated by other "people of color." Other "races," "nationalities," "ethnicities" co-exist, co-mingle, and intermarry in our society, as do blacks and whites, thus blurring definitions of race.

Before the 1995 U.S. Open Tournament, Tiger Woods, a young Stanford University student and the national amateur golf champion, distributed a prepared statement to journalists. It said, in part, "The various media have portrayed me as an African-American, sometimes Asian. In fact, I am both. Yet, I am a product of two great cultures. On my father's side, I am African-American. On my mother's side, I am Thai. That's who I am and what I am. Now with your cooperation, I can just be a golfer and a human being" (*Kansas City Star*, June 14, 1995). Mr. Woods chose to respond not simply in racial terms but in cultural, national, ethnic ones—African American and Thai. In addition, he recognized the power of the media to define people and announced two other identities—golfer and human being—as being more salient to him.

Our society is confounded by the meaning of race and ethnicity. Like many other social objects, we want them to be stable and objective. Yet both seem to change before our eyes and over time. In 1994, a Congressional subcommittee was reviewing the possible addition of a multiracial category to the year 2000 census in addition to the existing four—American Indian/Alaskan Native, Asian or Pacific Islander, black and white (broken down into Hispanic origin and not of Hispanic origin). Advocates of the multiracial category were seeking to legitimate a significant identity and to ratify a certain reality. One critic labelled the proposed multiracial change, "a postmodern conspiracy to explode racial identity." It could decrease the numbers of black Americans and thus affect voting rights, legislative implementation, and distributions of federal program dollars.

In response to the entire controversy, Rep. Tom Sawyer, the subcommittee chair stated:

We recognize the importance of racial categories in correcting clear injustices under the law. The dilemma we face is trying to assure the fundamental guarantees of equality of opportunity while at the same time recognizing that the populations themselves are changing as we seek to categorize them. It reaches the point where it becomes an absurd counting game. Part of the difficulty is that we are dealing with the illusion of precision. We wind up with precise counts of everybody in the country, and they are precisely wrong. They don't reflect who we are as a people. To be effective, the concepts of individual and group identity need to reflect not only who we have been but who we are becoming. The more these categories distort our perception of reality, the less useful they are. We act as if we knew what we're talking about when we talk about race, and we don't. (Wright, 1994: 55)

One example of this presumption of knowing and illusion of precision was reflected in a recent controversial book (Herrnstein & Murray, 1994) that argued genetic differences existed in intelligence and therefore, education and other social interventions had very limited effects on intelligence. However, scientists have rejected the validity of race as a biological determinant and its use to explain human variation. Human contacts have mixed gene pools, so no accurate taxonomy is possible. No single gene can define a race. Research often shows more variation within "racial" categories than among them. Research that shows differences can be explained by other factors. Yet the public and government continue to accept a concept that, to them, has an obvious reality and utility. It is a concept of great social power.

A recent work (Omi & Winant, 1994) argues that race is neither a scientific category nor simply illusory or inconsequential. Rather these authors see it is a social construction, a concept that attaches meaning to different types of bodies. The nature, importance, and consequence of the differences are created, maintained, contested and changed by social activities over time. Race, they say, is not reducible to ethnicity, class, or nation. The model for ethnicity, for example, is the experience of European immigrants who assimilated into American society and whose identities were hyphenated, adaptable, and contingent. Race is not that epiphenomenal.

A major reason for the difference is that race has served us historically as a fundamental element of our social structure and social categories. However, while grounded in power and inequality, it is also subject to permanent socio-political contestation. The society shapes the conditions and experiences that give meaning to those categories. The prevailing meanings are, however, constructed by actors from dominant groups. Those meanings, in turn, shape people's relations to the institutions and organizations of society. Over the past 50 years, for example, there have been efforts to challenge and change racial meanings, relationships, and American society. Omi and Winant call this sociohistorical process racial formation, where racial categories are created, inhabited, transformed, and destroyed. Today the racial order remains transient. It is not reducible to simply black and white because of the increasing presence of other people of color, the existence of multi-racial individuals, the changing meaning of "whiteness" to some whites and the continuing consciousness of race in society.

In contrast to race, ethnicity is generally viewed as a more transient or mutable category. The previous assimilation perspective on ethnicity, however, has been challenged by the resurgence of ethnic nationalism in the world and its changing but continuing importance in the United States. Ethnicity is thought to derive its existence from common languages, cultures, histories, nationalities, and religions. However, those presumed commonalities are also constructed by creating pasts and dismissing differences (Kornblum,

1974). As Nagel (1994) observes, ethnicity is best understood as a dynamic, constantly evolving property of both individual identity and group organization. Ethnic boundaries are constructed through individual identification, ethnic group formation, informal ascriptions, and official ethnic policies through processes of mobilization, negotiation, and attribution. External forces, however, shape the options, feasibility, and attractiveness of various ethnicities. Thus, we can see a process of ethnic formation akin to that of racial formation. Some parallels exist in the conditions, processes, and consequences of the recent constructions of "Latino" and "Asian American" identities and groups.

The reader should understand that racial and ethnic boundaries are fluid and their categorical meanings are dynamic. Their relevance to circumstances also can vary by society, situations, and actors. The concept of "situational ethnicity" has been proposed to explain these variations (Okamura, 1981). Within this framework, the context shapes or evokes the relevant roles/identities for actors. Okamura, like Omi and Winant, states there are structural and cognitive dimensions to situational ethnicity. The degree to which ethnicity (and race) is an organizing principle of society is the structural dimension. The cognitive dimension is represented by actors' perceptions and understandings of the situations and the attributes of self and others they deem necessary for making the situation work collectively and individually. The extent to which race and ethnicity are seen, announced, or defined is subject to the interplay between society, situation, and actors. In apartheid South Africa, race was clearly omnipresent. In a more democratic society with ideals about pluralism and equality, the place of race in any situation may be more problematic. Tiger Woods was "negotiating" with the media about these issues. In schools, teachers and administrators may claim to be color blind but act in ways that others see as invoking the categories. Students may segregate themselves by these categories or perhaps dismiss them as irrelevant as they assert their American identity or popular cultural/adolescent self (see Peshkin, 1991). Collective identities may transcend these racial/ethnic identities in behalf of some group or team effort. Individuals may be explicit in defining themselves in non-racial or ethnic terms.

In this chapter I will present race and ethnicity in a manner that gives them more stability, coherence, and concreteness than is valid or accurate. I would, given the ambiguity, disagreement, contradictions, and change in American society about the existence, significance, and consequences of these differentiations, place quotation marks around them each time they are used. On the other hand, as with other social constructions we create and use, they are not mere fantasies of the mind. They have real consequences for us because institutions and actors treat them as real. We see what we believe and we believe what we see. Data are collected on these categories. Legislation and court rulings are made about these categories. And many people define themselves and others in these terms.

AMERICAN SOCIETY AS CONTEXT

Bart Landry (1992) suggests that since our early colonial period there has been an ongoing reinforcing relationship between a social structure that produces inequality and a culture that promotes racism and the devaluation of people of color. The contemporary consequences of that relationship demonstrate patterns of inequality, exclusion, and adversity that create the context in which schools function. A brief examination of data about economic status, residential segregation, and family structure will illustrate some critical factors that shape differential educational opportunities for black Americans.

Economic Inequality

In 1989, reviewing the past 50 years, the Committee on the Status of Black Americans of the National Research Council (Jaynes & Williams, 1989) characterized the current situation as the proverbial half full-half empty glass. There has been considerable improvement in the economic status of the average black since 1939. This was due at first to northward migration and entry into nonagricultural employment in a period of national economic growth. After 1965 improvement was fostered by anti-discrimination policies, equal employment opportunity incentives, higher educational attainment and changing race relations. Even so blacks still lagged behind whites. Since the 1970s black economic gains stagnated or deteriorated.

For the period 1970-1990, there were greater median family income increases for whites (+$2,434) compared to blacks (+$172). Relative income for blacks dropped to $580 from $613 per $1,000 of white income during that time (Hacker, 1992). One of the notable developments in the post-1960 period was the increase in the size of the black middle class (Landry, 1987). In 1990, almost 30 percent of black families had incomes over $35,000 compared with 25 percent in 1970. (White families in this bracket went from 48 percent to 53 percent in that period.) However, Landry (1992) later observed that he had been too optimistic about future projections for the 1990s which were based on 1970s data, indicating the slowdown in growth. Blacks had made many of their middle class gains through public sector employment in the 1960s and 70s. However, there were growing *increases in income disparity* between blacks and whites in the 1980s in that sector (Zipp, 1994).

Offsetting improvements in the size of the black middle class were increases in the unemployment ratio of blacks to whites from 1970 to 1990, 1.86 to 2.76 (Hacker, 1992). This was disproportionately due to large numbers of young black males with limited economic opportunities and education. In addition, the data for this period show over one-third of black families, containing 40 percent of black children, were experiencing poverty compared to about 1 in 10 white families. The future, given national economic circumstances, may not be very optimistic. Jaynes and Williams (1989) indicate that, with lower real wages for black men and women, it is increasingly difficult to rise out of poverty through employment. Thus, while a larger black middle class exists, there are still high degrees of economic inequality, insecurity, and poverty among black Americans.

Residential Segregation
Myrdal (1944) wrote that residential segregation was a basic cause of racial inequality that exerted its influence in an indirect and impersonal way. If blacks did not live near whites, they could not encounter one another in ways typically associated with neighborhoods. Segregation then becomes reflected in schools, hospitals, and other institutions creating an "artificial city." A fair housing law was passed in 1968 to eliminate discrimination in housing and promote integrated neighborhoods.

Douglas Massey and Nancy Denton (1993) analyzed the 1980 census, focusing primarily on the 30 metropolitan areas with the largest black populations [over 50 percent of total U.S. black population] and showed that residential segregation for blacks remained extremely high. They believe it is the principal feature of American society responsible for the perpetuation of urban poverty and a primary cause of racial inequality. It is a structural condition, i.e., beyond the ability of any individual to change and constrains people's life chances. This residential segregation is not differentiated by socioeconomic levels among the black population. Thus, even the black middle class tends to live in segregated neighborhoods. This is due to widespread discrimination and prejudice that exists in urban housing markets and restricts mobility. Massey and Denton argue that this segregation did not occur by chance; but it is the ongoing result of purposeful institutional arrangements in real estate, housing, and financial sectors and reinforcing self-conscious actions. It has helped set into motion dynamic spirals of economic decline in central cities that affect community stability and cause the loss of commerce, jobs, investment, income and increases in social problems. The segregation and poverty also have significant political consequences since they unequally distribute the necessity for state assistance and other public services.

Reynolds Farley and William Frey (1994) conducted an extensive analysis of the 1990 census. They examined racial segregation in 232 metropolitan areas with substantial black populations. They argue that due to changes in federal housing policies, white racial attitudes, new housing construction, and the growth of the black middle class there were modest declines in segregation between 1980 and 1990. The declines were, *however*, unevenly distributed. In the Northeast and Midwest and some portions of the Old South, where most blacks reside, segregation and discrimination remain high(reinforcing the Massey-Denton analysis). However, in developing parts of the West and South, where new housing is being built, the declines are significant. The greatest declines occurred where blacks constitute *small minorities*, in small and mid-sized cities. Farley and Frey note that white attitudes indicate discomfort when too many blacks move into neighborhoods—thus limiting the desegregation that might occur. Finally, while they observe that the increasing number of middle-class blacks facing declining economic opportunities in the industrial north might migrate to the West and New South, they also see the possibility that those future moves might result in largely black suburbs and segregated neighborhoods. But because the state of the U.S. economy remains uneven and erratic, the growth of the black middle class may be halted. The ability of blacks to move may be limited, and thus continuing segregation will perpetuate isolation and inequality.

The Family

Current data show that most black families are not two-parent households. Today, "a majority of black children live in families that include their mothers and not their fathers; in contrast 4 of 5 white children under 18 live with both parents" (Jaynes & Williams, 1989, 544-545). Andrew Billingsley (1992) shows that this has not always been the case. In fact, between 1890 and 1960, almost four-fifths of black families were two-parent ones. In 1980, for the first time, less than half were two-parent families. That critical shift has occurred, then, over the last 30 years.

There are numerous possible explanations for this dramatic change. "The most powerful hypothesis is that the economic situation in the black community together with residential segregation not only affects the immediate living conditions of blacks, but also strongly influences family structures and thereby alters the social and economic prospects for the next generation" (Jaynes & Williams, 1989: 545). Billingsley shows the positive relationship between income and family structure; the higher the income, the greater the likelihood of two-parent families. To sustain that position generally requires a "working wife," given the disparity between black and white incomes. Joyce Ladner (1971) and Carol Stack (1974) showed that unemployment and low-paying insecure jobs discourage some black men from marriage. Women similarly may see risk and uncertainty in those prospects and not seek marriage. Robin Jarrett (1994) using focus groups of poor black women with children found that the women wanted marriage but were pessimistic about its success. Economic impediments were critical in their decisions to forego the institution. The women, Jarrett states, not only foresee lack of economic security through male partners but also viewed their *own* potentials for economic independence to be greater.

The concern about the family here is what effect it has on children who will come to school. Two-thirds of black children who were living in female-headed households in 1986 were below the poverty level. These conditions lead to many possible problems—lack of access to knowledge, poor physical and psychological health, and unsafe and unstable environments. Consequently, these children will start school from disadvantaged positions.

Culture and Structure

The previous paragraphs illustrate some basic aspects of social inequality. For many whites, these "facts" become defining for the character of black Americans and not for the processes and nature of social institutions that constitute that character. Bart Landry (1992) argues that racism and prejudice are not merely individual attitudes but cultural norms to which the dominant majority are socialized. Evidence for their beliefs then comes from the institutions and practices that produce the inequality. The beliefs are embedded in cultural expectations and norms that reinforce and sustain the structure. Thus, he notes that a 1990 NORC poll indicated over 50 percent of whites believed blacks were lazy and less intelligent than whites. White Americans tend to believe that poverty has individual causes rather than social ones—lack of effort, ability, proper skills, and loose morals (Kluegel & Smith, 1986). While public opinion polls may show increasing support for the principle of equality, more openness to public contact and even at some level, personal relationships, "principles of equality are endorsed less when they result in close, frequent, or prolonged social contact and whites are much less prone to endorse policies meant to implement equal participation of blacks in important institutions. In practice many whites refuse or are reluctant to participate in social settings (e.g., neighborhoods and schools) in which significant numbers of blacks are present" (Jaynes & Williams, 1989: 11). Class differences, residential isolation, perceptions of social problems, stereotypes, and media images together with differential experiences and perceptions reinforce the existing society and lead to polarization, particularly in a period where economic opportunities for all are perceived to be increasingly problematic.

It would be erroneous to suggest that American culture is an integrated, cohesive, consensual totality built around either racism or pluralism and equality. All coexist in some partial relationships to one another within individuals, collectivities, and society. In addition, blacks and whites are not objective monolithic realities but social constructions glossing variation and blurred boundaries that have been accepted as well as contested. Members of both social categories express commitments to the same society, goals, and values. Appeals, at times, to general democratic and egalitarian ideals have generated improvement in relationships and decreasing inequality. Nevertheless, both tend to have different perceptions and interpretations about societal history, events, and policies. Many whites believe equality of opportunity has been provided to blacks, who have failed to take advantage of the openings. Many blacks believe there has been and is continuing discrimination and racism. These beliefs and unequal/insulated circumstances thus constitute an important context for American public education both in terms of differential starting points due to economic inequality and residential segregation and differential expectations and interpretations due to culture and social conceptions of race.

EDUCATION AND SCHOOLING
This next section explores the educational outcomes of blacks in comparison with whites. In general the results show that minorities perform less well, and thus the inequality that was depicted in the previous section is reproduced. However, this is not a benign continuation, namely, that because of poorer socioeconomic conditions and less conventional family structures, these children lack some characteristics or qualities to do well in school so that schools simply do the best they can with youths who are not as prepared, motivated, and capable as white children. Indeed, I will argue that the structures, cultures, processes, and practices of school, what Hugh Mehan (1992) refers to as constitutive practices, significantly affect student academic careers.

In this section I explore first the data on educational attainment and performance and then see whether there are differences in values, motivation, or expectations that might lead to differential attainment or performance. Next I examine schooling contexts, practices, and expectations that might be factors in producing differential outcomes. Since human beings are not programmed robots, it is also critical to analyze how minority students respond to schooling, society, and themselves and how they influence the processes. Finally, I examine the question of cultural differences between population groups and the utility of multiculturalism for schooling.

Educational Attainment and Performance
In the past 50 years there has been a significant narrowing of the gap between blacks and whites in schools. Large differences in median years of schooling that once existed have almost disappeared. In 1991, for whites between ages 25 and 29, the median years of schooling were 12.9 and for blacks in the same bracket, 12.5 (NCES, 1993). Notable in producing this near-parity

was the increased number of blacks who had completed high school. However, the degree of high school completion by blacks remains less than that by whites. In 1991 among persons 16-24, the figures reported for dropouts were whites 9.0 percent, blacks 13.6 percent (NCES, 1993).

College entry and completion are critical factors for youth, as they are the routes to relative economic security. The percentage of blacks going to college increased dramatically after the 1960s. In 1977 about half of both black and white youth 18-24 had graduated from high school and enrolled in college (NCES, 1993). However, over the next 10 years that percentage drops significantly for blacks (36.5 percent) but rises for whites (56 percent). One possible factor for the developing disparity was a change in the mode of financial aid to students, from grants to loans (Jaynes & Williams, 1989). Since 1987, more blacks have entered college. In 1992 48 percent of black high school graduates enrolled in college compared to 62 percent of white high school graduates, so there still remains a substantial difference.

College graduation rates show disparities as well, indicating that higher education institutions do not retain minorities well. Persell et al. (1993) indicate that in 1992, 30 percent of whites 25-29 completed four or more years of college in comparison to 14 percent of blacks. Some of this difference is attributable to the types of higher education institutions attended by minorities compared to whites. Blacks are overrepresented at public two-year colleges and underrepresented in four-year institutions. Students who attend community colleges and intend to transfer to a four-year BA-granting institution are less likely to achieve that degree than are students with similar ambitions, academic ability, and social background who go to four-year schools. This is due to the lack of retention by two-year schools, obstacles to transferring to four-year institutions, and higher attrition rates of those who transfer (Dougherty, 1992). In addition, minority students are less likely to attend academically selective and prestigious universities or small liberal arts colleges that graduate higher percentages of students than the average public four-year institution.

Consequently, blacks are underrepresented in both associate and bachelor's degrees in comparison to whites. This difference is even greater for graduate degrees (Thomas, 1987). The author notes a 20 percent drop in black enrollment between 1976 and 1982 in comparison to a 9 percent drop for whites. In addition, of the Ph.D.s awarded in 1980-81, blacks received only 3.9 percent, exacerbating the degree of underrepresentation. Gail Thomas is particularly concerned about lack of graduate degree completion in the natural and technical sciences. Recent data indicate that of over 9,000 Ph.D.s awarded in natural sciences and engineering to U.S. citizens in 1991, only 130 went to black Americans (Drew, 1993). Thus, proportionately fewer blacks than whites graduate from high school, enter and complete college, and receive post-baccalaureate degrees.

Over the past 20 years, there has been a significant increase in the measured academic performance of black youngsters, and while there is a gap in relation to whites, it has diminished in reading, math, and science. This is due to large increases in the proportion of black youngsters who have mastered the basics and thus approach the percentage of mastery by whites at that level in those subjects. While decreased over time, there remain significant differences in measurements of higher-level knowledge in those fields. These differences in higher-level knowledge are probably related to differential entry into high school courses offering advanced material.

Examination of reading scores on the National Assessment of Educational Progress (NAEP) between 1970 and 1990 shows the overall gap between 17-year-old whites and blacks reduced from 44 to 30 scale points (NCES, 1993). (Gains over the 20 years for disadvantaged urban youth were over 90 scale points!) In addition, 13-year-old blacks show significant increases in the intermediate levels above the basics while 13-year-old whites' scores remained stable. There are, however, strong remaining differences at the highest levels between the two population categories.

The pattern is repeated for math with black gains over the 20 years exceeding white gains for 9-, 13-, and 17-year-olds (NCES, 1993). In the proficiency levels, blacks closely approximate whites at basic and intermediate but trail significantly at the two highest levels, e.g., for 17-year-olds in 1990: whites 63 percent and 8 percent respectively; blacks 33 percent and 2 percent respectively. However, the percentage gain for blacks over that period in those areas exceeds that of whites. Proficiency has a strong parallel with math courses taken, and blacks (as well as whites) who take geometry, algebra II, and calculus score higher. Examination of SAT scores between 1975-76 and 1991-92 shows black increases in verbal and math scores, while white scores decline slightly (NCES, 1993). Granted that taking this test is voluntary, the results are indicative of a growing pool of better-prepared youngsters. Some of the improvement in the 17-year-old math scores and the SAT might be attributed to increased course taking. Thus between 1982 and 1990 average math course taking by blacks increased from 2.44 to 3.09, science from 1.99 to 2.73, English 3.90 to 4.17, and overall from 20.5 to 23.4 (NCES, 1993). If minorities had equal access to courses that represented higher-level knowledge, their scores would increase and move toward closing the gaps with whites.

Sociocultural and Social Psychological Factors
If race and ethnicity are not biological, genetic, or clearly bounded homogeneous groups, then it might be argued that they are collectivities with particular unique and coherent cultures with distinctive value systems that shape their attitudes and behavior toward education. Survey research has consistently demonstrated that there is little difference between the value placed on education and the importance of doing well in school in order to do well in society by families of both white and black children (Epstein, 1995). Perhaps, then, black students, unlike their parents, do not value education. As Roslyn Mickelson (1990) notes, James Coleman and colleagues (1966) observed that black students held highly favorable attitudes toward education, irrespective of their performance, and this has been confirmed frequently and again by Mickelson herself.

Sandra Graham (1994) takes a different perspective when she reviews the literature on motivation among blacks. One could argue that some might value a goal but not exert the effort for attainment. Graham reviewed 140 studies and concluded that the evidence did not show that blacks lacked motivation to strive for success. [Significantly, she observes class was generally not included in this body of research but when it was, it was an important factor.] In terms of attributions about reasons for success and failure, both blacks and whites equally attribute success to one's ability and failure to lack of effort. Graham also finds that research does not indicate differences in expectancy for future success or academic self-concepts between blacks and whites, even when performance might indicate otherwise.

There is another way of exploring these issues. Graham recalls that Bernard Rosen (1959) made a distinction between achievement aspirations and expectations. John Ogbu (1978) took a similar position when he argued that blacks would scale down expectations in response to perceived labor market ceilings. Jay MacLeod (1987) ironically shows this to be the case for some white young men who "dropped out" and not true for a black group who perceived some windows of opportunity following the civil rights era and pursued education. Mickelson (1990) follows up on these suggestions by arguing that attitudes toward education are multidimensional. Black adolescents can have a very positive attitude about the value of education in the abstract, but, in concrete terms, they evaluate it in the contemporary social context and in terms that are derived from community and family experiences. The discrepancy between attitudes and achievement is explained by the effects of the concrete views of experience. As long as black youths do not see educational and employment opportunities after high school, they will not strive for success in high school.

School Segregation, Desegregation, and Resegregation
Earlier I presented evidence of significant residential segregation in the United States. Since school desegregation has been national policy for many years, it is useful to see whether it has offset residential patterns. Gary Orfield (1993) has recently shown that while desegregation was increasing in the 1960s and 1970s, it reversed course in the 1980s and is increasing in the 1990s. In the South, the focus of early efforts, segregation has shown a significant resurgence since 1988. School segregation across the U.S. is strongly related to segregation by poverty. It remains high in big cities and is substantial in midsized central cities. Even in suburbs of metropolitan areas, many blacks attend segregated schools. Schools in rural areas, small towns, small metropolitan areas, and suburbs of midsize metropolitan areas are likely to be more integrated, but these are also areas with generally small non-white populations. Steven Rivkin (1994) examines the demographic changes and integration efforts of 40 large urban school districts between 1968 and 1988. These districts contain a substantial proportion of blacks in the United States. Rivkin concludes that, given the decrease of resident white students, integrating those districts as fully as possible (with current enrollments) would not significantly reduce racial isolation. Indeed, only the movement of students *across* district boundaries would produce that. In addition, Orfield observes that it is states with more fragmented (smaller and more numerous) district structures that have higher levels of segregation. Given recent Supreme Court decisions and the current political climate, it is unlikely that more cross-district or metropolitan area desegregation patterns will be implemented. In addition, some voices of educators and minority communities have turned away

from desegregation efforts and are focusing on improving performance of minority students in neighborhood schools.

In the past 40 years of court-ordered desegregation, there has been a great deal of scholarship focusing on student achievement, self-esteem, and intergroup relations. The results are mixed but generally show positive effects. In regard to performance, for example, minority students generally improve while the process has no effect on whites. Black gains are greater in schools that are mostly white and when the plan is metropolitan in scope (more middle-class whites and across class lines). This is explained by increased access to knowledge and higher staff expectations for achievement. Reasons for mixed findings are attributable to research problems (Mahard & Crain, 1983) but also to the way in which desegregation is implemented (Longshore & Prager, 1985; Kazal-Thresher, 1994). It is a very complex process (Schofield, 1991). Desegregation has been hard to maintain over time as populations and proportions change. In addition, there is a second generation segregation in which minorities are resegregated in desegregated schools by tracking, ability grouping, special education assignment, and disciplinary measures (Meier et al., 1989).

Effects on achievement, self-esteem, and intergroup relations in school are short-term measurements. Jomills Braddock (1985) has focused his scholarship on long-term effects such as college attendance, adult employment, and interracial contacts. His conclusions are that, "As adults, all students who have experienced desegregated elementary-secondary schooling are more likely than students with only segregated schooling to voluntarily choose desegregated experiences in college, employment, and neighborhood settings as well as increased interracial contacts." [As adults, these students] are also more likely "to experience fairer and more equal access to adult career and employment opportunities, more prestigious and better paying jobs" (Braddock, 1994:2).

Braddock (1985) speaks of these effects as *structural* assimilation, positional integration without sacrificing a cultural identity. He argues that segregation tends to perpetuate or reproduce itself, *in part*, because minority students who have not regularly experienced desegregation may overestimate the degree of overt hostility or underestimate their skill at coping with strains in interracial situations. Thus, those students will avoid those contacts.

Amy Wells and Robert Crain (1992) also review this research and place it in a larger context. They find that desegregated black students set their occupational aspirations higher than segregated blacks. Desegregated black students' occupational aspirations are also more realistically related to their educational background and aspirations than those of segregated black students. They concur that black graduates of desegregated schools are more likely than those of segregated schools to attend desegregated colleges. Finally, they conclude desegregated black students are more likely to have desegregated social and political networks in later life, more likely to find positions in desegregated employment, and somewhat more likely to have private sector white-collar and professional jobs versus government or blue-collar jobs. Wells and Crain propose that the major influence here is structural and informational. Black students in white schools have greater access to information about colleges and careers than they would have in segregated schools. They may also receive assignment to college counselors who have ties to college admissions offices. In addition, they argue that for college-educated youth, many post-college positions are filled through referrals and social networks and that integrated social networks as consequences of desegregated education provide these connections. Wells and Crain argue that desegregation in the long term does meet the goals of providing blacks more equal access to important education and employment opportunities. Over time, support for continuing or beginning new desegregation efforts has diminished among white and black populations. Some members of black communities see children as taking the burden of the process. With cities becoming increasingly composed of minorities and strong external resistance to metropolitan desegregation, maintaining the policy/program is increasingly difficult. Retrospectively, many in black communities remember that their teachers and administrators lost their jobs during desegregation and their buildings were closed (Irvine, 1990). It is not uncommon to feel a loss of community, a loss of a center to hold the community together. This is vividly and movingly depicted in Dempsey and Noblit (1993). Irvine argues that desegregation increased discontinuity between black students and school because the desegregated schools were run by whites who had no sense of the black community or its culture.

One of the abiding interests in the desegregation process, given the history of discrimination, prejudice, and sometimes overt conflict, is whether relationships between majority and minority will improve. The underlying theory promoting this process was Gordon Allport's (1954) social psychological contact theory. Contact alone, however, may do nothing more than reinforce stereotypes or produce conflict. Allport said the situation needed to be structured so that majority and minority both had equal status and there was institutional support for positive relations. Elizabeth Cohen (1982) and Thomas Pettigrew (1986), however, point out that that larger context of status stratification and group relations strongly complicates producing equality and a sense of *similarity* in schools and classrooms. Indeed, *differences* are likely to remain present.

Thus, Janet Schofield's (1991) review of the literature in this area is to use her word "pessimistic." She finds much of the research weak. However, she does affirm the findings from the better qualitative studies of social processes in desegregated schools. As Schofield notes, these focused on "what's going on here" and "what works." These studies demonstrate the "remarkable, even daunting, complexities of the desegregation process" as well as some recurring problems and processes. Some significant amount of resegregation was found in a number of studies in the late 1970s (Wax, 1980). There was heightened attention to maintaining order and avoiding conflict and the presence of racial tension. Students generally dealt with difficult situations by avoidance or trying to "get along." *Class* disparities that manifested themselves in greater academic success for the middle class (whites) were interpreted as *racial* differences. Thus desegregation did not generally produce integration or improved intergroup relations.

Longshore and Prager (1985) observe that what stands out in their review of the literature is the "consistently favorable impact of cooperative learning." It does promote conditions (equal-status contact, favorable norms) that are otherwise difficult to achieve in desegregated schools, and, under those conditions, it produces improvement in achievement, self-esteem, and intergroup relations for both minority and majority children. Schofield notes that its main purpose has been academic, but it also has significant consequences for intergroup attitudes and relations. Cooperative learning and cooperation in general may work for a variety of reasons. They can generate task and reward interdependency. The process allows lower achievers to contribute to group goals and also to learn at higher rates. It may also be responsive to some ethnic/racial group norms of cooperation that contrast with presumed white competitive ones. Schofield (1995) extends the cooperative learning context to broader intergroup relations improvement by stating that it can occur through the following conditions equal status, cooperative interdependence, cross-cutting identities, personalization of the outgroup, creating affective positive environments, and support of authorities for positive relations. However, Schofield also observes that low priority has traditionally been given to these matters.

Schooling Practices and Teacher Expectations for Students and Families

It is crucial to examine the internal life of classrooms and schools to understand how student backgrounds interact with the perceptions, interactions, and practices of educators and differentially affect students' academic careers. The most prevalent and consequential of these practices is ability grouping and tracking. Many researchers have shown that track placement correlates with race (Alexander et al., 1978; Oakes, 1990). The consequences of these practices sort students into different learning environments. The results, *even* when controlling for student background, prior achievement and (often) achievement aspirations, are increased differences in achievement test performance, college attendance, educational aspirations, self-esteem, and perceived legitimacy of schooling (Persell et al., 1993).

The reasons for the differential performance as a result of tracking or ability grouping are found in the very different experiences children in lower groups have compared to higher ones. There is less instructional time, less material covered, lower difficulty of material presented, lower teacher quality and, even when the same teachers have both high and low tracks, the latter receive lower quality instruction. There are also lower teacher expectations and encouragement, more teacher interruptions of student responses and different advice about educational and occupational options. These results have been found to occur as early as first grade (Eder, 1981; Dreeben & Gamoran, 1986). Aaron Pallas et al. (1994) document that first grade placement can have persistent effects over several years and perhaps longer, partly because of teacher and parent expectations. But as Hugh Mehan (1992), Gary Natriello et al. (1993) and Pallas et al. (1994) all have observed the assignment to groups has numerous problems and inaccuracies: many children are miscategorized (students with identical abilities placed in widely varying groups or students' abilities miscalculated) or assignments vary by class size, school organizational processes and constraints. It is no wonder then that grouping and tracking rather than narrowing differences exacerbates them with major consequences over the length of students' academic careers.

Differential teacher expectations for students and their reinforcing ways of interacting with them produce different outcomes that correlate with race. Irvine (1990:61) in a review of the literature concludes:

> In summary teacher expectations are powerful contributors to the school achievement of black students but are mediated by factors such as the characteristics of the teacher and the students. It does appear that black children are particularly susceptible to negative teacher expectations because they differ from most teachers who are white and middle class; they are also more teacher dependent. Previous research, mostly naturalistic classroom studies, documents that white teachers are more likely to have more negative expectations than do black teachers (for black children).

One manifestation of these expectations can be on a collective as well as individual level. In "effective schools" serving primarily low-income black students, there may be a stress on the maintenance of order, disciplined student behavior, and the learning of basic skills (Jaynes & Williams, 1989; Hallinger & Murphy, 1986). Those schools, if serving white middle-class children, would stress different educational processes and outcomes. The goals of the school then are based upon the differential expectations for children.

Another manifestation of low expectations is how failure is explained. Irvine and York (1993) conducted an interesting study among some elementary teachers in the Southeast who were asked to attribute causes of failure for African American, Vietnamese, and Hispanic students. For African Americans, the primary reasons are family conditions and individual characteristics. For Hispanics the reasons are similar, but also include problems of language and poverty. The teachers see the Vietnamese as facing the greatest cultural and structural problems of the three groups—language, poverty, and racism. Teachers explicitly rejected negative teacher expectations, curriculum, or teacher training as major causes of black student's failure. This research also shows the connections between teacher expectations for students and those for families.

Some research in inner city schools (Epstein & Dauber, 1991; Dauber & Epstein, 1993) showed that teachers expected many activities from parents at home, e.g. assisting with homework, but, as a rule, had no program to inform parents how to engage in the activities. They blamed parents for low levels of involvement. Parents, in the meantime, said they were involved but wanted more information about how to help more effectively. In a study that compared teacher reactions to parent involvement by single-parent and two-parent households, Epstein (1990) found that teachers who were not active in parent involvement programming tended to devalue the quality of help to students from single-parent households as well as those students and their homework compared to two-parent households. (Two-thirds of the single parents were black.) Teachers who compartmentalized parent involvement to the home, not the classroom, tended to have stereotypes about single parents. Teachers who, however, structured parent involvement into their regular practice and into their classroom saw no difference between the amount and quality of the parental help from one- or two-parent households. Students generally did better in these classrooms with structured parent involvement. Teacher expectations for parents and students were matched with practices that created equal partnerships between teachers and parents (Epstein, 1995).

Tracking and ability group placement are based upon combinations of achievement test results, grades in classes, and teacher judgments. Gilmore (as cited by Irvine, 1990) stated, for example, that black students' "attitude" was used to keep them from high-track classes, illustrating the importance of subjective elements. But even "objective" achievement test evidence is subject to interpretation and has subjective and cultural assumptions built into its construction and use.

There is strong evidence that "African-American, Latino, Native American, and students for whom English is a second language do not, as a group, perform as well as Anglos on formal tests" (García & Pearson, 1994: 340). These are reduced but not eliminated when controlled for class and English proficiency. These tests were designed to produce differences although all differences are not always equal. The retained differences are those that match *developers'* cultural expectations of how intelligence and achievement ought to be distributed (Kamin, 1974). And while there has been an awareness of the limits of these tests, as late as 1993 the U.S. Government Accounting Office (U.S. G.A.O., 1993) reported that about three-fourths of the tests administered by districts were norm-referenced multiple choice tests. Speed and accuracy become the significant factors in these tests. García and Pearson present a strong and careful critique of these tests. The tests provide little analysis about student comprehension and reasoning. They have a norming bias in eliminating items on which low-scoring students do comparatively well. They have a content bias, reflecting the dominant culture's standards. They have linguistic and cultural biases including the testing event itself, the emphasis on speed, and differential interpretation of questions that affects results.

The authors point out that the tests have greater problems, not merely with the immediate results but with how they are used, what they refer to as "consequential validity." Chachkin (1989) said the use of test results had impeded desegregation for minority students and were used excessively in special education and low-track placements in secondary schools. The test results can have a disproportionate influence on curriculum where teachers in inner-city schools are more likely to rely on data from tests and then develop curriculum and instruction in order to improve test scores. Thus with more pressure for accountability, there will be more emphasis on testing; more classroom time would be spent on test preparation with less time for broader instruction on non-tested subjects and skills. Low-income students would continue to receive a fragmented, skills-based curriculum with little time to connect things to larger subjects.

In conjunction with a variety of recent reforms, alternative assessment strategies have emerged: e.g., authentic assessment and performance assessment. While there is little evidence about the development and consequences of these for minorities, García and Pearson suggest that authentic assessment has the *potential* to be responsive to cultural and linguistic diversity. However, since performance assessment is often constructed by those outside the classroom, there is no guarantee that assessment developers will be knowledgeable about or interested in language and cultural factors.

The authors cite some evidence that teachers may ignore potential information from alternative assessment and attribute low performance to home life or earlier schooling. Thus there remains uncertainty as to whether staff will accept these new forms and alter instruction in a congruent way. García and Pearson observed that the typical governance and instructional practices in schools with low-income and diverse children do not match those where the best use of portfolios, an alternative assessment strategy, for language arts occurs. Site-based decision making, whole language philosophy, and cooperative learning support the use of portfolios. If these assessment practices are to be successful there are numerous changes that need to be made in opportunities to learn, school governance, professional development for teachers, and the relationship of assessment to instruction in those schools.

Students—Identities, Peer Groups, Cultures, and Schooling
Students are not simply passive about schooling. They act individually and collectively to construct their educational careers and responses to the school context, albeit not necessarily with an equal degree of influence. Students develop and become changed during the schooling process and do react to and influence that process. Students are also not a monolithic category but exhibit tremendous diversity that affects schooling processes including their awareness, construction, and commitment to racial/ethnic, student, and adolescent identities.

Patricia Phelan et al. (1993) make this vividly clear in their presentation of a multiple worlds model of self, family, peers, and school. Individuals must negotiate border crossings between those worlds, which, given their degree of difference or congruence with the developing self, are differentially successful. The authors indicate four types of student adaptation to the multiple worlds—I. Congruent Worlds/Smooth Transitions; II. Different Worlds/Border Crossings Managed; III. Different Worlds/Border Crossings Difficult; IV. Different Worlds/ Borders Impenetrable. Type I is represented by an Anglo, middle-class adolescent in high school—who the authors note has little contact with students from other ethnic/racial groups who are bused in and whom s/he does not want to be there. For those from outside the mainstream, a Type II example is a Latina who adapts situationally by conforming in school when in a minority and returns to home patterns when with friends and family. This type of student, the authors state, suffers the least psychosocial stress of those from minority backgrounds and is able to fit in and operate successfully in a variety of settings. Type III students cross borders only under certain conditions and are caught between engagement and withdrawal. This is exemplified by a Latina who does well in student-centered classrooms but performs poorly in teacher-dominated ones. A Type IV example could be a black female who is immersed in her peer group and who commits herself to a culture that is contrary to school expectations and behaviors.

Alan Peshkin (1991) describes a high school that is at once quite surprising and quite expected. It is a comprehensive high school in a solidly working class but extremely diverse small California city. Its community and high school contain no dominant or majority groups but large proportions of blacks, Hispanics, Filipinos, Asians, and whites, Sicilians and non-Sicilians. The community has seen its political institutions open up to this diversity and its school respond to black and Hispanic protests. Peshkin observes that to these high school students in the 1980s, "ethnicity" (including race) was not "a big deal." The students' primary identity was adolescent, and they mingled relatively freely across ethnic and racial boundaries according to their social interests, preferences, and activities. (Some exceptions occurred when black males were in interracial cross-gender relationships). The students had norms about the situational relevance of ethnicity and race. Indeed, for many, the primary goal was assimilation into American mass culture and being "American." In some situations, there was also acknowledgment of and adaptation to the home culture of parents. Within school, however, preoccupations with or strong assertions of ethnic or racial identity were discouraged.

This remarkable racial/ethnic social harmony and interaction was facilitated by the school's fostering of this climate and its acceptance of poor academic performance by many of its students, particularly blacks and Hispanics. Fitting many of the patterns of *The Shopping Mall High School* (Powell et al., 1985), low academic expectations and reinforcing practices were schoolwide. Attributions of responsibility were put on the students and their families. While the staff asserted a color-blind philosophy and denied the relevance of race/ethnicity for schooling, they voiced a race-conscious explanation of poor performance and ability. John Ogbu (1978, 1992) argues that the circumstances of black and Hispanics and Native Americans as coerced and colonized minorities are different from those of European Americans, Filipinos, and Asians who voluntarily came to the United States and expect to accommodate to the dominant society and become accepted and successful. Signithia Fordham and Ogbu (1986) assert that blacks resisted this coerced colonized status through an inversion of the dominant society, its institutions, and the routes to assimilation and success including schools. To be successful in the .U.S. then, blacks must "act white," which means negating their race, losing their identity and connections to community and culture. Fordham (1991) argues that there are strong cultural differences between the black community and white society that include contradictory values and practices. Thus "acting black" expresses this identity, resists white society, and leads to rejection by whites and thus failure in schools. Fordham offers alternatives that would allow success without identity loss by focusing on peer group sanctioned learning and pedagogical practices that are congruent with local culture. Ogbu (1992) also offers strategies involving accommodation without assimilation by separating the worlds of school and community such as Phelan et al.'s Type II.

In contrast, William Cross, Jr. (1995) takes issue with Fordham and Ogbu. He suggests that their oppositional identity represents only one variant of several oppositional identities of blacks in America, an alienated version. Rather than assume a separatist, rejectionist stance, Cross argues that some blacks develop a defensive identity that was founded on an awareness of American racism but also on an active involvement in and efforts to change social institutions. He concurs that, given current structural and political developments, Fordham and Ogbu may represent trends in identity among some segments of the black population but those cannot be generalized to all. Cross suggests rather that attention must be paid to the existence of both oppositional identities and their consequences.

While Fordham makes clear the consequences of her small sample for generalizing purposes, she clearly asserts the pervasiveness of the cultural differences and the essentialism of the black community and identity, at least in the inner city. While Peshkin found *some* elements of the beliefs about acting black or white and the existence of some duality between school and community, others have not shown extensive evidence of it. Philip Wexler (1992), while focussing on class, acknowledges the impact of race on student self-images in an inner-city high school. Students felt an absence of self and the need to seek respect and assert self and become "somebody." They recognized that school and society saw them as *bad* and they wanted and sought self-respect. Farrell (1994) observes in the selves of *successful* inner-city high school students that they may have repressed their "peer self" in the struggle between student self and peer self, opting for the former while surrounding themselves with a *few* friends who had congruent values. Success for these students came in integrating their selves and their multiple worlds so they led congruently to success. More complicated are the circumstances offered by Shirley Brice Heath and Milbrey McLaughlin (1993). Heath (1995) sees inner-city youth consciously defying categorization and defining themselves in terms of multiple networks of family and friends that are individualized and contain cross-racial/ethnic categories.

Gonzales and Cauce (1995) report that ethnic pride, ethnic social involvement, and bicultural competence (the perceived ability to fit into either a black or white group comfortably) were associated with perceived self-competence, emotional and behavioral adjustment. Black youngsters can succeed in schools by learning how to negotiate multiple worlds so that they can situationally present their race/ethnicity as necessary. The ability to "do as in Rome," according to Phelan et al., prompted the least psychosocial stress. One might raise the question about why that strategy is necessary and whether accommodation devalues an identity and culture? It is clear, however, that a color-blind approach does not work. Race is invoked even as people say it is not. There are directions to follow here. One is to explore whether there are significant cultural differences between racial and ethnic groups that can be documented. The other is to explore multiculturalism in a way that values diversity/difference, rather than compartmentalizing it. This also means explicating the nature of culture. Finally, it should now be evident that the definitions and development of identities as well as cultures are dynamic and variable. Much of the way people act toward others ignores these processes and forces individuals into categories not of their choosing, which they, in turn, sometimes resist.

Possible Racial/Ethnic Cultural Differences
The expanding literature on cultural differences on learning has three related themes—that learning styles may vary by collectivity, that there is a discontinuity between the culture of the home and the school, and effective African American teachers of African American students are successful because they make explicit connections to local culture.

Irvine and York (1995) report that scholarly literature suggests that black learners are field dependent as opposed to the field independent style of majority whites. That means that blacks tend to respond to objects as wholes instead of isolated parts, prefer inferential reasoning as opposed to deductive or inductive reasoning, focus on people rather than things, and prefer learning characterized by variation and freedom of movement. Hispanics are said to prefer group learning situations to individual ones, concrete representations to abstract ones, and to learn by doing as opposed to memory. Native Americans tend to prefer visual and spatial information to verbal, to learn privately rather than in public, to watch and then do rather than by trial and error. To the extent that these tendencies are valid, they should lead to the differential structuring of learning situations.

Irvine and York are aware that this literature must be interpreted cautiously for a number of reasons. One is that culture affects individuals differently. It is shaped by socialization, identity, and commitment that vary. Cultural differences are, in addition, mediated by other factors such as gender and class. There are great dangers in generalizing to all assumed members of a category. No single learning style is isomorphic with any particular defined cultural group. This literature suggests that teachers must contextualize their teaching by being sensitive to their students as individuals as well as "members" of cultural categories.

Hugh Mehan (1992) summarizes the literature on the discontinuity between the language of home and school of students from certain low income and linguistic minority backgrounds that is congruent with the learning styles scholarship. Shirley Brice Heath (1982), for example, compared the way white middle-income teachers talked to black low-income elementary children with the way they talked to their own children. Much of their talk to both was in the mode of the traditional question-response-evaluation of classroom lessons (Mehan, 1979). This was what these teachers used in the classroom with the black children. This, however, is a discourse that differs for black children at home. Questions at home called for nonspecific comparisons or analogies as answers. These children then were not prepared for the style of their classroom. Ann Piestrup (1973) showed the other side of the Heath finding by observing in predominantly black first grade classrooms. When teachers used the speech patterns of the community, performance improved. These patterns included rhythmic language, rapid intonation, repetition, alliteration, call and response, variation in pace and creative language play. Similarly, Etta Hollins (1982) concludes that Marva Collins' famed success in Chicago was not due to the phonics curriculum but rather to synchrony between her interactional pedagogical style and the children's cultural experience.

The conclusion drawn from this research by Mehan is not to treat the students as if they are deficient or to defer to the cultural background but to mutually accommodate the differences. As Mehan along with Irvine and York (1993) argue, one major implication is to remove the source of school failure from children and family and recognize school responsibility in the process. "The problems that lower-income and ethnic minority children face in school must be viewed as a consequence of institutional arrangements that do not recognize that children can display skills differently in different types of situations" (Mehan, 1992:8).

Meier et al. (1989) demonstrated that the proportion of black teachers in a district was the single most consequential factor for black student schooling careers. They find that the more black teachers in a district, the fewer black students are placed in special education classes, corporally punished, suspended or expelled and the more black students are placed in gifted classes and graduate from high school. Examination of the research on effective black teachers presents a rationale for these findings. Michele Foster (1995) indicates that cultural solidarity is important, that these teachers have a strong attachment to the community and consider themselves part of it. They view their students in kin terms and exude a sense of interpersonal caring. Foster, however, wants to make clear that this relationship is neither permissive nor authoritarian and controlling. Rather it represents an authoritative parenting style that balances toughness and tenderness (Baumrind, 1978). It is that of an adult who commands respect, is respectful of students, and who through caring requires all students to meet high academic and behavioral standards. There is a connectedness that is pervasive. Classrooms have co-membership. Ladson-Billings (1990, 1992) observes that student-teacher interaction was equitable, and teachers shared power with students. Students interacted collaboratively and accepted responsibility for each other's education. In addition, there is a conscious attempt to link classroom content to students experiences. For example, Ladson-Billings illustrates the use of common cultural background, political history, and racial identity by the teachers with their students. Teachers also do not silence student voices; they focus on the whole child, use familiar cultural patterns, and incorporate culturally compatible communication patterns.

One perspective on this literature is that it emphasizes student-centered classrooms with engagement and high energy (Cuban, 1993). This is what works generally and is too sadly lacking in many classrooms. In addition, it also focuses on what white students frequently have, teachers from their communities and culture and classrooms with congruent curriculum and pedagogy. The issue is how to do that for minorities and not diminish it for whites who could also benefit from different forms of instruction and curriculum.

Multicultural Education

One response to the kinds of information presented in previous sections detailing inequities in schooling for racial and ethnic minorities has been to move toward multicultural education. This movement had its earlier roots in the intergroup relations efforts of the 1940s to early 1960s focussing on changing attitudes towards minority groups and facilitating cross-group interaction *and* the separate ethnic studies program developments of the 1960s and 1970s. As James Banks (1993) indicates, this was deemed inadequate and as with gender, a movement occurred to expand the coverage in the curriculum and representation in instructional materials of racial and ethnic groups as well as women. Part of the argument here was to legitimate the existence and aspirations of these categories, to provide role models and improve self-esteem and to educate all students about past, present, and possible futures.

For many then, multicultural education was defined by a curriculum orientation and content infusion. As Banks (1993) observes, the initial and perhaps continuing emphasis here has been a *contributory* approach or what has been labelled "holiday and heroes" celebrations. A spin-off has been the *additive* approach in which a section of a course or textbook is devoted to the topic rather than integrated throughout. Proponents of multicultural education have argued that these curriculum approaches are insufficient. Far from providing just content integration and altering attitudes, the goals of contemporary proponents are to reform schools so that students from racial, ethnic, class and gender groups experience educational equality. This requires much more than curriculum change.

However, the focus of the debate has been on curriculum and instructional materials. Cornbleth and Waugh (1995) detail controversies in California and New York about the social studies curriculum. In both cases, they indicate the failure of these states to develop a consensus about what shall be taught and how. Their discussion illustrates the political context of curricular knowledge and the accepted definitions of "America." Some defenders of the traditional order want to maintain "the Western tradition," the idea of an American consensus, a relatively benign view of our history, and they want to reduce race to ethnicity to create a pluralist view of the society. Many multicultural and minority proponents seek to revise the history, grant greater space for the experience of minorities, and contest the traditional power to define what is accepted knowledge.

Thus at issue here is, in fact, the nature of knowledge and truth. Many social scientists and philosophers as well as feminists and racial/ethnic studies scholars have demonstrated and argued the relationship between knowledge and power. They have examined the processes of social construction of knowledge and the use of knowledge to discipline or to liberate. This entails critical analyses of the assumptions, perspectives, interests, implications/ consequences of texts, knowledge, and knowledge construction. Indeed the arguments made by social scientists about race, ethnicity, and gender reflect this point of view. The approach questions the existence of objectivity in science, culture, and curriculum. Just as many recognize that history and science are continuously being revised, students can learn how the process occurs and how it is influenced by sponsorship, power, curiosity, and marginality as well as logic, argument, and evidence. Thus multicultural education would also include a dimension that would focus on knowledge construction.

Multicultural education has increasingly been about more than the social psychological consequences of curricular content, whether for majority or minority children. While there are important benefits if majority children gain understanding of other cultures and become sensitive to the consequences of power and if minority youth can see themselves in the curriculum, given all that we have discussed, there is a strong need for incorporating practices that produce equity for *all* children. Thus the multicultural education movement has incorporated the concept of *equity pedagogy*, namely, modifying classroom discourse for cultural compatibility. Additionally, attention would be given to the unequal effects of the existing sorting practices and the development of strategies that provide success, elimination of ability grouping and tracking, and cooperative learning. James Banks (1993) has suggested that the multiple dimensions of multicultural education and the significant inequities require substantial restructuring of schools. He has stated that the entire school, structurally and culturally, needs to be altered in order to empower staff, parents, and students to achieve multiculturalism and equity.

CONCLUSION AND INTRODUCTION TO THE SYMPOSIUM

In this chapter I have argued that racial (and ethnic) categories and their meanings are the result of human activities, unequal power, and historical, structural, and cultural contexts. As a grounding for exploring the relationship between race, ethnicity, and schooling, the contemporary societal context has been described to show the disadvantaged status that children from these categories face upon entering educational institutions. The remainder of the chapter has summarized how the structures, cultures, and practices of schooling further and perpetuate that inequality. At the same time, I argued it is important to take into account how youth collectively and individually respond to these categories and act toward the institution of schooling. Finally issues of cultural differences and multicultural education were introduced to reflect some alternative perspectives and possibilities.

The chapters that follow not only elaborate and deepen those topics but also offer options currently in process which can contribute to the alteration of the inequality. The symposium that provided the basis for this volume was organized by a systematic logic. First the broad *societal* context is depicted and its consequences for education stated. Next within that context the degree of influence that *family* has on primary, secondary, and tertiary education is empirically considered. Then we go inside schools to focus on *classroom teachers* and their pedagogy as they learn about racial and ethnic families and communities. The following chapter addresses the *structure and practice* of tracking by examining a program designed to reverse its typical consequences. *School*wide change is explored next in terms of organizational culture and discourse. Finally there is an analysis of *district* multicultural education policy formation. In the final chapter I will bring together change suggestions offered by the authors and provide a conclusion that integrates these reforms with broader restructuring efforts.

In chapter 2 Bart Landry provides a sharp image of diversity in American society and consequent issues and prospects. He offers a concise history of immigration to the United States and the political and ideological responses it produced. Landry illustrates how the unique post-1965 immigration has led to the first multicultural society. He poses some alternative models, based upon our past and other societies, that might characterize how we as a nation respond to this multicultural diversity. Reviewing our past and the ideological rationale for tracking and testing, Landry wonders whether we can overcome this legacy and provide a democratic society. His conclusion offers a sociologically grounded rationale for multicultural education.

Aaron Thompson and Reid Luhman in chapter 3 examine family influences on educational attainment for African Americans and European Americans. Using data from a longitudinal survey, they analyze whether the attainment gap can be explained better by family economic, occupational, and educational factors or structural barriers represented by institutional factors. In general, they find that family factors, particularly a mother's education, is a strong predictor of a child's attainment for both races but is more powerful for K-12 attainment and for blacks in the South. However, family factors have a much weaker influence on post-secondary attainment, particularly in the North and for African Americans. This evidence clearly indicates to the authors that extrafamilial factors, i. e., discrimination in the economy and lack of retention in four-year colleges, are responsible for creating the post-secondary attainment gap.

Luis Moll and Norma González present an exciting and valuable method to develop partnerships between teachers and families which significantly affects teacher practice, classroom pedagogy and parent involvement in chapter 4. They demonstrate how a collaborative teacher-researcher project can dissolve myths and stereotypes about minority communities through teacher home visits to gather data about household funds of knowledge and community social networks. Such visits, premised upon a dynamic and contextual idea of "culture" and focused on asking questions, not giving information, provide the bases for curriculum themes and units, student and teacher learning, and parent participation. Teachers also become part of the household networks in the community. The knowledge gained by teachers comes to mediate how they think about the community and how they think about teaching children from the community. This occurs in a collaborative teacher study group that greatly facilitates teacher reflexivity and successful practice.

In chapter 5 Hugh Mehan confronts tracking and its consequences for post-secondary enrollment of minorities. He focuses on an untracking program in the San Diego City Schools that places low-track, low-income, minority youngsters in a college preparatory curriculum and provides them with additional resources. College enrollment data by program participants compared to those who leave the program, San Diego high school graduates, and U.S. graduates show significantly higher rates for the participants. Mehan goes beyond the statistics to reveal the program processes and practices that make it effective and successful. Program staff provide information, skills, and strategies for high school success and college enrollment that is taken for granted by affluent majority youth but is otherwise unavailable to program students. In addition, the program staff develop a system of social supports for the students by serving as mentors and advocates within the school and externally as sponsors to colleges and universities. The program thus provides both cultural and social capital to the students.

Eugene Eubanks, Ralph Parish, and Dianne Smith in chapter 6 argue that producing necessary schoolwide change requires a new perspective, culture, and discourse. Practitioners must become aware that their typical way of thinking and talking about school problems and change focuses on symptoms, not causes, and externalizes responsibility to bureaucratic/political "theys" or families and children. In addition, they must consciously reject participating in structures and processes that reproduce inequality. Based upon their work in schools, the authors assert that the first step toward substantial change is the introduction of a new critical discourse that promotes a "learning organization culture." The discourse brings to the fore uncomfortable issues around class, race, and gender; takes seriously the belief that all children can learn at high levels; and offers no packaged solutions or prescribed change processes. Rather they say schools must take time (and it is a long time) to find their ways to what works in their context.

In chapter 7 Margaret Placier, Peter Hall, and Barbara Davis present a case study of multicultural education policy creation in a local school district. Using a processual and political analysis they show how the district's history, structure, and culture shaped the process and privileged the upper administration. At the same time, they document how the topic's ambiguity, community involvement and participation intentions and actions led to unanticipated policy outcomes and well as conflict. While the district administration regained control, they also had to introduce some changes that brought more potential consequences than initially planned. The authors compare these results with two other case studies and offer observations about constraints on developing policy.

In the final chapter, I review the policy suggestions offered by the other authors. The strength of these recommendations, I argue, can be greatly increased if they are part of an overall transformation of schooling, a restructuring process that fully integrates multicultural education within its goals and processes. In the same sense, schools alone cannot generate equity or demonstrate the benefits of diversity. Rather, the conclusion is that other social institutions must be venues of change to create a more affirmative and equitable society.

REFERENCES

Alexander, Karl, Martha Cook, and Edward McDill. 1978. "Curriculum Tracking and Educational Stratification: Some Further Evidence." *American Sociological Review* 43 (1):47-66.

Allport, Gordon. 1954. *The Nature of Prejudice*. Garden City, NY: Doubleday.

Banks, James. 1993. "Multicultural Education: Historical Development, Dimensions and Practice." *Review of Research in Education* 19:3-49.

Baumrind, Diana. 1978. "Parental Disciplinary Patterns and Social Competence in Children." *Youth and Society* 9(3):239-276.

Billingsley, Andrew. 1992. *Climbing Jacob's Ladder: The Enduring Legacy of African-American Families*. New York: Simon and Schuster.

Blauner, Robert. 1989. *Black Lives, White Lives: Three Decades of Race Relations in America*. Berkeley, CA: University of California.

Braddock, Jomills. 1985. "School Desegregation and Black Assimilation." *Journal of Social Issues* 41(3):9-22.

Braddock, Jomills. May, 1994. "The Impacts of School Desegregation." Fact Sheet for American Sociological Association Briefing on "Revitalizing Public Education: The Relation Between Resources and Learning." Washington, DC: American Sociological Association.

Chachkin, Norman. 1989. "Testing in Elementary and Secondary Schools: Can Misuse be Avoided?" Pp. 163-187 in *Test Policy and the Politics of Opportunity Allocation: The Workplace and the Law*, edited by Bernard Gifford. Boston: Kluwer.

Cohen, Elizabeth. 1982. "Expectation States and Interracial Interaction in School Settings." *Annual Review of Sociology* 8:209-235.

Coleman, James, Ernest Campbell, Carol Hobson, James McPartland, Alexander Mood, Frederic Weinfeld, and Robert York. 1966. *Equality of Educational Opportunity*. Washington, DC: U. S. Government Printing Office.

Cornbleth, Catherine, and Dexter Waugh. 1995. *The Great Speckled Bird: Education Policy-in-the-Making*. New York: St. Martin's.

Cross, William, Jr. 1995. "Oppositional Identity and African American Youth: Issues and Prospects." Pp. 185-204 in *Toward a Common Destiny*, edited by Willis Hawley and Anthony Jackson. San Francisco: Jossey-Bass.

Cuban, Larry. 1993. *How Teachers Taught: Constancy and Change in American Classrooms 1880-1990* (second edition). New York: Teachers College.

Dauber, Susan, and Joyce Epstein. 1993. "Parents' Attitudes and Practices of Involvement in Inner-City Elementary and Middle Schools." Pp. 53-71 in *Families* and *Schools in a Pluralistic Society*, edited by Nancy Chavkin. Albany, NY: State University of New York.

Dempsey, Van, and George Noblit. 1993. "Cultural Ignorance and School Desegregation: Reconstructing a Silenced Narrative." *Educational Policy* 7(3):318-339.

Dougherty, Kevin. 1992. *The Contradictory College: The Conflicting Origins, Impacts, and Futures of the Community College*. Albany, NY: State University of New York.

Dreeben, Robert, and Adam Gamoran. 1986. "Race, Instruction and Learning." *American Sociological Review* 51(5):660-669.

Drew, David. 1993. "Mathematics, Science and Urban Education." Pp. 297-315 in *Handbook of Schooling in Urban America*, edited by Stanley Rothstein. Westport, CT: Greenwood.

Eder, Donna. 1981. "Ability Grouping as a Self-Fulfilling Prophecy: A Micro-Analysis of Teacher-Student Interaction." *Sociology of Education* 54(3):151-162.

Epstein, Joyce. 1990. "Single Parents and the Schools: Effects of Marital Status on Parent and Teacher Interactions." Pp. 91-121 in *Changes in Social Institutions*, edited by Maureen Hallinan. New York: Plenum.

Epstein, Joyce. 1995. "School/Family/Community Partnerships: Caring for the Children We Share." *Phi Delta Kappan* 76(9):701-712.

Epstein, Joyce, and Susan Dauber. 1991. "School Practices and Teacher Practices of Parent Involvement in Inner-City Elementary and Middle Schools." *Elementary School Journal* 91(3):289-305.

Farley, Reynolds, and William Frey. 1994. "Changes in the Segregation of Whites From Blacks During the 1980s: Small Steps Toward a More Integrated Society." *American Sociological Review* 59(1):23-45.

Farrell, Edwin. 1994. *Self and School Success: Voices and Lore of Inner-City Students*. Albany, NY: State University of New York.

Fordham, Signithia. 1991. "Peer-Proofing Academic Competition Among Black Adolescents: 'Acting White' Black American Style." Pp. 69-93 in *Empowerment Through Multicultural Education*, edited by Christine Sleeter. Albany, NY: State University of New York.

Fordham, Signithia, and John Ogbu. 1986. "Black Students' School Success: Coping with the Burden of 'Acting White.'" *The Urban Review* 18(3):176-206.

Foster, Michele. 1995. "African American Teachers and Culturally Relevant Pedagogy." Pp. 570-581 in *Handbook of Research on Multicultural Education*, edited by James Banks and Cherry Banks. New York: Macmillan.

García, Georgia, and R. David Pearson. 1994. "Assessment and Diversity." *Review of Research in Education* 20:337-391.

Gates, Henry Louis. 1994. *Colored People: A Memoir*. New York: Knopf.

Gonzales, Nancy, and Ana Cauce. 1995. "Ethnic Identity and Multicultural Competence: Dilemmas and Challenges for Minority Youth." Pp. 131-162 in *Toward a Common Destiny*, edited by Willis Hawley and Anthony Jackson. San Francisco: Jossey-Bass.

Graham, Sandra. 1994. "Motivation in African Americans." *Review of Educational Research* 64(1):55-117.

Hacker, Andrew. 1992. *Two Nations: Black and White, Separate, Hostile, Unequal*. New York: Scribner's.

Hallinger, Phillip, and Joseph Murphy. 1986. "The Social Context of Effective Schools." *American Journal of Education* 94(3): 328-354.

Heath, Shirley Brice. 1982. "Questioning at Home and at School: A Comparative Study." Pp. 102-131 in *Doing the Ethnography of Schooling*, edited by George Spindler. New York: Holt, Rinehart and Winston.

Heath, Shirley Brice. 1995. "Race, Ethnicity and the Defiance of Categories." Pp. 39-70 in *Toward a Common Destiny*, edited by Willis Hawley and Anthony Jackson. San Francisco: Jossey-Bass.

Heath, Shirley Brice, and Milbrey McLaughlin (Eds.). 1993. *Identity and Inner-City Youth: Beyond Ethnicity and Gender*. New York: Teachers College.

Herrnstein, Richard, and Charles Murray. 1994. *The Bell Curve: Intelligence and Class Structure in American Life*. New York: Free Press.

Hollins, Etta. 1982. "The Marva Collins Story Revisited: Implications for Regular Classroom Instruction." *Journal of Teacher Education* 33(1):37-40.

Irvine, Jacqueline. 1990. *Black Students and School Failure*. New York: Praeger.

Irvine, Jacqueline, and Darlene York. 1993. "Teacher Perspectives: Why Do African-American, Hispanic, and Vietnamese Students Fail." Pp. 161-174 in *Handbook of Schooling in Urban America*, edited by Stanley Rothstein. Westport, CT: Greenwood.

Irvine, Jacqueline, and Darlene York. 1995. "Learning Styles and Culturally Diverse Students: A Literature Review." Pp. 484-497 in *Handbook of Research on Multicultural Education*, edited by James Banks and Cherry Banks. New York: Macmillan.

Jarrett, Robin. 1994. "Living Poor: Family Life Among Single Parent, African American Women." *Social Problems* 41(1):30-49.

Jaynes, Gerald, and Robin Williams, Jr. (Eds.). 1989. *A Common Destiny: Blacks and American Society*. Washington, DC: National Academy.

Kamin, Leon. 1974. *The Science and Politics of IQ*. New York: John Wiley.

Kazal-Thresher, Deborah. 1994. "Desegregation Goals and Educational Finance Reform: An Agenda for the Next Decade." *Educational Policy* 8(1):51-67.

Kluegel, James, and Eliot Smith. 1986. *Beliefs about Inequality: Americans' Views of What Is and What Ought to Be*. New York: Aldine de Gruyter.

Kornblum, William. 1974. *Blue Collar Community*. Chicago: University of Chicago.

Ladner, Joyce. 1971. *Tomorrow's Tomorrow: The Black Woman*. New York: Anchor.

Ladson-Billings, Gloria. 1990. "Like Lightning in a Bottle: Attempting to Capture the Pedagogical Excellence of Successful Teachers of Black Students." *The International Journal of Qualitative Studies in Education* 3:335-344.

Ladson-Billings, Gloria. 1992. "Reading Between the Lines and Beyond the Pages: A Culturally Relevant Approach to Literacy." *Theory into Practice* 31(4):312-320.

Landry, Bart. 1987. *The New Black Middle Class*. Berkeley, CA: University of California.

Landry, Bart. 1992. "The Enduring Dilemma of Race in America." Pp. 185-207 in *America at Century's End*, edited by Alan Wolfe. Berkeley, CA: University of California.

Longshore, Douglas, and Jeffrey Prager. 1985. "The Impact of School Desegregation." *Annual Review of Sociology* 11:75-91.

MacLeod, Jay. 1987. *Ain't No Makin' It*. Boulder, CO: Westview.

Mahard, Rita, and Robert Crain. 1983. "Research on Minority Achievement in Desegregated Schools." Pp. 103-125 in *The Consequences of School Desegregation*, edited by Christine Rossell and Willis Hawley.

Massey, Douglas, and Nancy Denton. 1993. *American Apartheid: Segregation and the Making of the Underclass*. Cambridge, MA: Harvard University Press.

Mehan, Hugh. 1979. *Learning Lessons*. Cambridge, MA: Harvard University Press.

Mehan, Hugh. 1992. "Understanding Inequality in Schools: The Contribution of Interpretive Studies." *Sociology of Education* 65(1):1-20.

Meier, Kenneth, Joseph Stewart, Jr., and Robert England. 1989. *Race, Class and Education: The Politics of Second Generation Discrimination*. Madison, WI: University of Wisconsin.

Mickelson, Roslyn. 1990. "The Attitude-Achievement Paradox Among Black Adolescents." *Sociology of Education* 63(1):44-61.

Myrdal, Gunnar. 1944. *An American Dilemma: The Negro Problem and Modern Democracy*. New York: Harper and Row.

Nagel, Joane. 1994. "Constructing Ethnicity: Creating and Recreating Ethnic Identity and Culture." *Social Problems* 41(1):152-176.

National Center for Education Statistics. 1993. *Digest of Education Statistics*. Washington, DC: U.S. Department of Education.

Natriello, Gary, Aaron Pallas, and Carolyn Riehl. 1993. *Executive Summary of Research Report: Matching School Resources and Student Needs: Scheduling and Assignment Problems in High Schools Serving At-Risk Youth*. New York: Teachers College.

Oakes, Jeannie. 1990. *Multiplying Inequalities: The Effects of Race, Social Class and Tracking on Opportunities to Learn Math and Science*. Santa Monica, CA: Rand.

Ogbu, John. 1978. *Minority Education and Caste: The American System in Cross-Cultural Perspective*. New York: Academic.

Ogbu, John. 1992. "Understanding Cultural Diversity and Learning." *Educational Researcher* 21(8):5-14, 24.

Okamura, Jonathan. 1981. "Situational Ethnicity." *Ethnic and Racial Studies* 4(4):452-465.

Omi, Michael, and Howard Winant. 1994. *Racial Formation in the United States: From the 1960s to the 1990s* (second edition). New York: Routledge.

Orfield, Gary. 1993. *The Growth of Segregation in American Schools: Changing Patterns of Separation and Poverty Since 1968*. Alexandria, VA: National School Boards Association.

Pallas, Aaron, Doris Entwisle, Karl Alexander, and M. Francis Stluka. 1994. "Ability-Group Effects: Instructional, Social or Institutional?" *Sociology of Education* 67(1):27-46.

Persell, Caroline, Kevin Dougherty, and Harold Wenglinsky. July 1993. "Equity and Diversity in American Education." Report from Round Table #1 of O.E.R.I. Conference on Equity and Excellence in Education: The Policy Uses of Sociology. Washington, DC.

Peshkin, Alan. 1991. *The Color of Strangers, The Color of Friends: The Play of Ethnicity in School and Community*. Chicago: University of Chicago.

Pettigrew, Thomas. 1986. "The Intergroup Contact Hypothesis Reconsidered." Pp. 169-195 in *Contact and Conflict in Intergroup Encounters*, edited by Miles Hewstone and Rupert Brown. Oxford, England: Basil Blackwell.

Phelan, Patricia, Ann Davidson, and Hank Yu. 1993. "Students' Multiple Worlds: Navigating the Borders of Family, Peer and School Cultures." Pp. 52-88 in *Renegotiating Cultural Diversity in American Schools*, edited by Patricia Phelan and Ann Davidson. New York: Teachers College.

Piestrup, Ann. 1973. *Black Dialect Interference and Accommodation of Reading Instruction in the First Grade* (monograph of the Language Behavior Research Laboratory). Berkeley, CA: University of California.

Powell, Arthur, Eleanor Farrar, and David Cohen. 1985. *The Shopping Mall High School: Winners and Losers in the Educational Marketplace*. Boston: Houghton Mifflin.

Rivkin, Steven. 1994. "Residential Segregation and School Integration." *Sociology of Education* 67(4):279-292.

Rosen, Bernard. 1959. "Race, Ethnicity and the Achievement Syndrome." *American Sociological Review* 24(1):47-60.

Schofield, Janet. 1991. "School Desegregation and Intergroup Relations." *Review of Research in Education* 17:335-409.

Schofield, Janet. 1995. "Review of Research on School Desegregation's Impact on Elementary and Secondary School Students." Pp. 597-616 in *Handbook of Research on Multicultural Education*, edited by James Banks and Cherry Banks. New York: Macmillan.

Stack, Carol. 1974. *All Our Kin: Strategies for Survival in a Black Community*. New York: Harper and Row.

Thomas, Gail. 1987. "Black Students in U. S. Graduate and Professional Schools in the 1980s: A National and Institutional Assessment." *Harvard Educational Review* 57(3):261-282.

U.S. Government Accounting Office. 1993. *Student Testing: Current Extent and Expenditures, with Cost Estimates for National Examination*. Washington, DC: US GAO, Program Evaluation and Methodology Division.

Wax, Murray (Ed.) 1980. *When Schools Are Desegregated: Problems and Possibilities for Students, Educators, Parents and the Community*. New Brunswick, NJ: Transaction.

Wells, Amy, and Robert Crain. August, 1992. "Perpetuation Theory and the Long-Term Effects of School Desegregation." Paper presented at the annual meeting of the American Sociological Association. Pittsburgh, PA.

West, Cornel, 1993. *Race Matters*. Boston, MA: Beacon.

Wexler, Philip. 1992. *Becoming Somebody*. London, England: Falmer.

Wright, Lawrence. 1994. "One Drop of Blood." *The New Yorker* 70(July 25):46-55.

Zipp, John. 1994. "Government Employment and Black-White Earnings Inequality, 1980-1990." *Social Problems* 41(3):363-382.

CHAPTER 2

Education in a Multicultural Society

Bart Landry

In the early 1970s, white Americans by the millions rediscovered their ethnic roots, and champions of ethnicity like Michael Novak (1973) sang the paeans of the "unmeltable ethnics." In the ensuing decades we went from melting pot to ethnic society, and closet ethnics became hyphenated Americans: Italian-Americans, Irish-Americans, Polish-Americans. It was suddenly no longer un-American to admit or even to be proud of one's foreign, read *European*, origins.

THE FIRST MULTICULTURAL SOCIETY

Today, however, we face an even more difficult issue, whether we can accept and manage what *Time* magazine has called "the World's First Multicultural Society" (Special Issue, Fall 1993). What do they mean by a "multicultural society"? And if we are a multicultural society, how did we get that way and what will we be in the future? In the first place, we seem to be talking about something more than "ethnicity" as it was defined in the 1970s—people of different European national origins. For all their historical differences white ethnics, several generations removed from the old country, are not so different after all. And if they were the only inhabitants of this country, there would be little debate about the composition of the United States. But, that is not the case. African-Americans have long been a significant part of the population—especially in the South and Latinos—though fewer in number—have also been an identifiable group. Together, they constituted almost 13 percent of the U.S. population in 1950 and had increased to one out of five Americans by 1987. Still, we did not talk about a multicultural society in the past but were focused on the so-called "racial division" or spoke of "minorities."

Why the new terminology? To understand this we need to take a quick look at immigration trends over the past two hundred years.

There have been three distinct immigration waves in the history of the republic. The first, extending roughly between 1820 and 1890, brought immigrants mainly from England, Ireland, Scotland, and Germany (Figure 2.1). These northwestern Europeans, numbering some 15 million, joined a population of native-born Americans whose roots also led back to the same areas of Europe. Starting in the 1890s, they were joined by a new wave of immigrants coming from southern and eastern Europe (Figure 2.2). It was at the beginning of this period that Ellis Island (1890) was opened as a processing center for immigrants following the dedication of the Statue of Liberty in 1886. At the base of this statue was an inscription, part of the famous poem of Emma Lazarus, "The New Colossus," which read in part:

Give me your tired, your poor
Your huddled masses yearning to breathe free,
The wretched refuse of your teeming shore.
Send these, the homeless, tempest-tossed to me.
I lift my lamp beside the golden door!

In the peak decade of immigration during this period, 1901 to 1910, over 8 million new arrivals entered through Ellis Island, most of them from southeastern Europe. Though also Europeans, these southern Italians, Poles, Bohemians, and Russian Jews were sufficiently different linguistically and culturally from those who came before to cause concern. Forgetting their own immigrant origins and the sentiment expressed on the base of the Statue of Liberty, many native-born whites felt that the American way of life would be threatened by what some called a "mongrel and degenerate breed" of immigrants. The result was the first comprehensive immigration bill of 1921, which set very low quotas for all areas of the world except northwestern Europe. Under this discriminatory immigration act as amended in 1924, Germany received a quota of 51,227, Great Britain and Northern Ireland 34,000, Italy 3,800, Greece and Turkey 100 each, all of Asia 1,424, and all of Africa and Oceania 1,821.

With the volume of immigrants greatly diminished now, most immigrants continued to originate from northwestern Europe in the ensuing decades. It was not until 1965 that we begin to see a major shift in the composition of the newcomers. Most analysts agree that it was provisions of the 1965 immigration bill, particularly the

Figure 2.1. Legal Immigrants Admitted to the U.S. by Region: 1820-1890

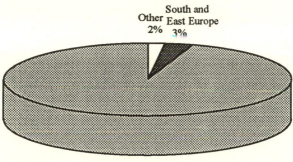

Other
2%

South and
East Europe
3%

North and West
Europe
95%

Figure 2.2. Legal Immigrants Admitted
to the U.S. by Region: 1890-1920

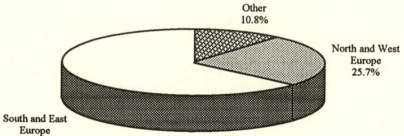

Other
10.8%

North and West
Europe
25.7%

South and East
Europe
63.5%

abolition of the quota system and the addition of the family reunification provision, that led to this change. By 1970, we find that about 40 percent of legal immigrants were coming from Latin America, 35 percent from Asia, and only 18 percent from all of Europe (Figure 2.3); by 1980, 35 percent arrived from Latin America, 48 percent from Asia, and only 11 percent from Europe. The volume of immigrants was once more high, rising from two or three million a decade in the period following the 1920s to over 6 million *legal* immigrants in the 1980s. The legal immigrant volume of the 1980s was second only to the peak decade of 8.8 million in the first decade of this century and probably was exceeded when you add illegal immigrants. In the early 1900s the immigrants were from southeastern Europe, despised but white. Now they were from Asia, Latin America, and other parts of the non-European world. This is indeed a new situation.

It has long been common for social scientists to call northwestern European immigrants of the nineteenth century, "old immigrants," and those from southeastern Europe at the turn of the century, "new immigrants." Scholars have not yet coined a term for this newest wave. Its impact on the demography of the population is unmistakable, however. In 1990 the U.S. population was 76 percent Anglo, 12 percent African American, 9 percent Latino, and 3 percent Asian (Figure 2.4). By the year 2050, it is projected that Anglos will be down to 52 percent of the population, African Americans will have increased to 16 percent, Latinos 22 percent, and Asians 10 percent (Figure 2.5). No longer is the ethnic debate of the 1970s relevant to this demographic profile. Just as we need a new term for this third wave of immigrants, so too, we need a new term for the society we have become. Multiculturalism will have to do for now.

But this is not the end of the story. Demographic projections for the last quarter of the twenty-first century—say somewhere around 2056—are for an Anglo population that is *49* percent or less of the total. To quote a 1990 *Time* magazine article: "By 2056, when someone born today will be 66 years old, the 'average' U.S. resident, as defined by Census statistics, will trace his or her descent to Africa, Asia, the Hispanic world, the Pacific Islands, Arabia—almost anywhere but white Europe" (April 9, 1990:31).

While this may be an overstatement, these demographics do point to a *new reality in American society* and also call for new terminology. In my course on American Society I have tended to use "ethnics" to refer to those groups of European origin and "ethnic minorities" for those from Third World countries.

**Figure 2.3. Legal Immigrants Admitted
to the U.S. by Region: 1971-1980**

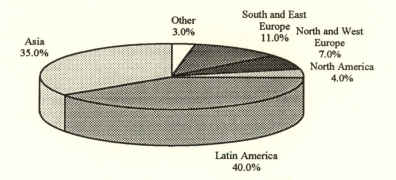

Figure 2.4. U.S. Racial and Ethnic Composition: 1990

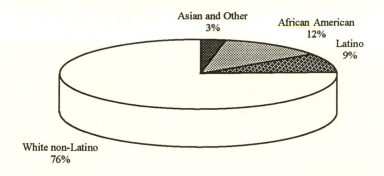

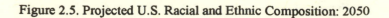

Figure 2.5. Projected U.S. Racial and Ethnic Composition: 2050

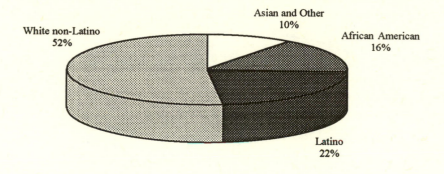

Asian and Other
10%

White non-Latino
52%

African American
16%

Latino
22%

White/non-white will hardly do anymore. There is too much diversity on both sides of the divide but especially among the "non-white" group. If those groups from Third World countries had been in a position to develop the nomenclature, they certainly would not have chosen the negative, "non" for themselves as in "non-white." And certainly, the term, "race" is obsolete and only persists through inertia.

What is so different about this "new" multicultural society? One is tempted to say everything; but that would be an exaggeration. So what *is* different about the United States prior to 1965 and after 1965? Consider composition. For all their historical differences, the German, the Englishman, the Irishman, or the Swede one generation removed from their roots blend together rather easily across the landscape of America. But three generations from their roots, the Chinese, the African, the Mexican, the Egyptian, or the Indian are in some real sense still Chinese, African, Mexican, Egyptian and Indian. Hyphenation does not have the same effect as among those of European origin. A hyphenated African-American or Korean cannot disappear into the crowd or melt into the suburban neighborhood landscape, nor can his or her children remain undetected in a classroom even if they should want to.

What else does it mean? Consider religion, one element of culture. For a long time there has been this mosque on Wisconsin Avenue in Washington, D.C. It blends in pretty well with the surrounding architecture. And you might pass it again and again and be only slightly curious about its appearance. But drive out New Hampshire Ave. into the suburbs today and you come across this imposing Buddhist temple. You are not on vacation in an exotic land or watching a travelogue. You are on your way home to suburbia, and it rises before you as unmistakably "different," even "strange" in this environment. A survey by Barry Kosmin and Seymour Lachman (1993) tells us that Buddhists make up .4 percent of the population, Muslims .5 percent, Hindus .2 percent. These might seem like small numbers. But Jews, according to the same survey, are only 1.8 percent of the population, Episcopalians and Anglicans, 1.7 percent, Pentecostals 1.8 percent and Presbyterians 2.8 percent. I asked my students what percentage of the U.S. population they thought was foreign born? And I received answers of 20 percent and even 30 percent. The percentage of foreign born today is actually only 8 percent. That seems very small, less than one in ten, nothing to get stirred up about. But tell that to the native-born residents of Miami which has a population that is 60 percent foreign born; to those in Union City, NJ, where the foreign-born population numbers 55 percent, or to those in Huntington Park, California and Santa Ana, California, where the foreign born are 59 percent and 51 percent, respectively, of the city's population.

Better still, visit schools in Los Angeles or Brooklyn where PTA meetings are conducted in three or four languages. Or consider the fact that in New York State, 40 percent of elementary— and secondary-school children belonged to an ethnic minority group in 1990 (*Time*, April 9, 1990) while in New York City school instruction is given in seven different languages (Kasinitz, 1987). In California, the school system is trying to adjust to the fact that slightly over half of elementary- and secondary-school children are not white. These are images of the new America. In our schools, we see already that the future is now.

DIVERSITY THEN AND NOW

Is this diversity really unprecedented? Well, yes and no. In the early twentieth century, two-thirds to three-fourths of public school children in northeastern and midwestern cities were either foreign born or the children of immigrants. Rather than Spanish, Chinese or Cambodian, they spoke Italian, Yiddish, Polish, or Russian. They lived in cities like Chicago and New York, where the foreign-born population in 1890 was about 41 percent, or Milwaukee, where it was 39 percent, or Lawrence, Massachusetts, where it was 47 percent. Teachers then as now struggled with the problem of educating students who spoke many different languages, as many as six in the same classroom.

We should not minimize the educational challenge that cultural and linguistic differences posed for early twentieth-century public school systems. Yet it is difficult not to conclude that the diversity of public school populations today is qualitatively and quantitatively different. There is, for one thing, a greater variety of cultures represented today, cultures that share little in common with European history. In the Washington, D.C., school system, students speak 127 different languages and dialects. In Fairfax County, Virginia, a Washington suburb, you can count 100 different languages and dialects among their public school students. Perhaps most significant of all, the *hues* of these immigrant children are black, yellow, and a variety of browns. In the 1890s and 1910s we set out to "Americanize" the newcomers and their children. Today, this approach is met with resistance. We have long debated the wisdom of integration versus assimilation when we saw diversity in black/white terms. We know now that diversity does not translate directly into integration. We see that clearly in city and suburban neighborhoods. We see it in our secondary schools and on college campuses. We are also aware that any mention of "assimilation" is met with shocking disbelief today, as an invitation to deny one's very identity. So where does that leave us?

MODELS OF THE FUTURE

Before going on to the implications of multiculturalism for education, let us briefly consider a number of models of our future society. There are the proponents of multiculturalism versus the advocates of what might be called the "new Americanization." The latter tend to see multiculturalism as "balkanization" of our society. They are afraid that its unity and cohesion will be undermined. Alan Bloom (1987) is one of the spokespersons for this group. Of multiculturalism, Bloom says: "Obviously, the future of America can't be sustained if people keep only to their own ways and remain perpetual outsiders. The society has got to turn them into Americans. There are natural fears that today's immigrants may be too much of a cultural stretch for a nation based on Western values" (*Time*, April 9, 1990). Or hear Norman Podhoretz, editor of *Commentary*, who wrote: "A lot of people are trying to undermine the foundations of the American experience and are pushing toward a more Balkanized society. I think that would be a disaster, not only because it would destroy a precious social inheritance but also because it would lead to enormous unrest, even violence" (*Time*, April 9, 1990). Then there is the *New York Times* editorial that read: "There is a limit to our powers of assimilation, and when it is exceeded the country suffers from something very like indigestion" (*Time*, Fall 1993). That quote from a *New York Times* editorial comes from an issue in May 1880, a decade when 72 percent of immigrants were still coming from northwestern Europe. How similar is the ring of these quotes from 1880 and 1990, a hundred years apart. It is from this group that calls for laws establishing English as the official language come today. For Bloom and other proponents of the new Americanization, American culture is a given, and must not be tampered with. Immigration and multiculturalism are seen as threats to national cohesion.

Those who favor multiculturalism see it as an enrichment of our society, or at least as no threat. Thomas Bender, a historian at New York University, argues that the cultural center should be "the ever changing outcome of a continuing contest among social groups and ideas for the power to define public culture" (*Time*, April 9, 1990). Julian Simon of the University of Maryland, who has done much research on immigrants, believes that: "The life and institutions here shape immigrants and not vice versa. This business about immigrants changing our institutions and our basic ways of life is hogwash. It's nativist scare talk" (*Time*, April 9, 1990).

And who are these nativists? Throughout the nineteenth century there were those who saw immigrants as a threat to American society. They agitated against them in the press, took violent action sometimes and won their supreme victory in the immigration bill of 1921. That legislation capped their earlier victory in 1884 when Congress passed the first immigration bill limiting access of a particular group. It was called the Chinese Exclusion Act and barred Chinese workmen from immigrating to the United States for the next 10 years. It was subsequently twice renewed. They and other Asians were also denied the right of citizenship, a prohibition that lasted until 1943, when China became an ally of the United States in the Second World War. The 1921 immigration act went even further. It set quotas which discriminated against those nations that were viewed as "undesirables," those from southeastern Europe and all of the Third World. Today, many are again questioning the wisdom of immigration. A recent *Time*/CNN telephone poll in September 1993 found 73 percent of respondents in favor of strictly limiting immigration and only 24 percent believing that we should keep the doors open to immigration (*Time*, Fall 1993).

From a political point of view, what we are becoming may lie somewhere between Belgium and the Old South. Belgium is divided geographically between French-speaking Belgians and Flemish-speaking Belgians. This is not the same as ethnic or ethnic-minority neighborhoods. The geographical division of Belgium into these two linguistic-ethnic groups is recognized by law. Sociologist Milton Gordon (1981) calls this "corporate pluralism." Under corporate pluralism, the government gives legal recognition to an ethnic group's identity and subscribes to *group* rights. In addition, as in Belgium, there are sometimes territorial divisions. Seats in national legislatures are usually based on proportional represen- tation of the population. This system sees further value in cultural and linguistic diversity and acts to preserve it.

The system of the Old South, on the other hand, was discriminatory in principle and legal fact. One group was denied rights held by another. The former's culture was viewed as valueless and inferior. Lying somewhere between these two patterns is what Gordon calls "liberal pluralism." Liberal pluralism gives legal recognition to the existence and rights of *individuals* rather than groups. Individuals can, if they wish, band together voluntarily, but cannot lay legal claim to any part of the national territory, including neighborhoods. While not giving legal recognition to group cultures and identities, individuals under liberal pluralism have the legal right to preserve their cultural heritage or to jettison it if they choose. They are neither rewarded nor punished for their choice.

Milton Gordon thinks that we are faced with the choice of deciding which form of pluralism we want in the United States today, corporate or liberal. Multiculturalism may actually be a new model that is drawing from both corporate and liberal pluralism. Gordon's views would appear to account for some of the occurrences today. From this point of view, for instance, those who call for laws making English the official language can be seen as attempting a preemptive strike on the multiculturalists whom they fear are moving the country toward corporate pluralism. From their perspective, America should remain focused on the individual and ethnic and ethnic minority groups should not be recognized or encouraged to maintain their unique identities. They should Americanize and assimilate.

What is the future of American society, then; corporate pluralism, liberal pluralism, a new Americanization, multiculturalism or something else? The cover of the 1993 special *Time* magazine issue featured a picture of a woman. Brown skinned with dark hair, she could have come from any number of Third World countries. She was, in fact, created on a computer out of various groups already in the society, to represent the possible future face of America. She was 15 percent Anglo-Saxon, 17.5 percent Middle Eastern, 17.5 percent African, 7.5 percent Asian, 35 percent Southern European and 7.5 percent Latino. The creator of this "new Eve" was Kin Wah Lam, himself an Asian computer specialist. As the image of the woman began to appear on the computer screen, one *Time* staff member remarked: "It really breaks my heart that she doesn't exist." This is what some have referred to as "the browning of America," a statement that strikes fear in the hearts of some and rejoicing among others. Is this the ultimate victory of multiculturalism? It is certainly not what we think of as assimilation. Assimilation involves a minority group assuming the culture of the preexisting majority group. This is something for which we do not yet have a name, unless its name is multiculturalism. Should we decide to choose multiculturalism, and the arguments in its favor are powerful, how will we institutionalize it? Are we, in fact, prepared historically and culturally for this challenge?

THE HISTORICAL CHALLENGE OF DIVERSITY

Writing about the viability of white ethnicity in the United States, Stephen Steinberg (1989) suggests that proponents of ethnicity have largely ignored "the essentially negative basis on which pluralism developed historically," a history of "conquest," "slavery," and "exploitation of foreign labor." From the very beginning, religious intolerance and national rivalries were commonplace within the colonies, transferred from a fractious Europe to these shores. Before, and even after the Revolution, many of the revered "fathers" of American democracy took a dim view of the diverse groups entering the society through immigration.

Benjamin Franklin, Thomas Jefferson, Alexander Hamilton, and even George Washington repeatedly questioned the wisdom of further immigration. "Why should the Palatine boors be suffered to swarm into our settlements ....," wrote Franklin in 1751, and "Why should Pennsylvania, founded by the English, become a colony of aliens, who will shortly be so numerous as to Germanize us, instead of our Anglifying them ...?" (Steinberg, 1989:11) Writing shortly after the Revolution, Thomas Jefferson also opposed further immigration, which he clearly viewed as a danger to the type of society that was developing. Of these immigrants, he wrote:

> In proportion to their numbers, they will share with us the legislation. They will infuse into it their spirit, warp and bias its directions, and render it a heterogeneous, incoherent, distracted mass (Steinberg, 1989:16).

It is not surprising, then, that from the very beginning an initial harmonious relationship of white settlers with Native Americans soon gave way to open warfare and a landgrab that rivaled the most notorious in human history. To rationalize the obvious injustice, the colonists developed a strategy of justification that became a pattern when later enslaving Africans in the South and Mexican-Americans in the Southwest.

As Steinberg notes, in the case of Native Americans, eviction from their lands was premised upon the principle that "the soil was destined to be tilled." Added to this presumption was the growing view of Native Americans as uncivilized savages. Theodore Roosevelt was to later combine both views when reflecting on this experience in *The Winning of the West*, writing that "the settler and pioneer have at bottom had justice on their side; this great continent could not have been kept as nothing but a game preserve for squalid savages" (Steinberg, 1989:22).

The principle of "Manifest destiny" became the ideological framework for further expansion and the annexation of Mexican territory after a war was deliberately provoked by the United States in 1846. Specific justifications for this action were carbon copies of those used for defrauding Native Americans. Mexicans, also, were said to be "a degenerate and backward people who wasted land and resources," and in the words of one politician in 1859, "no nation had the right to hold soil, virgin and rich, yet unproducing ...." (Steinberg, 1989:22).

Running contemporaneously with the despoliation of Native Americans and Mexicans was the experience and justification of slavery that was to sink deep into the psyche and culture of white Americans and to continue to pollute the American Experience. Slave holders took the lead in justifying what one historian has called "the peculiar institution" (Stampp, 1956). Justifications ran from the alleged inferiority of slaves to the *benefits* slavery offered for an inferior race. Both arguments can be seen combined in the famous "mudsill" speech given in the U.S. Senate in 1858 by James Hammond, a planter and senator from South Carolina:

In all social systems there must be a class to do the menial duties, to perform the drudgery of life. That is a class requiring but a low order of intellect and but little skill. Its requisites are vigor, docility, fidelity. Such a class you must have .... It constitutes the very mud-sill of society .... Fortunately for the South we have found a race adapted to that purpose to her hand .... We do not think that whites should be slaves either by law or necessity. Our slaves are black, of another, inferior race. The *status* in which we have placed them is an elevation. They are elevated from the condition in which God first created them by being made our slaves (Frederickson, 1988:23).

We might dismiss such racism as the rationalization of self-interested planters attempting to preserve the economic advantage afforded them by the slave system were it not for the continuation of such views long after emancipation. There was neither economic nor psychological gain for the negative stereotypes offered by Howard Odum in his doctoral dissertation at Ivy League Columbia University in 1910. Odum, who was to later become a prominent sociologist, wrote:

The Negro has little home conscience or love of home, no local attachments of the better sort .... He has no pride of ancestry, and he is not influenced by the lives of great men .... He has little conception of the meaning of virtue, truth, honor, manhood, integrity .... He does not know the value of his word or the meaning of words in general .... Their moral natures are miserably perverted (Gutman, 1976).

Such views are echoed in negative stereotypes of blacks that whites have continued to hold throughout this century (Jaynes & Williams, 1989). While public opinion polls appear to document some decline in these negative attitudes over time, a recent *Washington Post* article summarized a current poll in the following words:

A majority of whites questioned in a nationwide survey said they believe blacks and Hispanics are likely to prefer welfare to hard work and tend to be lazier than whites, more prone to violence, less intelligent and less patriotic (January 9, 1991:A1).

The article went on to cite statistics from the National Opinion Research Center (NORC) poll supporting the above statement: "62 percent [of whites] said blacks are more likely to be lazy," "53 percent said they [blacks] are less intelligent," "50 percent thought them [Hispanics] to be violence-prone." While few whites today might actually affirm their agreement with Odum's statement, results from the NORC poll suggests that deep down a majority of whites have not moved far from Odum's position. The racism expressed by Odum in 1910 lives on in the culture and continues to impede efforts at genuine multicultural education, since one of the prerequisites of success is mutual respect for the members and cultures of other ethnic groups.

Because of these stereotypes, perhaps, recent research reveals that a large percentage of whites also continue to resist close interaction with blacks in neighborhoods, schools, and social settings. One such study (Massey & Denton, 1993) revealed that blacks and whites continue to be almost as residentially separate today as 20 or 30 years ago. Many whites are also prone to say that blacks have come far enough or are trying to go too fast today. In view of this past, we have to ask ourselves whether our history and the culture which emerged out of it preclude success in our effort to build a viable multicultural society.

WHOSE HEROES? COLUMBUS OR GANDHI?
It should not be surprising that education is seen by many as at the very heart and soul of this debate. Let us return again to the early

twentieth century for a parallel. As immigrant children from southeastern Europe poured into the schools of urban America, educators were struggling with the task of extending compulsory schooling to the secondary level. As difficult a task as this might have been for a school population of native-born Americans, it was made doubly difficult in the face of millions of new arrivals. Between 1880 and 1918 enrollment across the nation increased by over 700 percent. To accommodate the growth, "an average of more than one new high school was built for each day of each year between 1890 and 1918" (Oakes, 1985:19).

In the United States, we often think of education as the great equalizer. No matter what your class background, schooling is the supreme escalator. It offers opportunity to all to scale the heights, as long as they work hard and possess the right attitudes and aptitudes. There are those, however, who dispute this view of American education, arguing instead that it was never intended to give equal opportunity to all. Rather, they argue, education was, from the beginning of our secondary school system, intended to meet the labor demands of the economy and the socializing function of Americanization (Bowles & Gintis, 1976).

Around the turn of the century, the 1890s to 1920s, a great debate was raging among American educators on the shape of the expanding secondary school system. On one side was Charles Eliot, president of Harvard University and chair of the Committee of Ten on Secondary Studies of the National Education Association; on the other were the Social Darwinists represented by the psychologist G. Stanley Hall. In their report, Eliot and the Committee of Ten saw secondary education as preparation neither for the workforce nor for college but for *life*. The curriculum recommended would serve as the vehicle for producing an educated person, regardless of future plans. Intrinsic to their approach was the belief in the *educability of all students* regardless of class background or ethnic origin. To quote Eliot directly:

> It is a curious fact that we Americans habitually underestimate the capacity of pupils at almost every stage of education from the primary school through the university .... It seems to me probable that the proportion of grammar school children incapable of pursuing geometry, algebra, and a foreign language would turn out to be much smaller than we now imagine (Oakes, 1985:18).

According to Jeannie Oakes, Eliot's position "reflected the ideals of American schooling over the previous eighty years—the notion that from common and equal educational experiences would come an intelligent American citizenry" (Oakes, 1985:21). Unfortunately, not all shared Eliot's faith in the student. Fundamental to the views of Social Darwinists was a belief in the innate differences of people of various cultures which they called "races." The southeastern European immigrants represented to them "races" that were lower on the evolutionary scale than the Anglo-Saxons of northwestern Europe. A member of the Boston school committee in 1889 expressed this view in the following words:

> Many of these children come from homes of vice and crime. In their blood are generations of iniquity .... They hate restraint or obedience to law. They know nothing of the feelings which are inherited by those who were born on our shores (Oakes, 1985:21).

Hall proposed an evolutionary developmental framework in child psychology which gave "scientific" plausibility to Social Darwinist thought. His views stressed individual differences, and ridiculed the Committee of Ten for ignoring "the great army of incapables," as he called those whom he believed were unqualified to master the basic secondary school curriculum. Echoing the same theme as Hall, another prominent educator, Ellwood Cubberly, wrote in 1909:

> These southern and eastern Europeans are of a very different type from the north Europeans who preceded them. Illiterate, docile, lacking in self-reliance and initiative, and not possessing the Anglo-Teutonic conceptions of law, order, and government, their coming has served to dilute tremendously our national stock, and to corrupt our civic life .... Everywhere these people tend to settle in groups or settlements, and to set up here their national manners, customs, and observances. Our task is to break up these groups or settlements, to assimilate and amalgamate these people as a part of our American race, and to implant in their children, so far as can be done, the Anglo-Saxon conception of righteousness, law and order, and popular government, and to awaken in them a reverence for our democratic institutions and for those things in our national life which we as a people hold to be of abiding worth (Oakes, 1985:25-26).

In the end, it was the Social Darwinists who won the educational battle and provided the pseudo-scientific justification for the schools to treat the children of various cultures and classes differently. These views were institutionalized in the secondary school curriculum through the device of tracking. Immigrant children, with their "inferior genes" and cultures, would have to be Americanized (read civilized) and sent into the factories for they were not capable of mastering material that prepared students for college. The children, particularly the *sons*, of native-born white middle-class families, would be placed in college preparatory tracks that would lead to higher education and the emerging world of white-collar office work. Tracking, despite clear evidence that it represents bad pedagogy, remains with us today and continues to sort students into streams that lead to factory or office.

THE BATTLE OVER MULTICULTURAL EDUCATION

We are once more in the midst of redefining the curriculum of our public schools. And again, the debate is being shaped by our reactions to immigrants. Though today there are few who would espouse the beliefs of nineteenth-century Social Darwinists in the biological inferiority of some ethnic groups, there are many who fall into the category that Stephen Steinberg (1989) calls the "new Darwinist." These are people who believe in the cultural inferiority and superiority of groups. "According to this perspective," he writes, "differences in social class position among ethnic groups in America are a product of cultural attributes that are endemic to the groups themselves" (Steinberg, 1989:79). Out of this approach comes the culture of poverty thesis. Blacks do not know how to defer gratification; Latinos are lazy, and Asians are industrious. In the eyes of many teachers and educators, then, ethnics and ethnic minorities do not meet on the same footing within the classroom. Some are *better* material with which to work, and we continue to advantageously track them. The cultures are not of equal value. The idea of schools creating a level playing field never occurs because it is never tried. It is never tried because educators today, like educators in the early twentieth century, do not believe it is possible.

Multiculturalism is a challenge to the new Darwinism. Teachers and educators are called upon to place *equal* value on the cultures of all groups and to celebrate them in the curriculum. From this perspective, Ralph Ellison's *The Invisible Man* is as much a classic as Mark Twain's *Tom Sawyer*, Gandhi and Nkrumah as great heroes as George Washington or Columbus, and we may have as much to learn from Confucius as from Plato or Aristotle.

As educators we are aware that education is more than the three Rs. Indispensable as they are, the three Rs must be combined with the nourishment of each child's inner being who needs to see himself or herself reflected positively in the curriculum. Early in this century, the social psychologist Charles Cooley developed a theory of identity that he called the "looking glass self." It is only through interaction with others, he argued, that we learn who we are. Their reactions to us are the looking glass through which we form our own self-image. This insight was summarized in the brief phrase: "Self and society are twin-born" (Cooley, 1902). We can apply this analogy to the school curriculum. Children should find themselves reflected in the texts and experiences of the curriculum and classroom. How they are represented in textbooks and in the eyes, words, and expressions of teachers and classmates help mold their conception of self. We can rephrase Cooley's maxim by saying,"Self and the society of the school are twin-born." If they are not even represented in learning materials, what image do ethnic minority children form of themselves? If they are represented in negative stereotypes, how much damage is inflicted on their self-image and egos?

Fortunately, some schools are beginning to respond positively and creatively to the challenge of ethnic and ethnic minority diversity in their classrooms. In the schools of Garden City, Kansas with a population of 24,600, immigrant children find themselves reflected in the classroom through the celebration of different national holidays "including Mexican Independence Day, the Laotian New Year and Vietnam's Tet" (*Time*, Fall 1993). And Haitian children who make up one-third of one class at New York City's P. S. 189 recognized themselves in a class project about Jean-Jacques Dessalines, "the slave who freed Haiti from France"(*Time*, Fall 1993). Some argue that the time needed to implement a multicultural curriculum will impede students' learning of basic skills in math, science, and English. But how can young students absorb the intricacies of negative numbers, of algebra and science if they do not have confidence in their own abilities, if they do not see respect in the eyes of their teachers but rather see doubt about their abilities or, worse, scorn and disdain for their working-class or ethnic minority status?

If we accept the premise (as many do) that a Eurocentric education is at best incomplete, that other events than the Magna Charta and the French Revolution have had profound effects on the course of history, that Impressionists did not corner the market on artistic imagination, that Plato, Locke, and Rousseau were not the only great social thinkers and that history is not coterminous with European and American events, then we have to ask ourselves what needs to be added to the curriculum of our schools to provide *all* children (ethnic and ethnic minority) with a sound education.

Evidence from schools that have developed a multicultural curriculum reveals both academic and social benefits. A program called REACH (Respecting Ethnic and Cultural Heritage) which was prepared for middle schools has led to a variety of tangible benefits including "a greater acceptance of differences among the peer group and a reduction in ethnic put-downs and jokes" and "a greater interest and motivation in learning, particularly among non-achieving students" (Howard, 1989).

Education is slow to change. I have observed this inertia first hand as a PTA president and vice-president over the past seven years. But the education curricula and approaches developed at the turn of the twentieth century were fundamentally flawed and continue to be fundamentally flawed. Now the challenge is even greater. As we move to develop national academic standards in various subject areas, we must also devise pedagogical approaches and teacher training to meet the needs of a truly multicultural school population. We cannot wait. The future is now.

REFERENCES

Bloom, Alan. 1987. *The Closing of the American Mind*. New York: Simon and Schuster.

Bowles, Samuel and Herbert Gintis. 1976. *Schooling in Capitalist America*. New York: Basic Books.

Cooley, Charles, 1902. *Human Nature and the Social Order*. New York: Scribner's.

Frederickson, George. 1988. *The Arrogance of Race*. Middletown, CT: Wesleyan University.

Gordon, Milton. 1981. "Models of Pluralism: The New American Dilemma." *Annals of the American Academy of Political and Social Science* 454:178-188.

Gutman, Herbert. 1976. *The Black Family in Slavery and Freedom 1750-1925*. New York: Vintage.

Howard, Gary. 1989. "Multicultural Education in Action." *Middle School Journal* 21(1):23-25.

Jaynes, Gerald, and Robin Williams (Eds). 1989. *A Common Destiny: Blacks and American Society*. Washington, DC: National Academy Press.

Kasinitz, Philip. 1987. "The City's 'New Immigrants': Cultural Snapshots--From Koreans to Caribbeans." *Dissent* 34(4):497-506.

Kosmin, Barry, and Seymour Lachman. 1993. *One Nation Under God: Religion in Contemporary American Society*. New York: Harmony.

Massey, Douglas, and Nancy Denton. 1993. *American Apartheid: Segregation and the Making of the Underclass*. Cambridge, MA: Harvard University.

Novak, Michael. 1973. *The Rise of Unmeltable Ethnics: Politics and Culture in the Seventies*. New York: Macmillan.

Oakes, Jeannie. 1985. *Keeping Track*. New Haven, CT: Yale University.

Stampp, Kenneth. 1956. *The Peculiar Institution*. New York: Knopf.

Steinberg, Stephen. 1989. *The Ethnic Myth: Race, Ethnicity, and Class in America* (2nd edition). Boston: Beacon.

Time. 1990. 135(15). April 9.

Time. 1993. 142(21). Fall special issue.

CHAPTER 3

Familial Predictors of Educational Attainment: Regional and Racial Variations

Aaron Thompson and Reid Luhman

INTRODUCTION

Thurgood Marshall's death in early 1993, just missing the fortieth anniversary of his historic victory in *Brown v. Board of Education*, closes one era of civil rights in the United States while inviting a reappraisal of equal opportunity in American education. Marshall's decades-long struggle with the "separate but equal" precedent of *Plessy v. Ferguson* overshadowed larger, more basic questions about the potential of African Americans in an institution dominated by European American traditions, values, and people. And if those questions were left unexplored on the road to *Brown*, it is not surprising that the larger issue of racial stratification and the structure of opportunity in the United States remained unexamined. Ironically, we have yet to see significant racial integration in American schools, but the larger questions of African American educational attainment and economic opportunity have received considerable research attention in recent years.

African American educational attainment has clearly improved since 1954, but the rate of that improvement has just as clearly decreased since the 1960s. By virtually any measure employed, the continuing gap between African American and European American educational attainment is unmistakable. In 1990, for example, the high school dropout rate (grades 10-12) was 3.8 percent for European Americans compared to 5.1 percent for African Americans (U.S. Bureau of the Census, 1992a). In that same year, among 24- to 25-year-olds, 90.4 percent of European Americans had completed high school compared to 82.2 percent of African American students (National Center for Education Statistics, 1992b). Turning to college enrollment rates of 1991, 41 percent of European American high school graduates entered college compared with 28.2 percent of African American high school graduates (National Center for Education Statistics, 1992a). Considering that a smaller percentage of African Americans graduate from high school, this lower college enrollment percentage is particularly troublesome.

The gap in postsecondary African American and European American student participation continues to widen after enrollment. In 1991, 54.9 percent of European American high school graduates (age 25-29) had completed one or more years of college compared with 42.5 percent of African American high school graduates. From that same cohort, the figures for those completing four or more years of college drop to 29.7 percent and 13.6 percent, respectively (National Center for Education Statistics, 1992b). We note similar figures in comparing postsecondary degrees awarded in the United States during 1989-1990. African American students received 7.9 percent of the associate degrees compared to 82.1 percent received by European American students. Of bachelor degrees, however, African Americans received only 5.8 percent compared to 84.3 percent awarded to European Americans. While percentages for both groups begin to drop for master's degrees and doctor's degrees (due to increasing numbers of non-resident aliens in the student population), African American students who attained the Ph.D. in 89-90 received only 3.0 percent of those awarded compared to 67.9 percent awarded to European Americans (National Center for Education Statistics, 1992a). In short, African American students in the United States can be expected to attain less than European American students *at every level* of education.

Statement of Purpose
Our intent in this paper is to examine an important subset of the explanations for differential educational attainment by focusing on the impact of family variables (parental income, occupational status, and education) as predictors of educational attainment for both European Americans and African Americans. The analysis presented explores the relative importance of those variables in predicting educational attainment with the following foci: (1)

What are the relative strengths of different family characteristics in predicting educational attainment? (2) For family characteristics that appear to be strong predictors, does the strength of that prediction vary (a) by race, (b) by region, and (c) by the ultimate level of education attained?

Before turning to the analysis, however, research on educational attainment must be placed in theoretical context. The continuing gap in educational attainment between African Americans and European Americans raises questions about the structure of opportunity in American society; who achieves upward mobility and do all those who are successful use the same ladder? These questions have generated two dominant models that focus respectively on "cultural deficiencies" within the African American population and structural barriers inherent in American racial stratification. Explanations of educational attainment tend to have their roots in these two dominant models.

REVIEW OF THE LITERATURE
The Structure of Opportunity in the United States
The more traditional models of economic opportunity stress social class variables (with a particular emphasis on education) as providing routes for status attainment (see Blau and Duncan, 1967). Models which assume an open opportunity structure limited only by individual achievement tend to bypass questions of racial discrimination while focusing attention on individual factors which affect that achievement. A classic model within this tradition is the "cultural deficit" perspective. Popular in the 1960s and yet again in the 1980s with interest in the "underclass," the cultural deficit approach stresses value and behavioral orientations that work at cross purposes with achievement in lower-class family structure and relationships (see Moynihan, 1965). Most notably, orientations toward immediate gratification and low educational aspirations are singled out for attention. With regard to the African American family, the growth of single-parent families coupled with public assistance availability offers ample ammunition for making a cultural argument concerning lack of African American educational attainment. As Baca Zinn (1989) points out, the family and the welfare system upon which it is dependent become the villains that conspire to program children for a life of poverty. If the opportunity structure is indeed open, failure to succeed must be located elsewhere than in the workings of that structure.

If we shift our focus to an alternative model that stresses the structural barriers of racial stratification, a different picture of the African American family structure emerges. Beginning around 1890 when African Americans moved into the industrialized work force, they entered at a different pace and level than European Americans (Thernstrom, 1964; Wilkinson, 1991). Lack of occupational opportunities, particularly for African American males, coupled with nonexistent community support systems weakened the family structure and forced women to become economically independent (Smith & Smith, 1986; Staples, 1987). The lack of participation in the labor force by African American males led women to see marriage more as a liability than as an economic advantage (McAdoo, 1986). As a result of these economic circumstances, the African American family has developed a predominantly female-headed structure (Wilson & Neckerman, 1987). Unlike the key role that divorce plays as a cause for poverty status among female-headed *European American* families (see Weitzman, 1985), there is growing evidence that the poverty status of female-headed African American families is endemic to the African American community, equally present among never married and divorced mothers. For the latter, poverty is as likely a major *cause* of the divorce as a product of it (Bane, 1986). In short, this alternative model explains the structure of the African American family more as the product of historical and economic discriminatory forces than as the creator of pathological decision making among its members. And if we focus our attention on structural barriers to African American success, both educationally and economically, there is considerable evidence to support this latter model.

The growing urbanization of the African American population during the twentieth century has occurred along with major changes in the U.S. economy involving (a) a growth in the tertiary sector at the expense of the secondary sector, (b) a decline of entry-level jobs for unskilled workers (with the exception of low-level service work in the tertiary sector), and (c) a geographical shift of most employment away from central cities (except for the higher level of the tertiary sector such as finance and civil service). The late entry of African Americans in the industrialized labor force coincided with fundamental changes in the structure of economic opportunity; employment opportunities for African American workers are both less plentiful in core economic sectors and more common in unstable and low-wage sectors. When diminished opportunities are augmented by various forms of racial discrimination, the result for African Americans is a fundamentally different opportunity structure than that offered European Americans.

At every level of educational attainment in the United States, European Americans achieve higher mean incomes than African Americans. In 1989, for example, the income gap between 25- to 34-year-old European and African Americans with sixteen years of education was approximately $8,000; in 1991, African Americans with sixteen or more years of education faced a 4.5 percent unemployment rate compared to a 2.9 percent rate for similarly educated European Americans (U.S. Bureau of the Census, 1991). While educational level and gender are both stronger predictors of income than race, the fact that racial discrimination persists, even among African Americans at the highest educational levels, suggests a less than open opportunity structure.

While the above statistics only begin to describe the impact of racial discrimination upon African American opportunity, they should certainly be sufficient to indicate that the African American route to opportunity is circuitous indeed. Blaming the family for its members' failure to achieve educational success begs the question of limited opportunity that occurs even when those members *are* successful within American educational institutions. And if that opportunity is limited within the American economic system as a whole, we should certainly not be surprised to find that limitation is reflected in the workings of educational institutions that produce workers for that economy. While we have seen that success in education alone does not produce economic equality for African Americans, it nevertheless does have a direct connection to the marketplace. As we turn now to examine the route to educational attainment for African Americans, the mixed research results that appear are perhaps best understood when the complexities of the African American opportunity structure and the impact of educational attainment within that structure are kept in mind.

Research on Educational Attainment
Given its importance for economic advancement, it is not altogether surprising that educational attainment has been linked in research with virtually every measurable variable in hopes of finessing a correlation worthy of mention. The plethora of data produced provides insights into this relationship; it also clouds the

issue due to its sheer volume and conflicting results (White, 1982). Since we are about to add to this body of work through a closer examination of an edge of the research territory, its import would be best appreciated following an aerial survey of the terrain.

Educational attainment research logically breaks down into two substantive areas. One area focuses on characteristics students bring with them upon entering educational institutions. These characteristics range from family and community characteristics (e.g., voluntary organizations present, family socioeconomic status, parental educational attainment, encouragement, and aspirations) to individual characteristics (e.g., self-esteem, parental status, peer group orientations). The other area focuses on educational institutions and the internal factors most closely linked with subsequent student attainment. Individual schools, for example, may or may not employ racially biased tracking, provide college-oriented courses to African American students, or provide appropriate role models among their faculty or administrators. Having logically separated these two research arenas, however, it should also be noted that much research thrives on their intersection, tracing, for example, the interplay of family environment, educational achievement test results, and educational institutional structure.

Family and Community Factors in Educational Attainment
Turning first to the area of family and community characteristics, considerable research has been devoted to the connection between family socioeconomic status (S.E.S.) and student attainment. In his remarkable overview of some of this research, White (1982) concludes that the average correlation between S.E.S. and educational attainment is about .22 but that slight alterations in research procedure and (interestingly) the form or type of publications in which research appears affect this correlation greatly. Thomas et al. (1979) report that S.E.S. has a positive relationship with educational credentials (such as test results); however, this is truer for European American students than African American. They also note that S.E.S. has little effect on the institutional class ranking of students. Wilson-Sadberry et al. (1991) note a connection between family S.E.S. and African American educational attainment but find (through multiple regression) that factors such as educational attitudes and attendance plans explain more of the variance.

S.E.S., as commonly constructed for research, combines such easily ascertained variables as family income, parent's educational level and occupational prestige (see White, 1982). While such a combination seems to give us an easy operationalization of social class, the ease of access to that concept should make the self-critical researcher suspicious. Although the components of S.E.S. correlate highly with one another on a regular basis, those same components clearly play different roles in predicting the educational attainment of offspring. Porter (1974), for example, notes only a small correlation between the family head's occupation and educational attainment; in addition, the variable had no direct effect in multiple regression.

Other family characteristics have also been frequently studied. Blau (1981) finds a general connection between educational attainment and family involvement with religious and other voluntary organizations. Brown (1991) concludes this is also true for African Americans with regard to religious organization involvement although it explains only 10 percent of the variance. Wilson-Sadberry et al.'s (1991) findings concerning positive parental educational attitudes and children's attainment are corroborated by Watts and Watts (1991). [African American parents have equally high educational aspirations for their children as do European American parents (see Solorzano, 1992).] Research on the effects of single-parent families within the African American community has found no relation between father absence and educational attainment (Wasserman, 1972; Watts & Watts, 1991). Johnson (1992) widens the perspective on the single-parent family, noting that the degree of control that parents feel they have over their environment affects their children's achievement far more than the number of parents in the household. When the students themselves are parents, however, there is a negative effect on attainment (Wilson & Allen, 1987). In addition, Hare (1987) points out that parenthood is often perceived as an official entrance to adult status in the African American community, thereby carrying positive values in the eyes of teenagers. The implication of this finding is that European American teenagers can achieve adult status through a wider choice of means. Finally, family income is a factor in attainment, particularly at the post-secondary level. Not surprisingly, poverty keeps African American students out of colleges and, when enrolled, makes them more likely to be enrolled in two-year institutions (DeMott, 1991; Wilson-Sadberry et al., 1991).

Individual Student Characteristics and Educational Attainment
The characteristics of individual students have also received considerable attention, particularly with regard to psychological and social psychological variables. Brookover & Schneider (1975) report that a student's sense of futility regarding educational expectations explains 45 percent of the variance of educational attainment even when controlling for race and S.E.S. Hare (1987) continues in this tradition, noting that student self-esteem is identical in African American and European American students when S.E.S. is held constant but that African American students have a noticeably lower *school* connected self-esteem than European American students at similar S.E.S. levels. He also contends that African American students are more peer oriented and simultaneously less school oriented than European American students. In a similar vein, Clark (1991) singles out African American students with "oppositional social identities" that, she maintains, hinder educational attainment. Part of this negative attitude, as suggested by many researchers, is that African American students perceive educational success as requiring and/or indicating "acting white," perceived as mutually exclusive of maintaining solidarity with the African American community (see Feagin, 1992; Fordham and Ogbu, 1986; Hood, 1992; Ogbu 1988). If, as Hare suggests, African American students are more peer-oriented than European American students, such values would understandably be reinforced.

Student Characteristics and Institutional Structure
If we now move into the common research ground of the intersection of student characteristics and institutional structure, many of the above observations assume added significance in their role of affecting educational attainment. For example, African American students who view educational success as "acting white" are often responding quite logically to the educational world that confronts them. In both secondary and postsecondary schools, the absence of African American role models on the faculties can lead African American students to perceive academic success as unattainable for them (see Gilbert & Gay, 1985; Thompson, 1992). Clark (1991), in particular, argues for the presence of role models

and mentors for African American students to counteract the negative attitudes African American students bring with them to school.

If African American students do not identify with their teachers, what problems do they face identifying with student peers? We have already noted the apparent contradiction within the African American community between peer orientation and school orientation. Both this problem and the lack of role models discussed above would seem to be either eased or eliminated by black colleges; indeed, black colleges do have a record of higher attainment among students with fewer apparent college preparatory skills than do largely dominant group institutions (Garibaldi, 1991). Pascarella (1985) finds that black colleges alone are not significant for facilitating attainment but that the situations they foster, high levels of student social and academic integration within the school setting, are highly related to attainment. When dominant group institutions foster these experiences for African American students, attainment is equally high. In this latter situation, where African American students are a clear numerical minority, a critical factor is that African American students not perceive themselves to be token representatives of their group, unacceptable to dominant group students and restricted by those same students from expressing their cultural distinctiveness (Kanter, 1977).

The Structure of Educational Institutions
Moving now to research most clearly related to the structure of American educational institutions, a dominant theme is that decisions made within those institutions are based on assumptions detrimental to African American educational attainment. In particular, the practice of ability and achievement testing of students appears more clearly geared to dominant-group students than minority students and, even with the former group, the predictive power is not always clear. Hood (1992) reviews a number of studies on college entrance examinations that conclude that those tests provide some level of predictive power for European American attainment but not for African Americans. The latter group's success is more closely related to behaviors that focus on long-term behaviors such as perseverance. Wilson and Allen (1987) offer results suggesting that knowledgeable and committed high school counselors coupled with a good, college-focused high school curriculum predict African American success in postsecondary education. Other studies have noted the predictive power of high

school grades (or class standing) among African American students for future attainment (Hood, 1992; Slaughter & Epps, 1987). The irony of these results is that ability and achievement tests, which have less predictive power with African American students anyway, are often used to place those students in the lower (ranks) of "tracking" systems in high schools, denying them the very high school experiences shown by research to predict postsecondary attainment (Wilson-Sadberry et al., 1991).

The above overly brief and certainly overly simplified review at the least focuses attention on the complex nature of African American educational attainment. Perhaps most importantly, it makes clear that *factors that produce educational success for dominant group students cannot be depended upon to create similar results for minority students.* In tracing these differences, even the most closely focused social psychological studies of African American students must be viewed in light of the more general structure of opportunity in American society and its racial components. As we noted earlier, the economic gains typically available through increased education are muted for African Americans due to the employment discrimination they face. As the advantages of education lessen, so presumably would the motivation of students to achieve. And if this is indeed true of African American students, we would expect to find their ultimate achievement less clearly tied to educationally related skills available within the family environment.

RESEARCH QUESTIONS

The research reviewed above covers a remarkable amount of territory but contains two major shortcomings relative to African American educational attainment. First, little attention is paid to comparing primary and secondary with postsecondary educational attainment. Most research either combines them or focuses on one or the other. As suggested by the more focused research, very different factors appear as predictors of attainment at different levels of education for both African American and European American students. A comparison by level would provide us with a clearer view of how those predictors change at different levels *within* each racial group.

A second shortcoming of available research concerns lack of attention to historical and demographic differences between the African American and European American populations. Part of the differing structures of opportunity for these groups, as noted

72   THOMPSON AND LUHMAN

earlier, can be attributed to the relatively late migration of African Americans to the industrial urban north. Changes in the economy along with their urban location hinder locating entry-level jobs and gaining access to adequate education at all levels. Of equal importance, however, is the persistent concentration of the African American population in the South where levels of industrialization and educational attainment are both distinctively low. Any comparison of educational attainment by race must take region into account to control for the disproportionate residence of African Americans in the South.

The research presented here addresses these questions by comparing the importance of family characteristics by race on educational attainment with a particular focus on (a) primary and secondary attainment vs. postsecondary attainment, and (b) regional differences, allowing us to control the impact of the large percentage of the African American population at the low educational levels characteristic of the South. Our two hypotheses are:

1. Family variables are less important predictors of postsecondary educational attainment than of primary and secondary educational attainment. We expect this to be true for both European Americans and African Americans because older students are less closely connected to their family of origin while simultaneously more influenced by a wider variety of other factors such as income, residence, their own marital status and other demands of adulthood. It follows that family variables will be more important in the American South where a higher percentage of the student population abandons its efforts short of postsecondary education.

2. Family variables will be stronger predictors of educational attainment for European Americans than for African Americans at *all* levels of education. This second hypothesis stems from the minority status and differing structure of opportunity faced by African Americans. Research reviewed earlier suggests that family background advantages for these students will be muted at the lower levels by factors such as school quality and bias coupled with community and peer group influences. At postsecondary levels, educational institutional factors will be joined by the demands of adulthood noted above. In addition, African American adults understand that postsecondary educational success does not automatically allay the impact of employment discrimination.

METHODS
Sample
The sample for this research was drawn from the national General Social Surveys (GSS) data set from the years 1972-1990. The GSS is one of the most widely used data sets in the social sciences that provides a random sample of Americans responding to the same questions year after year. A cumulative data set was created which merged seventeen yearly surveys into a single file (N=26,265). With the exception of a few years in which African Americans were oversampled (e.g., 1982), the relatively small numbers of African Americans in each yearly sample (which were further diminished due to the deletion of missing items) made the use of this larger merged data set of particular importance for this research. The overall sample was reduced to two regions of the eastern United States that allowed a comparison between the traditional agricultural southern states and old industrial northeastern states. These two regions not only contain the majority of the African American population but also contain significant differences in overall educational levels. The southern region states include Mississippi, Alabama, Georgia, Florida, South Carolina, North Carolina, Tennessee, Kentucky, West Virginia and Virginia. The northern region states include Maine, New Hampshire, Vermont, Massachusetts, Rhode Island, Connecticut, New York, New Jersey, Maryland, Delaware, Pennsylvania, Ohio, Michigan, Indiana, Illinois and Wisconsin.

Dependent Variable
The dependent variable examined in this analysis is the respondent's educational attainment. Each respondent to the GSS was asked to list the highest year of attainment, ranging from 1-12 in primary and secondary education or 1-8 years of post-secondary education. This response produced a continuous variable that ranged from 0 to 20. The variable was used in that form in multiple regression analysis and in a more simplified ordinal form (0-7;8-11;12;13-15;16;17+ years) for crosstab analysis.

Independent Variables
Four family history variables were selected from the GSS to be utilized as predictors of educational attainment. These variables included (a) the prestige of the respondent's father's occupation at the time the respondent was 16 years old, (b) the educational attainment level of the respondent's father, (c) the educational

level of the respondent's mother, and (d) the income of the respondent's family at the time the respondent was 16 years old. Father's occupational prestige was measured by asking the respondent to select a three-digit code that best fit his or her father's occupation. These codes were derived from the occupation code classifications distributed by the U.S. Bureau of the Census in 1970. The educational attainment of the respondent's parents was measured in the same form as the respondent's educational attainment. The final variable, family income when the respondent was 16 years old, was created by asking each respondent to evaluate his or her family's income level on a five-item ordinal scale ranging from 1 (far below average) to 5 (far above average).

Other variables used in this analysis acted as control variables. The region of the country in which the respondent lived at age 16 was used to create the two composite regional variables described above. A second variable, race, was also used to separate the sample into racial groups for purposes of comparison.

Analysis and Results

The effect of the four independent variables on the dependent variable was assessed through multiple regression analysis. Multiple regression was selected for this purpose because it analyzes the association between several independent variables and one dependent variable simultaneously, showing the relative impact of each independent variable on variation in the dependent variable. Three models were compared. The first model consisted of parallel multiple regression analyses in which the sample was separated by race. The second and third models were identical to the first except that the sample was further divided into northern and southern regions.

The independent variables used in this analysis presented a problem of multicollinearity. This occurs when two or more independent variables are highly associated with each other. If two highly associated variables are found to predict variation in the dependent variable, it is difficult to know whether one or both are important as predictors. Before the regression was conducted, a test of collinearity for the variables was performed. As expected, most were intercorrelated. As a result, the independent variables were analyzed simultaneously to reduce confusion in interpreting the models. Our interpretation is necessarily limited to each model's explanatory power (the R square) and not to separate partial coefficients (or betas). For example, Tables 3.1 through 3.3 show

Table 3.1
Multiple Regression of Family History Variables with Education by Race

Family History Variables	European Americans (N=15,531)		African Americans (N=1,725)	
	B's (Betas)	Mean (SD)	B's (Betas)	Mean (SD)
Father's Prestige	.022 (.088***)	40.29 (12.39)	-.018 (-.061**)	33.87 (12.27)
Father's Education	.180 (.245)	9.86 (4.26)	.214 (.269***)	.02 (4.45)
Mother's Education	.244 (.286***)	10.11 (3.66)	.302 (.340***)	9.05 (3.99)
Family Income at Age 16	.014 (.004)	2.90 (.97)	.050 (.017)	.48 (1.18)
Respondent's Education		12.26 (3.13)		11.04 (3.54)
R Square		.29		.31

F=1548.02 Sig F=.0000 F=190.07 Sig F=.0000
[*P < .05 **P < .01 ***P < .001]

high betas for both mother's and father's education. It is hard to know, however, which is more important since people typically marry others of similar education.

Table 3.1 includes the means, standard deviations, and multiple regression analysis of the variables used in the model for the entire sample. The independent variables used in the first model were significant predictors for the European American respondent's educational attainment (F=1548.02, p < .001) and for the African American respondent's educational attainment (F=190.07, p < .001). The relatively large size of this sample makes those levels of significance not particularly noteworthy. Our analysis will focus more attention on fluctuations in the percent of variance explained in various models. The full model presented here offered little difference between the two groups, explaining approximately 30 percent of the variance for each group. We can therefore conclude that family background has a sizable impact on educational attainment but that an additional 70 percent of that attainment must be explained by other factors.

Table 3.2 includes the means, standard deviations and multiple regression analysis of the variables used in the model for the southern region sample. The same independent variables used in the first model were significant predictors for European American respondent's educational attainment (F=442.34, p < .001) and for African American respondent's educational attainment (F=97.47, p < .001). Explained variance, as indicated in the tables, was 37 percent and 32 percent, respectively. While the southern region is more extreme than the overall sample in almost every way, it clearly parallels that overall sample, again showing little difference in the importance of various predictors and little difference between the two racial groups.

Table 3.3 includes the means, standard deviations, and multiple regression analysis of the variables used in the model for the northern region sample. The independent variables used in this model were significant predictors for the European American respondent's educational attainment (F=546.42, p < .001) with 24 percent of the variance of the dependent variable explained. The independent variables predicting African American respondent's educational attainment were also significant predictors (F=12.59, p < .001), but only 10 percent of the variance was explained in this model. This drop in the explained variance coupled with noted

Table 3.2

Means, Standard Deviations, and Multiple Regression Analysis for the South Region

Family History and Dependent Variables	European Americans (N=3024)			African Americans (N=828)		
	Mean	SD	B's	Mean	SD	B's
Father's Prestige	40.33	11.58	.011 (.039*)	33.68	11.50	-.017 (-.053)
Father's Education	9.15	4.44	.244 (.319***)	6.71	4.25	.195 (.218***)
Mother's Education	9.61	3.75	.280 (.309***)	8.11	4.02	.373 (.394***)
Family Income at Age 16	2.84	.93	.096 (.026)	2.27	1.23	-.019 (-.006)
Respondent's Education	11.53	3.4		10.30	3.80	
R-Square			.37			.32

F=442.34 Sig F=.0000   F=97.47 Sig F=.0000
[*P<.05 **P<.01 ***P<.001]
Betas in parentheses

Table 3.3
Means, Standard Deviations, and Multiple Regression Analysis for the North Region

Family History and Dependent Variables	European Americans (N=7031)			African Americans (N=450)		
	Mean	SD	B's	Mean	SD	B's
Father's Prestige	39.62	12.54	.032 (.142***)	32.48	12.89	.009 (.049)
Father's Education	10.09	4.03	.141 (.198***)	9.78	.026	3.80 (.135*)
Mother's Education	10.25	3.50	.197 (.239***)	10.47	3.24	.151 (.202***)
Family Income at Age 16	2.91	.95	.055 (.018)	2.68	1.07	.041 (.018)
Respondent's Education	12.51	2.88		12.30	2.41	
R-Square		.24			.10	

F=546.42 Sig F=.0000   F=12.59 Sig F=.0000
[*P<.05 **P<.01 ***P<.001]
Betas in parentheses

drops in betas suggests a major difference by race in explaining educational attainment in the northern region.

The regional variation and racial variation apparent in the multiple regression results suggested the utility of a closer look at one of the more significant variables, mother's educational attainment, and its relationship to the respondent's attainment. The drop in beta values by region for mother's education prompted correlational and crosstab analysis to more accurately track the relationship of that variable to respondent's education. Not surprisingly, those two variables correlated strongly in the southern region (Pearson r = .546 for African Americans and .556 for European Americans) but dropped in the northern region (.284 for African Americans and .427 for European Americans). The far more significant drop for African Americans by region hints at what will become a major focal point of this analysis.

Crosstab analyses for the two variables across the two regions provided a more complete statistical description of both the above associations *and* the regional mean differences in educational attainment for both mothers and respondents (see Tables 3.2 and 3.3). For both racial groups in the southern region, it became clear that the strength of the correlational relationship stemmed from the large percentage of the population with less than a high school diploma. For those lower levels of educational attainment, there was indeed a relatively strong relationship between mother's and respondent's education; southern mothers with less than 7 years of education seldom had children who achieved 12 years while mothers with 12 years of education regularly had children who achieved 12 years and more.

The crosstab analysis for both racial groups in the northern region presented a very different picture (and important enough for us to offer it graphically in Figures 3.1 and 3.2). Since crosstab analysis is essentially a relational frequency distribution and the two groups under comparison differed greatly in sample size, each box in the analysis was converted from a raw frequency count to its proportion of the overall sample. Thus, in Figures 3.1 and 3.2, the vertical dimension for any box represents the *percentage* of respondents at a given level of education whose mothers achieved a given level. The drop in correlation can be perceived visually as both samples tended to cluster towards the middle, this being particularly true for African Americans.

Figure 3.1. Northern African American Educational Attainment (in percentage of sample) by Mother's Educational Attainment (N=716; Pearson r=.284).

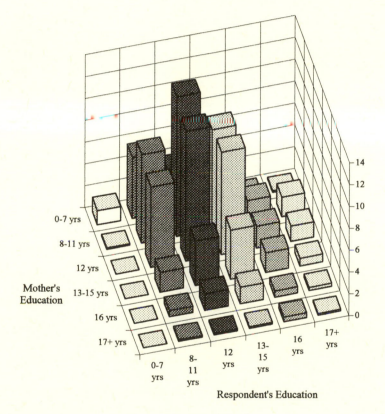

Figure 3.2. Northern European American Educational
Attainment (in percentage of sample) by Mother's
Educational Attainment (N=8350; Pearson r=.427).

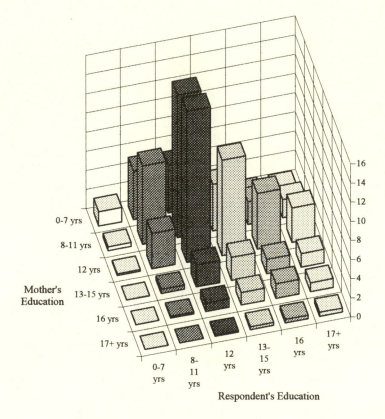

One of the most striking characteristics of Figure 3.1 is the concentration of northern African American students at the 13-15-year level in educational attainment. In the northern region, equal percentages (approximately 40 percent) of both African American and European American students venture into further education beyond their high school diploma. But among African Americans, 60 percent attain no more than 14 years while only 40 percent of the European American sample remains at that level. To better understand these northern postsecondary students, the association of independent variables employed earlier was measured to discover their association with the educational attainment of northern students who completed 13 or more years. The correlation of father's education with this more select group of African American and European American respondents dropped from .255 to .042 and from .433 to .137, respectively. The variable of mother's education showed similar movement, dropping from .284 to .126 and from .427 to .108, respectively. These statistics bear out the graphic depiction of a declining association between these variables at postsecondary levels.

DISCUSSION

Table 3.1 offers results both comforting and unsettling to the complacent researcher. On the one hand, regression analysis results confirm the importance of familial factors such as parent's educational attainment in predicting similar success in children. The relatively high 30 percent of explained variance with so few independent variables suggests a strong relationship and, more important, the similarity across racial lines invites speculation that racial discrimination may no longer be an important factor in limiting educational success. On the other hand, however, family variables such as father's occupational prestige and early family income levels are less significant in predicting a child's educational attainment. At the very least, these results should prod researchers into using extreme care in making assumptions of unidimensionality when combining variables to create a composite measure such as socioeconomic status. Intercorrelations among those separate variables notwithstanding, they cannot be depended upon to act in unison regardless of the dependent variables under study.

Tables 3.2 and 3.3, which present regression analysis data for the southern and northern regions respectively, suggest that the overall results presented in Table 3.1 are largely a compromise between the two regions with most of the strength of the relationships being contributed from the South. Neither race's educational attainment in the North approaches the level of explained variance found in the South. An explanation for this difference is suggested by the crosstab analysis of mother's education and respondent's education across race and region. There is a strong positive linear relationship in the South which, while skewed toward the lower end of both scales, nevertheless holds together as each rises. A reasonable conclusion is that parental education is indeed a strong predictor of a child's educational attainment *at the lower levels* of education where most parents and respondents in the southern region are located. By contrast, a far larger proportion of both races in the northern region are found at some level of postsecondary education, while virtually none are found at the lowest level. Given the relative dearth of cases at the lowest level for both mothers and respondents in the North, the degree of association between the variables could remain as high as in the South *only if* that association continued into those postsecondary levels. But for both races (and especially for African Americans), a relatively high level of parental education is no guarantee of equal attainment by a child. Indeed, we find an equal proportion of northern African Americans with high school dropout mothers attaining 17+ years of education as we find high school dropout respondents whose mothers have received postsecondary education. As higher levels of social industrialization produce higher levels of educational attainment, this general change in the relationship between parent's and child's educational attainment at postsecondary levels suggests a growing need for alternative models of explanation.

Perhaps the most striking finding apparent in Figures 3.1 and 3.2 is the proportional dominance of African Americans, both mothers and respondents, at the educational attainment level of 13 to 15 years. Among respondents, for example, around 30 percent of the African American northern region sample is located at that level compared with 20 percent of the European Americans. While the European American subsample (Figure 3.2) depicts a gentle stair- step progression in the respondent's attainment from the popular high point of 12 years on through postsecondary education, the African American subsample of respondent's attainment (Figure 3.1) shows a sharp drop off between 13 to 15 years and again, at 16 years. Considering that approximately 40 percent of each racial group in the northern region attains 13 or more years of education, the inability of African Americans to reach 16 or more years carries considerable economic significance for competition in the occupational marketplace. African American students are more likely to be enrolled in two-year colleges due to both the institution's physical accessibility and the financial limitations of the students. While students who graduate from two-year institutions can transfer to four-year institutions, African American students are less likely to do so than European American students. In addition, African American students who enroll initially in four-year institutions are less likely to complete their programs than are European American students at the same institutions (Wilson-Sadberry et al., 1991). These students are clearly facing limitations to their educational success that cannot be overcome by familial advantages stemming from high parental educational attainment. As we have seen, that relationship all but breaks down in the northern sample of African American respondents. Part of that change is due to the general changing relationship between parent and child attainment when the attainment level reaches the postsecondary level, northern European American respondents show a drop as well when compared with their southern counterparts, but part of the result is unique to African Americans.

For all intents and purposes, African American students appear to be hitting a "glass ceiling" in higher education, positioned just below a four-year degree and not easily broken through in spite of high parental education achievement. The research reviewed earlier in this article was included primarily to highlight some of the structural factors that collectively might produce such a ceiling. The tendency for northern African Americans to enroll in 2-year institutions noted above is obviously a starting point as it leads us to explore some of the reasons for that tendency. In particular, such schools are typically conveniently located and inexpensive. Clearly, more research needs to be conducted on the financial options of African American students. But even when transfer to (or enrollment in) four-year institutions is possible, graduation rates continue to be low. As indicated by research reviewed, numerous answers to this phenomenon are located in the cultural intersection between dominant group institutions and minority students. The lack of a minority peer community among students as well as the lack of significant minority role models among the faculty have been regularly shown to be related to retention. The often-noted cultural clash between African American students (particularly males) and institutional educational values undoubtedly has its roots in this larger conflict. Finally, we should note that African Americans will earn less than their European American counterparts even at the same levels of education (U.S. Bureau of the Census, 1992b). The incentive to excel in a system with discrimination waiting in the wings must understandably be muted.

IMPLICATIONS FOR SOCIAL POLICY

The results of this study have implications for family life educators, teachers, community educators, college administrators, lawmakers, researchers, and others who are concerned about "equal" education in our society. These findings suggest the need for extending the research reported in the initial sections of this paper on the importance of racial discrimination in its various forms for explaining the failure of African American students to either attend or be retained by four-year institutions of higher education in the United States. While it should clearly be noted that the research reported here shows a decreasing influence of familial factors in explaining that attainment without simultaneously shining a spotlight on other, presumably more influential factors, those familial factors are significant enough in the research literature to be worthy of this scrutiny. Their assumed importance in explaining educational attainment at all levels of education has prevented many researchers from distinguishing relative effects at different levels and turning their attention to other (and presumably more fruitful) models of explanation for postsecondary educational attainment among African Americans.

We suggest a more holistic approach to studying educational attainment. Research focusing on the interaction between the educational institution, family structural conditions, cultural norms and values, and community variables will likely provide the validated knowledge that a more comprehensive educational system can be provided to reach our increasing diverse population.

REFERENCES
Baca Zinn, Maxine. 1989. "Family, Race, and Poverty in the Eighties." *Signs: Journal of Women in Culture and Society* 14:856-874.
Bane, Mary J. 1986. "Household Composition and Poverty." Pp. 209-231 in *Fighting Poverty*, edited by Sheldon H. Danziger and Daniel H. Weinberg. Cambridge, MA: Harvard University Press.
Blau, Peter M., and Otis D. Duncan. 1967. *American Occupational Structure*. New York: Wiley.
Blau, Zena S. 1981. *Black Children/White Children: Competence, Socialization, and Social Structure*. New York: The Free Press.

Brookover, Wilbur B., and Jeffrey M. Schneider. 1975. "Academic Environments and Elementary School Achievement." *Journal of Research and Development in Education* 9(1):82-91.

Brown, Diane R. 1991. "Religious Socialization and Educational Attainment Among African Americans: An Empirical Assessment." *Journal of Negro Education* 60(3):411-426.

Clark, Maxine L. 1991."Social Identity, Peer Relations and Academic Competence of African American Adolescents." *Education and Urban Society* 24(1):41-52.

DeMott, Benjamin. 1991. "Legally Sanctioned Special Advantages are a Way of Life in the United States." *The Chronicle of Higher Education* 27(February):A40.

Feagin, Joseph R. 1992. "The Continuing Significance of Racism: Discrimination Against Black Students in White Colleges." *Journal of Black Studies* 22(4):546-578.

Fordham, Signithia, and John U. Ogbu. 1986. "Black Students' School Success: Coping with the Burden of 'Acting White.'" *Urban Review* 18(4):176-206.

Garibaldi, Antoine M. 1991. "The Role of Historically Black Colleges in Facilitating Resilience Among African-American Students." *Education and Urban Society* 24(1):103-112.

Gilbert, Shirl E., and Geneva Gay. 1985. "Improving the Success in School of Poor Black Children." *Phi Delta Kappan* 67(2):133-37.

Hare, Bruce. 1987. "Structural Inequality and the Endangered Status of Black Youth." *Journal of Negro Education* 56(1):100-110.

Hood, Denice W. 1992. "Academic and Noncognitive Factors Affecting the Retention of Black Men at a Predominantly White University." *Journal of Negro Education* 61(1):12-23.

Johnson, Sylvia T. 1992. "Extra-School Factors in Achievement, Attainment, and Aspiration Among Junior and Senior High School-age African American Youth." *Journal of Negro Education* 61(1):99-119.

Kanter, Rosabeth M. 1977. *Men and Women of the Corporation.* New York: Basic Books, Inc.

McAdoo, John L. 1986. "A Black Perspective on the Father's Role in Child Development." *Marriage and Family Review* 9(3-4):117-133.

Moynihan, Daniel P. 1965. *The Negro Family: The Case for National Action.* Washington, DC: Department of Labor, Office of Policy Planning and Research.

National Center for Education Statistics. 1992a. *Digest of Education Statistics, 1992.* Washington, DC: U.S. Department of Education.

National Center for Education Statistics. 1992b. *The Condition of Education,1992.* Washington, DC: U.S. Department of Education.

Ogbu, John U. 1988. "Class Stratification, Racial Stratification, and Schooling." Pp. 163-182 in *Class, Race, and Gender in American Education* edited by Lois Weis. Albany, NY: State University of New York Press.

Pascarella, Ernest T. 1985. "Racial Differences in Factors Associated with Bachelor's Degree Completion: A Nine-year Follow Up." *Research in Higher Education* 23(4):351-373.

Porter, James N. 1974. "Race, Socialization, and Mobility in Educational and Early Occupational Attainment." *American Sociological Review* 39(3):303-16.

Slaughter, Diane T., and Edgar G. Epps. 1987. "The Home Environment and Academic Achievement of Black American Children and Youth: An Overview." *Journal of Negro Education* 56(1):3-20.

Smith, Eleanor J., and Paul M. Smith. 1986. "The Black Female Single-parent Family Condition." *Journal of Black Studies* 17(1):125-134.

Solorzano, Daniel G. 1992. "An Exploratory Analysis of the Effects of Race, Class and Gender on Student and Parent Mobility Aspirations." *Journal of Negro Education* 61(1):30-44.

Staples, Robert. 1987. "Social Structure and Black Family Life." *Journal of Black Studies* 17(3):267-286.

Thernstrom, Stephen. 1964. *Poverty and Progress: Social Mobility in a Nineteenth Century City.* Cambridge, MA.: Harvard University Press.

Thomas, Gail E., Karl L. Alexander, and Bruce K. Eckland. 1979. "Access to Higher Education: The Importance of Race, Sex, Social Class, and Academic Credentials." *School Review* 87(2):133-56.

Thompson, Aaron. 1992. "Views on Affirmative Action Inside the University: The Relationship Between Authority and Attitudes." Unpublished doctoral dissertation, Department of Sociology, University of Kentucky.

U.S. Bureau of the Census. 1991. Current Population Reports, Series P-20, No. 451, *Educational Attainment in the United States: March 1989 and 1988.* Washington, DC: U.S. Government Printing Office.

U.S. Bureau of the Census. 1992a. Current Population Reports, Series P-20, No. 460, *School Enrollment—Social and Economic Characteristics of Students: October 1990.* U.S. Government Printing Office, Washington, DC.

U.S. Bureau of the Census. 1992b. Current Population Reports, Series P-20, No. 462, *Educational Attainment in the United States: March 1991 and 1990.* U.S. Government Printing Office, Washington, DC.

Wasserman, Herbert L. 1972. "A Comparative Study of School Performance Among Boys from Broken and Intact Black Families." *Journal of Negro Education* 41(2):137-141.

Watts, David, and Karen M. Watts. 1991. "The Impact of Female-headed Single Parent Families on Academic Achievement." *Journal of Divorce and Remarriage* 17(1-2):97-114.

Weitzman, Lenore. 1985. *Divorce Revolution: The Unexpected Social and Economic Consequences for Women and Children in America.* New York: Free Press.

White, Karl R. 1982. "The Relation Between Socioeconomic Status and Academic Achievement." *Psychological Bulletin* 91:461-481.

Wilkinson, Doris. 1991. "The Segmented Labor Market and African American Women from 1890-1960: A Social History Interpretation." *Research in Race and Ethnic Relations* 6:85-104. Greenwich, CT: JAI.

Wilson, Karen, and Walter R. Allen. 1987. "Explaining the Educational Attainment of Young Black Adults: Critical Familial and Extra-familial Influences." *Journal of Negro Education* 56(1):64-76.

Wilson, William J., and Katherine Neckerman. 1987. "Poverty and Family Structure: The Widening Gap Between Evidence and Public Policy Issues." Pp. 63-92 in *The Truly Disadvantaged*, edited by William J. Wilson. Chicago: University of Chicago Press.

Wilson-Sadberry, Karen R., Linda F. Winfield, and Deidre A. Royster. 1991. "Resilience and Persistence of African-American Males in Postsecondary Enrollment." *Education and Urban Society* 24(1):87-102.

Chapter 4

Teachers as Social Scientists: Learning about Culture from Household Research[1]

Luis C. Moll and Norma González

The most basic of pedagogical principles is for teachers to build on the experiences and abilities that students bring to class. An extension of this principle, especially in contemporary multicultural contexts, is that teachers must come to "know" the "cultures" from which their students emerge. The point, of course, is that students' cultural characteristics, including their language and literacy experiences, must be treated as resources, not as impediments to their schooling (e.g., Moll, 1992a; Moll & González, 1994). Indeed, as Ferreiro (1994) has recently suggested, transforming students' diversities into pedagogical assets may be the foremost educational challenge for the future (p. 25).

Although this "multicultural" approach is laudatory in its conceptualization, the application has run aground on at least two key issues. The first issue concerns the manner in which teachers' awareness of diversity is pre-packaged and pre-digested for inservice consumption. Typically, inservices or after-school meetings are held in which experts transmit to practitioners certain traits or attributes of "Culture X" or "Culture Y." Rather than grappling with the complexities of the movements of peoples, a historical consciousness of how these groups came to exist in their present circumstances, and what they do and know to survive or get ahead, inservices often offer an homogenized and standardized prescriptivism for dealing with children of the "other." Indeed, these approaches may simply succeed in forming new sets of stereotypes, albeit more positive or benign ones, to replace previous sets of stereotypes. Practitioners thus are forced to rely on a "transmission" model for learning about their students: disengaged from first-hand experience and with information often boxed into pre-existing molds and generalizations.

A second issue that proves problematic is dealing with the notion of "culture." Prevailing trends in anthropological or ethnographic literature have moved away from univocal and harmonious visions of an integrated version of culture. Yet, the prevailing notions of "culture" in the schools center around observable and tangible surface markers: dances, food, language, folklore, ethnic heritage festivals, and international potlucks. Although these affirmations are undoubtedly positive in fostering tolerance, there is an unspoken assumption of a normative and clearly defined culture "out there" that may not take into account the everyday lived experiences of students and their families (González, 1995).

In the work described in this chapter, we present a qualitative approach to addressing these two issues. We are participants in a collaborative research project involving teacher-researchers from elementary schools and university-researchers from the disciplines of anthropology and education (see González et al., 1995; Moll et al., 1992). The basic premise of this project is that classroom learning can be greatly enhanced when teachers learn more about their students and about their students' households. In our particular version of how this learning can come to be accomplished, teachers venture into their students' households and communities, not as "teachers" attempting to convey educational information, as valuable as that role may be, but as "learners" seeking to understand the ways in which people make sense of their everyday lives. Ethnographic research methods involving participant-observation, interviewing, elicitation of narratives, and reflection on field notes, flesh out the multidimensionality of student and family experiences. Although the concept of making home visits is not new, entering the households of Mexican origin, African American or Native American students with a "theoretical" eye towards learning from households is a radical departure from traditional school home-visits (González et al., 1995).

Drawing from ethnographic and qualitative methods, the goal is for teachers to tap into the reservoirs of accumulated knowledge and strategies for survival that households possess, which we refer to, following Greenberg (1989) and Vélez-Ibáñez (1988), as "funds of knowledge." Teachers are not given second-hand generalities about Mexican, or African American, or Native American culture by academic researchers; they are learning, as ethnographers would, directly from interviews and other first-hand experiences. Our claim is that these qualitative methods of study can become the "tools" necessary for the teachers' development of "theoretical" knowledge that, in turn, helps them formulate a pedagogy specific to their situations and that builds strategically on the social relations and cultural resources of their school's community.

ANALYZING FUNDS OF KNOWLEDGE

The project consists of three main interrelated activities: 1) a qualitative analysis of the strategies, uses, and development of knowledge among households in Latino and other communities in Tucson, Arizona; 2) creation of after-school sites where researchers and teachers meet to think about their joint research and to determine how to use pedagogically what we are learning; and, 3) classroom observations to examine methods of instruction and explore how to produce positive change by integrating what is learned from the households and at the after-school site. This three-part design—household analysis, the creation of study groups or lab settings with teachers, and the development of pedagogy—is, with considerable variability, our basic framework for conducting research. This design allows for the flexible but continuous analysis of three important domains of practice (households, labs, and classrooms), and for the exploration of interconnections (theoretical and practical) that may benefit classroom instruction (Moll, 1992b).

In previous studies we have documented how every household contains accumulated "funds of knowledge" (skills, abilities, ideas, practices), in short, those bodies of knowledge that are essential to the households' functioning and well-being (Greenberg, 1989; Moll & Greenberg, 1990). We have also emphasized how each household is interconnected with other households (and other institutions and individuals) for the purpose of garnering or exchanging these funds of knowledge. In fact, these social networks represent a flexible mechanism that allows households to adjust to changing (and often difficult) social and economic circumstances (see Vélez-Ibáñez, 1988). These funds of knowledge and the social networks have been the main focus of our household studies.

The centerpiece of our work, however, has become the collaboration with teachers in conducting household research (González et al., 1995; Moll et al., 1992). We emphasize this point because it has been such a significant change in our work. It is no longer the case of the researchers providing the teachers with "data," or the analysis of such data, and asking them to do something interesting with the information. It is now the case that the teachers themselves are creating new knowledge based on their own household observations. This change has had major consequences on our working relationships with teachers and on the relationship of teachers with families, as well as on how we think about the pedagogical consequences of our work, a point we will discuss later in this chapter.

We base the work on the assumption that there are important (cultural) resources for teaching in the school's immediate community but that one needs both theory and method to locate, identify, and document these resources. Furthermore, we also assume that these cultural resources (funds of knowledge) can be fruitfully imported into classrooms but only under the teachers' direction and control. In contrast to other efforts at teacher research (e.g., Lytle & Cochran-Smith, 1990), our starting point is not the study of classrooms but the analysis of household history and practices. One of the teachers in the project put it as follows:

> Like many other teacher-research projects, this project is a collaborative endeavor, carried out jointly by university- and school-based researchers. However, unlike most teacher-research, which has come to be synonymous with classroom research, the teachers working on this project have not been confined to research in their classrooms alone. Where teacher-research in general subscribes to the notion that teachers are more effective when they "closely observe individual students in their classrooms" (Bissex, 1987, p. 16), the benefits of closely observing their students in other contexts, such as their home, have been left unidentified (Amanti, 1994:2).

There are some compelling reasons for taking this "community-mediated" approach. For one, as Goodson (1991) has pointed out, having strangers scrutinize one's teaching is not a very good way of creating a working relationship between teachers and researchers. In contrast, the initiation of teachers into household, rather than classroom, analysis provides the context for collaboration in a number of overlapping arenas (see Moll & González, 1994). For example, as we discuss below, teachers are presented with a body of social theory that helps them reconsider the households of "minority" children from a different theoretical perspective. In addition, by approaching these households as qualitative researchers, teachers are offered a non-evaluative framework that helps them to go beyond surface images of families. The household analysis also serves as a way to learn to study, in general, unfamiliar settings that they cannot assume they know or understand. Not coincidentally, the contrast between the known or familiar (the classroom) and the unknown or unfamiliar (the households), especially when teachers do not live in the community in which they teach, is analogous to an anthropologist entering an unknown setting or community. This contrast becomes an issue even when the teachers are themselves members of the community. In such cases, the task becomes that of "making the familiar strange" in order to observe and document processes that are less salient or "visible" to the "insider." All teachers, minority or otherwise, have found that entering the households as researchers, rather than as "teachers," produces a discernible reorientation to household dynamics and processes and to the formation of qualitatively new social relations with families (González & Amanti, 1997; González et al., 1995).

The theoretical orientation of our fieldwork, then, is towards documenting the productive (and other) activities of households and what they reveal about families' knowledge. Particularly important in our work has been the analysis of households as "strategizing units": how they function as part of a wider economy and how family members obtain and distribute their material and intellectual resources through strategic social ties or networks or through other adaptive arrangements. We have learned that in contrast to classrooms, households never function alone or in isolation, they are always connected to other households and institutions through diverse social networks. These social networks not only facilitate different forms of economic assistance and labor cooperation that help families avoid the expenses involved in using secondary institutions, such as plumbing companies or automobile repair shops, but serve important emotional and service functions, providing assistance of different types, for example, in finding jobs, with child-care and rearing, or other problem-solving functions.

It is primarily through these social networks that family members obtain or share what we have termed "funds of knowledge." We have defined funds of knowledge as those historically accumulated and culturally developed bodies of knowledge and skills essential for household or individual functioning and well-being (Greenberg, 1989; Moll & Greenberg, 1990). As households interact within circles of kinship and friendship, children are "participant-observers" of the exchange of goods, services, and symbolic capital that is part of each household's functioning.

What is the source of these funds of knowledge? We have concentrated primarily on documenting the social and labor history of the families. Much of a household's knowledge is related to its origins and, of course, to family members' employment, occupations, or work, including labor specific to household activities. To make this discussion more concrete, consider the following case example drawn from one of our studies (adapted from Moll & Greenberg, 1990; names are pseudonyms)[2]:

> The Zavalas are an urban working-class family, with no ties to the rural hinterland. They have seven children. Their eldest daughter, however, no longer lives at home but with her boy friend and son. Mr. Zavala is best characterized as an entrepreneur. He works as a builder, part time, and owns some apartments in working-class neighborhoods in Tucson and properties in Nogales. Mrs. Zavala was born in Albuquerque, New Mexico, in 1950 but came to Tucson as a young child; she left school in the 11th grade. Mr. Zavala was born in Nogales, Sonora in 1947, where he lived until he finished the 6th grade. His father, too, was from Nogales. His father had little education, and began to work at the age of 9 to help support the family. His family, then, moved to Nogales, Arizona, where he went to school for another two years. When he was 17, Mr. Zavala left home and joined the army, and spent two years stationed on military bases in California and Texas. After his discharge, he returned to Nogales, Arizona, and worked for a year installing TV cable and installing heating and cooling ducts. In 1967, Mr. Zavala came to Tucson, first working as a house painter for six months, then in an airplane repair shop for three years. In 1971, he opened a washing machine and refrigerator repair shop, a business he had for three years. Since 1974, Mr. Zavala works in construction part time, builds and sells houses, and he owns four apartments (two of which he built in the backyard of his house).

Everyone in the Zavala's household, including the children, is involved in informal sector economic activities to help the family. Juan, for example, who is in the sixth grade, has a bicycle shop in the back of the house. He buys used bicycle parts at the swap meet and assembles them to build bicycles, which he sells at the yard sales his family holds regularly. He is also building a go-cart and says he is going to charge kids 15 cents per ride. His sisters, Carmen and Conchita, sell candies that their mother buys in Nogales to their schoolmates. The children have used the money they have earned to buy the family a VCR.

In Tucson, Mr. Zavala also has a set of younger brothers, who live in a house owned by his mother. Ana Zavala, an older sister, also rents a house (at a discount) from her grandmother on the same block. As is typical of such household clusterings of kin, Mr. Zavala's youngest brother and Ana are very close, and he does many favors for his niece, such as grocery shopping. As well, one of Mr. Zavala's sisters is married to a junior high school teacher. When his children have difficulties with their homework, they often seek assistance from their uncle. Although most of Mrs. Zavala's relatives live in California, she also has a brother in Phoenix. When he comes to visit, because he knows of Juan's interest in building bicycles, he buys parts for him.

Reading and writing are an integral part of the Zavalas' daily activities. Although much of what Mr. Zavala reads and writes is work related—blue prints, lists of materials, trade books and manuals—in his spare time, he also reads *National Geographic, Newsweek*, books on history, and enjoys browsing through the encyclopedia. Mrs. Zavala's use of literacy is more varied. She is in charge of reading and signing school papers. She writes greeting cards, shopping lists, recipes, notes to remind her children of household chores and family members of appointments. She reads *Time, Life, Good Housekeeping*. Her reading also includes a lot of self-improvement books on parenting, such as *How to Build Self Esteem in Your Child, Read Out Loud to Your Child, How to Put Brain Power into Your Child, Classics to Read to Children*, and *Loving Each Other*.

Mrs. Zavala is one of the most literate persons in the sample, and her reading reflects her concerns with her children's well-being. The Zavalas are committed to schooling. Both parents are deeply involved in school activities. Mrs. Zavala assists in preparing food for various school events, attends PTA meetings; Mr. Zavala is similarly involved with the school. He participates in school field trips, in the "story-telling" program at the public library, and has attended several computer workshops held for parents so they may assist their children with computer work. As well, both parents read stories to their children. Mr. Zavala often takes the three younger children to buy books at book fairs. Mrs. Zavala takes them to the public library at least once a week, she reports. School work is taken very seriously. Homework must be done before they are allowed to play. Both parents assist the children with their assignments. For example, when Juan does not understand the Spanish instructions, he will ask his mother to translate them into English. If they are no clearer to him in English than in Spanish, she will rephrase them in various ways until she is sure he has grasped the meaning. What is interesting here is that even though Juan asks for help, Mrs. Zavala does not take over the assignment but limits her role to assisting the child's performance.

Notice that even this cursory and superficial example reveals substantial funds of knowledge that a teacher could document, as well as knowledge about the family's strategies to cope with economic circumstances. We can specify that this family has knowledge about the purchase, construction, rental, and maintenance of apartments (business knowledge), installation of cable TV and heating and cooling ducts, the repair of washing machines, refrigerators, and even airplanes, and professional knowledge about the painting of houses; the father and son (and uncle) also have knowledge about the building and repair of bicycles, and the mother and daughters about sales (of candy purchased in Mexico) and savings. The family history also reveals the cross-border character (and knowledge) of the family, typical of many Mexican families in Tucson. Their social network places them in contact with considerable knowledge about other matters—in the example above, knowledge about formal schooling from the brother-in-law, who is a teacher, as well as knowledge gained from their own intimate involvement with schools and library, including the management of their children's homework tasks and knowledge about computers. We also learn about some of the family's uses of literacy, in both English and Spanish, ranging from job-related reading to reading for recreation, self-improvement, and child rearing and education.

The case example above, obviously, does not exhaust this household's funds of knowledge or the forms of exchange that the household is capable of producing. The knowledge and skills that such households and their networks possess are extensive. For example, many of the families know about repairs, carpentry, masonry, electrical wiring, fencing, and building codes—in general, knowledge related to jobs in the working-class segment of the labor market. Some families have knowledge about the cultivation of plants, folk remedies, herbal cures, midwifery, and first-aid procedures, usually learned from older relatives in rural settings. Family members with several years of formal schooling have knowledge about (and have worked in) archaeology, biology, education, engineering, and mathematics.

Our analysis also suggests that each exchange of information, or of other resources, includes a didactic component that is part of the activity of sharing. Sometimes this teaching is quite explicit, as when teaching someone how to build a room or a machine (such as a bicycle) or how to use a new gadget; at other times it is implicit and depends on the participation or observation of the learner, as when the children assist the father in the building of an addition to the house. What we are calling a didactic component of the exchange is part of any household's pedagogy. People must teach and learn new knowledge and skills to deal with a changing reality. In many instances the children are involved in these activities, they may be the recipients of the exchange, as observers or participants. However, just as literacy is embedded and found directly or indirectly in most funds of knowledge activities, this didactic component is not neatly separable from the exchange of knowledge: it is contextualized; it is found within the activity, and it occurs often. These households, then, as should be obvious, are not socially or intellectually barren: they contain knowledge; people use reading and writing; they mobilize social relationships, and they teach and they learn. From the documentation and (theoretical) analysis of funds of knowledge, one learns not only about the extent of the knowledge found among these working-class households but about the special importance of the social and cultural world, and of social relations, in the development of knowledge (Moll et al., 1993).

PEDAGOGICAL CONSEQUENCES

Teachers have reported to us the transformative potential of viewing households from a funds of knowledge perspective (see González et al., 1995). One implication, and a most important one, is debunking ideas of working-class, language-minority households as lacking worthwhile knowledge and experiences. These households, and by implication, these communities, are often viewed solely as places from which children must be saved or rescued rather than places that, in addition to problems (as in all communities), contain valuable knowledge and experiences that can foster the children's educational development.

Each teacher, as she or he came to know the households personally and emotionally, came away changed in some way. Some were struck by the sheer survival of the households against seemingly overwhelming odds. Others were astonished at the sacrifices the households made in order to gain a better education for their children. They all found parents who were engineers, teachers, and small business owners in Mexico, who pulled up stakes and now work in jobs far below their capabilities in order to obtain a "better life and education" for their children. They found immigrant families living with fifteen people in a household, with all adult males and females working, in order to pay rent and everyday necessities. The teachers not only documented family histories and activities and related these to the concept of funds of knowledge but established enduring social relationships with the families. It was common for teachers to be invited not only for dinner but to important family functions such as weddings, or *quinceañera* (debutante) celebrations, a prominent cultural activity for many families in this region. Parent visits to the schools or phone calls to the teachers also became common, as the parents sought to stay in touch with the teachers. In short, teachers became part of the families' social networks, signaling that   relationships of mutual trust *(confianza)* had developed.

Our work also involved the incorporation of household knowledge into tangible curricular activities within the classroom. For example, one teacher learned that many of her students' households had extensive knowledge of the medicinal value of plants and herbs. She was able to draw on this ethnobotanical knowledge in formulating a theme unit that reflected local knowledge of the curative properties of plants. Another teacher, after visiting a household that regularly participated in trans-border activities in northern Mexico, discovered that her student commonly returned from these trips with candy to sell. Elaborating on this student's marketing skills, an integrated unit was spun around various aspects of candy and the selling of candy. Students adopted an inquiry-based approach to investigate the nutritional content of candy to make a comparison of U.S. and Mexican candy and sugar processing, and to develop a survey and graphing unit on favorite candies. In both instances, individuals met during the household visits became participants, visiting the classrooms to contribute (in either English or Spanish) their knowledge or experiences (González et al., 1994; Moll et al., 1992; see also Moll & Greenberg, 1990).

In other cases, the involvement of the parents has followed an unexpected trajectory. In one special case involving an African American household, the research visits revealed that the father, in addition to his regular job as a gardener, had a wealth of musical and theatrical knowledge that was tapped for the production of a full-scale musical in the school. This father wrote lyrics and composed music and a script that featured eight original songs, described by the teacher as "songs that these children will carry with them for the rest of their lives" (Hensley, 1995). Other than the skills learned in staging the musical, a unit on sound and music was developed that focused on the acoustical properties of sound, the construction of various musical instruments, and ethnomusicology. Interestingly, a written survey sent by the school inquiring about household skills had not been returned by this family, but the personal and interested contact of the teacher was key in revealing and using this storehouse of talents.

One further development marks this case study as illustrative of the "catalytic" potential of this method. During an initial interview, the Johnsons (a pseudonym for this family) had indicated disinterest in the school's PTA. However, as Mr. Johnson became a frequent school visitor (on his weekly day off, we should add), carrying his musical instruments, other teachers noticed him and asked about his presence. Soon they were requesting that he visit their classrooms, and his visibility extended into other areas of school life. By the end of the school year, Mr. Johnson had been elected PTA president, proposing an ambitious agenda of community involvement in school matters. This case example effectively points out yet another area of potential that can be harnessed by transcending the boundaries of the school and making inroads into the funds of knowledge of the community (Moll & González, 1994).

Another implication, and one we want to highlight in this article because of its relevance for multicultural education, is in understanding the concept of culture from a more dynamic, "processual" view, not as a group of personality traits, folk celebrations, foods, or artifacts but as the lived practices and knowledge of the students and their families. The fact that many minority students live in ambiguous and contradictory circumstances favors a perspective in which attention is directed towards the interaction between individual agency and received structures. In this way, the actual and everyday experiences of students' lives are privileged over uniform, integrated and standardized cultural norms. Cathy Amanti (1994), a teacher-researcher, explains it as follows:

The impact of participating in this project went far beyond my expectations. My approach to curriculum and my relationship with my students are two areas where the impact was most profound. In the area of curriculum, as a teacher of predominantly Mexican and U.S. Mexican students, I believed in the importance of acknowledging and including aspects of my students' culture in my classroom practice. However, though teachers are trained to build on students' prior knowledge, they are given no guidelines for how to go about eliciting this knowledge. Also, the multicultural curriculum available in schools perpetuates an outdated notion of culture as special and isolated ritual events and artifacts, the kind featured in *National Geographic*. Its focus on holidays, "typical" foods and "traditional" artifacts covers a very narrow range of my students' experiences and ignores the reality of life in the borderlands, which often falls outside the norms of traditional Anglo or Mexican culture.

Participating in this project helped me to reformulate my concept of culture from being very static to more practice-oriented. This broadened conceptualization turned out to be the key which helped me develop strategies to include the knowledge my students were bringing to school in my classroom practice. It was the kind of information elicited through the questionnaires that was the catalyst for this transformation. I sought information on literacy, parenting attitudes, family and residential history, and daily activities. But I was not looking for static categories, or judging the households' activities in these areas according to any standards —my own or otherwise. I simply elicited and described the context within which my students were being socialized. What this meant was that if the father of one of my students' did not have a "job," I did not stop the inquiry there. The format of the questionnaires encouraged me to continue probing to discover any type of activity that the father and mother were doing to ensure the survival of the household.

If we were simply eliciting labor history associated with categories of work in the formal economic sector, we would risk both devaluing and missing many of the experiences of our students and their families. This has clear implications for how we approach culture. If our idea of culture is bound up with notions of authenticity and tradition, how much practice will we ignore as valueless and what will this say to our students? But if our idea of culture is expanded to include the ways we organize and make sense of all our experiences, we have many more resources to draw upon in the classroom (see also Amanti, 1995).

Viewing households within a processual view of culture, rooted in the lived contexts and practices of their students and families, engendered a realization that "culture" is a dynamic concept and not a static grab bag of *tamales*, *quinceañeras* and *cinco de mayo* celebrations. Instead, teachers learned how households network in informal market exchanges. They learned how cross-border activities made "mini-ethnographers" of their students. And most importantly, that students acquired a multi-dimensional depth and breadth from their participation in household life (Moll et al., 1992).

Once teachers entered households as "learners," as researchers seeking to construct a template for understanding and tapping into the concrete life experiences of their students, the conventional model of home visits was turned on its head. No attempt would be made to "teach" the parents or to visit for other school-related reasons. This shift constituted a radical departure from the household visits in other programs that incorporate the "home visit" concept. The after-school labs were restructured to accommodate these shifts, and the ethnographic method emerged as the vehicle for participant-observations, rather than "household visits." Within the lab setting, ethnography surfaced as more than techniques. It became the filter through which the households were conceptualized as multi-dimensional and vibrant entities. This new perspective reflected a corresponding shift in teacher's theoretical paradigms. As has been noted, in teaching anthropology "a state of mind is more important than specific techniques" (Spindler & Spindler, 1990:20).

Throughout the study groups, anthropological inquiry was presented as more of a state of mind than a technique. However, the theoretical implications of technique became conspicuous in several ways, and an effort to systematize reflexivity emerged. As part of the ethnographic experience, teachers were asked to select two to three students from their classrooms. Students were selected at the teacher's discretion, and no formal attempt at representativeness was made. Households were visited three times and the interviews lasted an average of two hours each. An interview of the target child was also conducted. Ages of the students ranged from kindergarten through fifth grade. Teachers were asked to taperecord the interviews (if the family was comfortable with it) and to conduct the interview as conversationally as possible. Teachers were paid (when possible) as project participants for their "extra duty" time.

Following their forays into the field, teachers were asked to write up fieldnotes based on each interview, and these fieldnotes became the basis for the study group discussions. Teachers overwhelmingly remarked on the time-consuming nature of this process. After a hectic school day, conducting interviews that often stretched into two or three hours and later investing several hours in writing field notes was an exacting price to pay for a connection to the households. They cited this one factor as precluding wholesale teacher participation in this project. Yet, in spite of the strain of the task, the teachers felt that the effort was "worth it." In the reflexive process involved in transcription, teachers were able to obtain elusive insights that could easily be overlooked. As they replayed the audio tapes and referred to notes, connections and hunches began to emerge. The household began to take on a multi-dimensional reality that had taken root in the interview and reached its fruition in reflexive writing. Writing gave form and substance to the connection forged between the household and the teacher.

A second ethnographic technique involved the writing of a personal field journal. Not all teachers opted to do this. One teacher who kept an extensive journal noted: "Transformation occurs over a long period of time and is quite subtle in its nature. Elements of my transformation would have been elusive had I not documented them along the way. I recognize this as I look back and cannot remember having those feelings/beliefs." Another teacher lamented the fact that she had not kept the journal. She did not follow the suggestion and bemoans the fact in retrospect. She relates, "I don't remember when I stopped feeling and thinking this way or that way. I don't think it was an overnight thing. I think all of that is just changing little by little. If I had kept a journal, I could go back and read and say, 'OK, this is where I first started thinking about it.'" These comments highlight that an awareness of the documentation of the reflexive process began to take shape.

A third field technique involved the questionnaires. Teachers felt that the use of questionnaires signaled a shift in approaching the households as "learners." Entering the household with questions rather than answers provided the context for an inquiry-based visit, and the teachers considered the questionnaires a meaningful resource. They addressed such diverse areas as familial histories, family networks, labor history, educational history, language use, and child-rearing ideologies. Within each topic, questions were left open-ended, and teachers probed and elicited information as the interviews proceeded. Interviews were, as teachers commented, more of a conversation than an interview, and one teacher noted that with the audiotaping of the interview, she was free to be a conversational partner without the task of furious notetaking. Teachers used the questionnaire as a guide rather than a protocol, suggesting possible areas to explore and incorporating previous knowledge into formulating new questions. Interviews were not conducted as a unilateral extraction of information, as teachers were encouraged to make connections with their own lives and histories as they elicited narratives from the families.

These issues illustrate the critical effect that methodology had in learning a different way of visiting homes. Teachers often voiced the notions that "methodology helps to implant theory and represents its embodiment, particularly in this project which is very experiential." The theoretical orientation to the households as containing funds of knowledge was critical in teacher transformation. But equally as important in the transformative process was the reflection generated by the collaborative effort of a collective ethnographic experience.

Through the mediating structure of the after-school study groups, teachers were provided with the forum to engage in reflexive thought. Although specific techniques in participant-observation, fieldnote writing, interviewing, and elicitation of life histories were presented and discussed, the focus was continuously on the discourse, on the joint construction of knowledge. Ethnographic fieldwork became not one lone researcher grappling with overwhelming data but a collaborative and reflexive process in which teachers and researchers shared insights and information.

Household research, however, is not unproblematic. Indeed, one of the missions of the study groups became to provide a setting to discuss problems or ethical considerations. The teachers sometimes felt overwhelmed with the sheer complexity of the task. Anna Rivera, one of the teacher-researchers, reported feeling "like a private investigator—like you're watching everything. What are they cooking? How do you make this, how do you do that? The home visit was totally different from what I had done before" (González et al., 1995). The requirements of participating and observing, of interviewing and audio-recording and note-taking, of being both the teacher and ethnographer, was at the outset for teachers a numbing experience. This hesitance soon wore off as teachers became more comfortable with the process. Martha Floyd-Tenery, for example, reported after her series of interviews, "I remember at first I was scared to death. Would the family be skeptical? What would they think of me? Would they feel uncomfortable? I remember thinking all kinds of things. And now, it seems, like, what is the big deal? I can do this, and I can do it well" (González et al., 1995).

Participants in the study groups were able to voice their changing ideas about households and the subsequent transformation that the observations and reflection provoked. In the face of the sometimes overwhelming social and structural factors that face the students and their families, it would be easy to simply "give up." One teacher, Floyd-Tenery, voiced this sentiment as she reflected on her initial pessimism: "I did not realize it at the time, but I used to believe that my students had limited opportunities in life. I thought that poverty was the root of many of their problems, and that this was something too big for me to change as a teacher." Through the reflexive discourse of the study groups, this hopelessness was short-circuited. The teachers no longer felt isolated from each other or the community, as this same teacher explains: "This fatalistic obsession of mine has slowly melted away as I have gotten to know my students and their families. I believe this transformation is the most important one I have made. Its ramifications have reached far beyond the classroom" (González et al., 1995).

THE POWER OF SOCIAL NETWORKS

So far we have highlighted pedagogical consequences that have to do with transformation in teachers, their views and work and instructional activities that can be developed by combining academic tasks with household funds of knowledge. In this section we want to address the enormous potential of the social relationships developed through the sorts of qualitative household analysis we advocate for creating structural support for the teachers' and students' work. James Coleman (1987, 1988; see also, Coleman & Hoffer, 1987), based on his sociological analysis of schools, has proposed the concept of "social capital" to capture something similar to what we mean.[3] Coleman explains it as follows: "What I mean by social capital in the raising of children is the norms, the social networks, and the relationships between adults and children that are of value for the child's growing up. Social capital exists within the family, but also outside the family, in the community" (1987:36). He suggests that social capital comes about through the social relations (and mutual trust) among persons that facilitate action, "social capital inheres in the structure of relations between actors and among actors. It is not lodged either in the actors themselves or in the physical implements of production" (1988:98). Social capital, then, is not a possession or a trait of people but social (and cultural) resources for persons, resources that can be used, mobilized, to achieve certain interests or goals.

As an example Coleman (1987) cites his analysis of the reasons why the dropout rate is much lower in Catholic schools than in public or other private schools. He points out that the lower drop-out rate is not the result of a better curriculum or other factors within the school but of the social capital available in the relation between school and community. He explains it as follows:

We concluded that the community surrounding the Catholic school, a community created by the church, was of great importance in reducing the dropouts among students at risk of dropping out. In effect, this church-and-school community, with its social networks, and its norms about what teenagers should and should not do, constituted social capital beyond the family that aided both family and school in the education of the family's children (1987:36).

Religious organizations are among the few remaining organizations in society, beyond the family, that cross generations. Thus, they are among the few in which the social capital of an adult community is available to children and youth (1987:37).

There are several important points in Coleman's (1987, 1988) analysis that relate to our work. One is that social capital is not found in individuals but in relations among individuals. In fact, he emphasizes the very same reciprocal social networks that we are studying as facilitating the development of social capital. The key to the social networks is that it allows the resources of one relationship to be harnessed and appropriated for use in others. It is the flexibility of the social networks that permits resources used for a purpose in one situation to be redirected to assist in another context. This means that social capital from outside the school can be used, often in combination with other resources, to influence the structure and outcomes of education, as Coleman (1987, 1988) has suggested and as our case studies of teachers illustrate.

Thus, Coleman's work makes a case for the importance of the families' and community social capital in shaping educational outcomes, namely, staying in school or not dropping out. The analysis also highlights the importance of channeling social capital through an academic curriculum (Coleman & Hoffer, 1987). Their comparative analysis of public and Catholic schools indicated that black and Hispanic students not only did not drop out but performed much better in the Catholic schools even when the analysis controlled for background variables. In fact, as they have pointed out, "on most dimensions of academic demands, blacks and Hispanics in Catholic schools realize greater advantages than Catholic school non-Hispanic whites compared to their public school counterparts" (Coleman & Hoffer, 1987:144). These advantages, they specify, were non-trivial; they involved placement in academic programs of study which required homework, English courses, and a number of advanced science and mathematics courses. The key difference between public and Catholic schools in facilitating the superior academic performance of Hispanics and blacks was the greater academic demands placed on the students (stronger discipline, we should note, explained little of the achievement advantages of minority students).

The ability of the school to make academic demands upon these students, it turns out, was intimately related to the community's social capital. That is, social capital in terms of the social integration of the Catholic community in support of the academic demands and activities placed on the students. Schools and families constituted a functional community around social and academic matters. In the case of the Catholic schools, this functional community, this social integration, was based on religious participation coupled with academic interests. The effects of the functional community were indirect; that is, it was not that the parents helped the children with their academic work, although that is certainly probable, but that the parents constituted a community outside the school; a community in the sense that there was frequent social contact among the parents of the students and intergenerational contact between adults and students and with teachers.

Our analysis complements the concept of social capital by bringing it to life concretely in the form of household funds of knowledge that teachers can document and analyze. From our perspective, social capital, as well as funds of knowledge, is a useful theoretical concept made pedagogically relevant only through the actions of teachers. Our work shows how funds of knowledge are constituted through the historical experiences and productive (and other) activities of families and shared or distributed through the creation of social networks for exchange. These productive and exchange activities involve or influence children in a variety of ways and are often intergenerational and transnational, as we have discussed. There are abundant and wide-ranging funds of knowledge in the community, social and intellectual resources that can become social capital and applied to education. Our analysis of household social networks and funds of knowledge points to the potential for establishing a similar support community to the one described by Coleman and colleagues but based on neighborhood or residence: social relations among parents and among parents and teachers that facilitate intergenerational contacts with students about academic and social matters.

There is one final point from Coleman's analysis that we should mention. It seems that the social capital of the community, as with the Catholic, church-based community in his analysis, compensates in part for its absence in specific families (Coleman & Hoffer, 1987). In our terms, that means that it may be more important for the teachers to develop social relations with a few "case study" families in the classroom's community, "thick" relations of the type fostered by a funds of knowledge approach, than attempt to visit all of their students' homes without the time or effort to develop and sustain relations of trust. As our work with teachers has shown, a strong social bond develops rapidly between the teachers and the families. Creating a social network with a few "core" families may be important as well in helping the teacher develop the theoretical and methodological wherewithal to capitalize on the funds of knowledge of the households not studied but now considered as containing valuable resources as well.

CONCLUSION

We have argued in this paper for an approach in which teachers become qualitative researchers of local households as part of their pedagogy. This approach is based on teachers themselves redefining the resources available for teaching through the documentation and analysis of the funds of knowledge available in their students' households. The insights gained by understanding, through systematic inquiry, household life and dynamics, and the resources available within and among these households, come to mediate in important ways (we claim) how teachers think about local communities and how they think about teaching the children from those communities.

How can this project be implemented elsewhere? Our basic recommendation to teachers and administrators is to start with the formation of teacher study groups. These study groups (we suggest meeting weekly) are the key for the intimate involvement of teachers. As Sarason (1982) has emphasized, no innovation has a realistic chance of succeeding unless teachers are able to express, define, and address problems as they see them; unless teachers start defining, through their intellectual involvement and contributions, the innovation as their own.

In our work these study groups rapidly became the "center of gravity" of the project. The initial training of teachers in ethnographic methods took place in these settings. This later included the selection of households, the development of strategies for approaching families, discussions and interpretations of findings, and problem solving as we progressed with the work. The discussions of theory, readings, and the planning of activities also took place in the study groups.

In addition, these settings became the "mediating structure" between households and classrooms. This is where we discussed how to use in classrooms what we were learning in households. All teaching innovations and attempts to integrate funds of knowledge into instruction were initiated in these study groups. As teachers implemented new activities, they were discussed here, as were the discussions of conference presentations and articles written by the project participants, including teachers.

These study groups were also the place for developing the relationships among the project participants. As soon as teachers made their initial visits to a household and had data that they collected themselves, the relationships between teachers and researchers became more symmetrical, a relationship among peers doing research. It was no longer the case of university-based researchers bringing into the discussion "their data" to impress upon teachers the importance of household resources. The household research and the identification of resources now became a "joint activity," a collaborative effort. We should add that in no case did the researchers relinquish their expertise in these research matters, no more than the teachers relinquished their expertise on teaching. We continued to take the lead in discussions of household theory and research methods; the teachers took the lead in discussion of teaching and learning in classrooms. But we forged the project together.

Furthermore, these settings became the place to educate others about the project. The principals were invited to attend and learn more about the work. One of the principals not only conducted her own household visits but accompanied reluctant teachers on their initial visits. A district superintendent visited a study group a few times to hear the teachers describe their work and the conditions they needed to continue their involvement. Teachers and researchers visiting from other states or countries were also invited to the study group. And the study group became the model for a graduate course on field research methods for teachers.

Through our collaboration with teachers we also understood better the difficulties of sustaining the project in a school and of introducing innovations based on the project into practice. As is well known, teachers face various constraints including district goals which must be accomplished, a curriculum to follow, tests to administer, in-services to attend, and what seems an overwhelming amount of paper work to complete. We do not underestimate the difficulty of the process we have undertaken and the time needed to sustain, develop, and improve the work. A major problem with projects such as ours, as Sarason (1982) has emphasized, is assuming that one can program change by the calendar. There is often an unrealistic time perspective of the difficulties of obtaining positive change in places as complex as schools and classrooms. Researchers are notorious for underestimating the difficulties of going from a good idea or promising results to sound classroom practice (Gallimore, 1985).

So, without doubt, time is a crucial element. Teachers need the time to meet and think as well as the time to conceptualize and conduct the household research and consider the implications for their practice. Gaining additional time for teachers usually implies some sort of restructuring of the school day, where teachers can have a reasonable amount of time during the week to meet. In our school systems, especially those serving working-class students, teachers as well as students are tracked, and neither have much control of or say about their work and their goals. The formation of study groups to collaborate with others, indeed, to form a community with others, is a strategy to provide teachers with the autonomy to be active thinkers about their work and, with support, make change a possibility.

And now a word about money. We paid the teachers in the project for their participation. They were remunerated for their participation in the study groups and in any other activities related to the project. Did paying the teachers make a difference in their rate of participation and in their willingness to try out a new approach? We assume it did. The teachers were pleased that they were getting paid, after all, they are professionals participating in a research project, but they were also strongly motivated to participate by the opportunity to learn more about the families in ways that may benefit their students. If our experience is any indication, most teachers are concerned about the students in their class, want them to do better, and are willing to put in the time and effort to assist them. If they receive money or academic credit, it is a welcome change but not a necessary one to get teachers to meet, conduct household research, share data, ideas, and opinions, and try to improve the ways they are teaching. Most teachers still work in relative isolation from their peers. They want and appreciate the opportunity to meet with other teachers to discuss and deal with substantive issues in education.

What are the next steps in our research? We are considering several activities. One is to develop the work in other communities, especially major urban centers. Is this project, with teachers making household visits for research purposes, feasible in a place like Chicago or New York City? We certainly think so. After all, other researchers and educators, although with a different emphasis, have been doing community-based work in these communities for many years. We also think that the theoretical concept of funds of knowledge and the emphasis on households as units of study will travel well. Regardless of ethnic background or social class, families will organize into household units, although, of course, with considerable variability. And these households will be developed and maintained through the productive activities of its members, where funds of knowledge will be used to exist, to make a go of it in life. So that regardless of community or household characteristic, funds of knowledge will play a central role in the life of families. And it is these funds of knowledge, the concrete manifestations of cultural practices within specific conditions of life, not culture in the abstract, that is of interest here, and of immediate relevance for teaching. Nevertheless, whether our approach is feasible in a major urban center, and with a variety of cultural groups, remains an empirical question.

We are also interested in specifying more carefully the curricular implications of our work. We are better at organizing systematic inquiry into household dynamics than at creating systemic links to classroom practice. For example, can we document mathematical funds of knowledge that are of practical relevance for classrooms in elementary or middle schools? How can we assess the effectiveness of instructional innovations developed through household analysis? To provide convincing evidence that our approach has a positive influence on classroom learning is one of our highest priorities.

We would also like to pay more attention to the role of children in household life and in the development of funds of knowledge. We are aware that knowing a lot about adults in households does not necessarily tell us anything important about children or about how to teach children in schools. Children's social worlds, to a great extent, may be independent from those of adults yet mediate their relationships with adults and adult institutions, such as schools (see Andrade & Moll, 1993). It is important to balance the data collection efforts in households between adults and children.

Finally, there is also the possibility of training pre-service teachers in our methods, so that when they enter schools they have both theory and methods to approach local communities. These novice teachers now have the vaguest notions of community, especially if they have never lived in the school's community, much less concrete ideas about how to turn community information into assets for their teaching. Perhaps we can learn together.

NOTES
1. Portions of this article have appeared in González, Norma. 1995. "Processual Approaches to Multicultural Education." *Journal of Applied Behavioral Science* 31(2):234-244. Portions of this research were funded by the National Center for Cultural Diversity and Second Language Learning, through the Office of Educational Research and Improvement (OERI) of the U.S. Department of Education, under Co-operative Agreement No. R117G10022. The findings and opinions expressed here are those of the authors and do not necessarily reflect the positions or policies of OERI.
2. This case example was developed by James Greenberg and borrows from the household research of Javier Taipa (1991).
3. We should point out that there are many differences in the concepts of social capital and funds of knowledge, most having to do with the theoretical and methodological underpinnings of the concepts. Funds of knowledge is an anthropological concept developed from ethnographic field research on household and community dynamics (see Greenberg, 1989; Vélez-Ibáñez, 1988); social capital is a sociological concept based on statistical, comparative analyses of school achievement, based primarily on test scores.

REFERENCES
Amanti, Cathy. 1994. "Teachers Doing Research: Beyond Classroom Walls." Paper presentation, Society for Applied Anthropology, Cancun, Mexico.
Amanti, Cathy. 1995. "Teachers Doing Research: Beyond Classroom Walls." *Practicing Anthropology* 17(3):7-10.

Andrade, Rosi, and Luis C. Moll. 1993. "The Social Worlds of Children: An Emic View." *The Journal of the Society for Accelerative Learning and Teaching* 18(1&2): 81-125.

Bissex, Glenda L. 1987. "Why Case Studies?" Pp. in 7-19 in *Seeing for Ourselves: Case-Study Research by Teachers of Writing*, edited by Glenda L. Bissex and Richard H. Bullock. Portsmouth, NH: Heinemann.

Coleman, James. 1987. "Families and Schools." *Educational Researcher* 16(6):32-38.

Coleman, James. 1988. "Social Capital in the Creation of Human Capital." *American Journal of Sociology* 94(Supplement):95-120.

Coleman, James, and Thomas Hoffer. 1987. *Public and Private High Schools: The Impact of Communities*. New York: Basic Books.

Ferreiro, Emilia. 1994. "Diversidad y Proceso de Alfabetizacin: De la Celebración a la Toma de Conciencia." Opening plenary session, International Reading Association, 15th World Congress, Buenos Aires, Argentina.

Gallimore, Ronald. 1985. "The Accommodation of Instruction to Cultural Differences." Paper presented at the University of California Conference on the Underachievement of Linguistic Minorities, Lake Tahoe, CA.

González, Norma. 1995. "Processual Approaches to Multicultural Education." *Journal of Applied Behavioral Science* 31(2):234-244.

González, Norma, and Cathy Amanti. (1997). "Teaching Anthropological Methods to Teachers: The Transformation of Knowledge." Pp. 353-359 in *The Teaching of Anthropology: Problems, Issues, and Decisions*, edited by Conrad Kottak, Jane White, Richard Furlow, and Patricia Rice. Mountain View, CA: Mayfield.

González, Norma, Cathy Amanti, and Martha Floyd. 1994. "Redefining 'Teachers as Researchers': The Research/Practice Connection." Unpublished manuscript.

González, Norma, Luis C. Moll, Martha Floyd-Tenery, Anna Rivera, Patricia Rendon, Racquel Gonzales, and Cathy Amanti. 1995. "Funds of Knowledge for Teaching in Latino Households.." *Urban Education* 29(4):443-470.

Goodson, Ivor. 1991. "Teachers' Lives and Educational Research." Pp. 137-149 in *Biography, Identity and Schooling: Episodes in Educational Research*, edited by Ivor Goodson, and Rob Walker. London: Falmer.

Greenberg, James B. 1989. "Funds of Knowledge: Historical Constitution, Social Distribution, and Transmission." Paper presented at the Annual Meeting of the Society for Applied Anthropology, Santa Fe, NM.

Hensley, Marla. 1995. "From Untapped Potential to Creative Realization: Empowering Parents of Multicultural Backgrounds." *Practicing Anthropology* 17(3):13-17.

Lytle, Susan, and Marilyn Cochran-Smith. 1990. "Learning from Teacher Research: A Working Typology." *Teachers College Record* 92(1):83-103.

Moll, Luis C. 1992a. "Bilingual Classrooms and Community Analysis: Some Recent Trends." *Educational Researcher* 21(2):20-24.

Moll, Luis C. 1992b. "Literacy Research in Community and Classrooms: A Sociocultural Approach." Pp. 211-224 in *Multidisciplinary Perspectives in Literacy Research*, edited by Richard Beach, Judith Green, Michael Kamil, and Timothy Shanahan. Urbana, IL: National Conference on Research in English.

Moll, Luis C., Cathy Amanti, Deborah Neff, and Norma González. 1992. "Funds of Knowledge for Teaching: Using a Qualitative Approach to Connect Homes and Classrooms." *Theory into Practice* 31(2):132-141.

Moll, Luis C., and Norma González. 1994. "Lessons from Research with 'Language Minority' Students." *Journal of Reading Behavior* 26(4):439-456.

Moll, Luis C., and James Greenberg. 1990. "Creating Zones of Possibilities: Combining Social Contexts for Instruction." Pp. 319-348 in *Vygotsky and Education*, edited by Luis C. Moll. Cambridge: Cambridge University Press.

Moll, Luis C., Javier Tapia, and Kathy Whitmore. 1993. "Living Knowledge: The Social Distribution of Cultural Resources for Thinking." Pp. 139-163 in *Distributed Cognitions: Psychological and Educational Considerations*, edited by Gavriel Salomon. Cambridge: Cambridge University Press.

Sarason, Seymour. 1982. *The Culture of the School and The Problem of Change.* Boston: Allyn & Bacon.

Spindler, George, and Louise Spindler. 1990. "The Inductive Case Study Approach to Teaching Anthropology." *Anthropology and Education Quarterly* 21(2):106-112.

Tapia, Javier. 1991. "Cultural Reproduction: Funds of Knowledge as Survival Strategies in the Mexican American Community." Unpublished doctoral dissertation, University of Arizona.

Vélez-Ibáñez, Carlos G. 1988. "Networks of Exchange Among Mexicans in the U.S. and Mexico: Local Level Mediating Responses to National and International Transformations." *Urban Anthropology* 17(1):27-51.

CHAPTER 5

Tracking Untracking: The Consequences of Placing Low-Track Students in High-Track Classes

Hugh Mehan

INTRODUCTION

Students from linguistic minority and ethnic minority backgrounds and low-income families do poorly in school by comparison with their majority and well-to-do contemporaries. They drop out at a higher rate. They score lower on tests. Their grades are lower. Most importantly, for the topic of this paper, they do not attend college as often (Carter & Wilson, 1991; American Council on Education, 1989). African American and Latino students have been enrolling in college increasingly, but not at the same rate as white students. In 1970, 26 percent of African American high school graduates enrolled in four-year colleges. This rate reached a high of 34 percent in 1976, declined to 31 percent in 1989, and rose to 33 percent in 1990. In 1972 (the first year data were available), 26 percent of Latino high school graduates enrolled in college, while only 29 percent enrolled in 1990. Although these college enrollment figures are improving, they are still well below those of white students; 33 percent of white high school graduates enrolled in college in 1970, and 39 percent enrolled in college in 1989 (Carter & Wilson, 1991: 36-37).

Untracking: An Alternative to Compensatory Education

"Compensatory education" has been the prevailing strategy employed by public schools throughout the United States to deal with educational inequality. Proponents of compensatory education say educational inequality is the result of a failure on the part of underachieving linguistic and ethnic minority youth. Compensatory education is designed to overcome their failure through remedial programs. Students who have been unsuccessful in school are placed into special programs. The curriculum in compensatory education programs is reduced in scope, content, and pace. Students receive a reduced curriculum, delivered in simpler form at a slower pace. Proponents of compensatory education believe that underachieving students will develop academic skills and will be promoted to "regular education" or even college-bound programs.

Research has shown, however, that the schools' practices of tracking, ability grouping and testing contribute to inequality (Rosenbaum, 1978; Cicourel & Mehan, 1983; Oakes, 1985; Page & Valli, 1991; Mehan, 1992; Oakes et al., 1992). Students placed on remedial tracks seldom catch up to their peers. They seldom receive equivalent curriculum or instruction. Furthermore, they often suffer the stigmatizing consequences of negative labeling (Mercer, 1974; Mehan et al., 1985). Placement in vocational and non-college-prep classes can trap ethnic and linguistic minority students despite their good achievement in school, as this comment by a Latina high school student illustrates:

My first day signing up for high school . . . my Dad had been working in the fields, but he came home early this day to take me so I could get registered . . . there was a counselor . . . and I took my eighth grade diploma which was straight As, and I was valedictorian of my eighth grade . . . and I told him I would like to go to college and could he fit me into college prep classes? And he looked at my grades and everything, and said, well, he wasn't sure I could handle it. My dad didn't understand. He was there with me. And this counselor put me in non-college prep classes. I remember going home and feeling just terrible (Gándara, 1995:73-74).

Recognizing the inequities caused by compensatory education, tracking and ability grouping, educators are exploring alternatives to these practices (Wheelock, 1992). "Accelerated Schools" (Levin, 1987), "cooperative learning" (Slavin et al., 1989), "restructured schools" (Sizer, 1992), "School Development Programs" (Comer, 1988) and "detracking" (Oakes et al., 1993) are just some of the reform efforts under way. In San Diego, one effort to break down the barriers erected by school sorting practices is to "untrack" students."

The AVID Untracking Program
The San Diego approach to "untracking" places previously low-achieving students (who are primarily from low-income and ethnic or language minority backgrounds) in the same college-prep academic program as high-achieving students (who are primarily from middle- or upper-middle income and "Anglo" backgrounds). "Untracking," then, is different from "detracking." Untracking is the process of assisting a small number of students to move from general and vocational tracks to the college-prep track. Detracking, as Oakes et al. (1993) explain it, refers to the process of dismantling the tracking system in one comprehensive effort. As I discuss in the conclusion of this paper, untracking has the potential to be the first step in a detracking effort.

The "Achievement via Individual Determination" (AVID) untracking program shifts education policy for underachieving students away from compensatory or remedial instruction. Instead of simplifying instruction or reducing the curriculum for underachieving students, AVID attempts to maintain a rigorous curriculum for all students while adding increased support for low-achieving students.

The idea of untracking low-achieving students was introduced to the San Diego City Schools in 1980 at Clairemont High, a predominantly white school, by Mary Catherine Swanson, a member of the English Department. Untracking became a way to educate minority students bused to Clairemont from predominantly ethnic minority schools in southeast San Diego in response to court-ordered desegregation. Unwilling to segregate African American and Latino students into a separate, compensatory curriculum, Swanson and the Clairemont faculty placed the bused students in regular college-prep classes. The expressed goals of the program are to motivate and prepare underachieving students from underrepresented linguistic and ethnic minority groups or low-income students of any ethnicity to perform well in high school and to seek a college education.

AVID soon spread beyond Clairemont High School. One of Swanson's colleagues went to Madison High School; she helped introduce AVID there in 1984. In 1986, Swanson was called to the San Diego County Office of Education and charged with the responsibility of implementing the AVID untracking model county-wide. Three other schools within the San Diego Unified School District adopted the AVID model of untracking low-achieving students between 1986 and 1989. The School Board of the San Diego City Schools mandated the adoption of AVID in every high school in the spring semester of 1987. By 1991, eleven other city schools, two schools in nearby districts, 50 high schools in San Diego County, and 84 high schools outside the county had introduced AVID programs.

AVID coordinators select students for the program. Low-income, ethnic and linguistic minority students with average to high scores on the "Comprehensive Test of Basic Skills" (CTBS), and "C" level junior high school grades are eligible for AVID. Once these high potential/low performance students are identified, parents are advised about the program. Those parents who agree to support their children's participation in the academic program sign contracts to have their children participate in AVID in high school.

Students are placed in a special AVID course which they take as an elective in three of their four high school years. This class meets every day for a regular class period. Within this special elective course, AVID advocates a distinctive approach to curriculum and instruction; the acronym for this approach is "WIC"—which stands for writing, inquiry and collaboration (Swanson, no date).

"Writing" is seen as a tool of learning. In the AVID classroom, students are taught a special form of note-taking, called the Cornell system. Students are instructed to jot detailed notes from their academic classes in a wide right-hand margin of a notebook and, as homework, develop questions based on the notes in a narrow left-hand column. These questions are to be used the following day in the AVID class. In addition to note-taking, the students are to keep "learning logs" (thoughts and reactions to the classes, learning and studying) and practice "quick writes" (thoughts about a poem or story written quickly without editing) (Swanson, no date).

"Inquiry" refers to the relationship between tutors (students recruited from local colleges) and the students in the elective AVID class. The program provides tutors to the AVID teacher who works in the AVID classroom. Tutors are trained to lead study groups in such subjects as math or English, based on the students' notes and questions. Tutors are trained not to give answers. AVID students clarify their thoughts based on their questions with help from their tutors. AVID insists on the inquiry method to keep the AVID class from becoming a glorified study hall or homework session and to help students become independent thinkers (Swanson, no date).

"Collaboration" is the instructional strategy of having students work together to achieve instructional goals rather than having them work in isolation. Collaborative groups or study teams enable students to serve as sources of information and feedback for each other. Collaboration, AVID asserts, shifts the responsibility for learning from the teacher who directs lessons to the students who participate with each other and the teacher (Swanson, no date).

AVID promotes the integration of WIC methodologies into the academic classes that AVID students take. To facilitate this diffusion of effective teaching strategies, AVID conducts summer institutes. Each school that is implementing AVID is invited to send an interdisciplinary team to the workshop. The team consists of the school principal, the head counselor, the AVID coordinator, and instructional leaders from the English, foreign language, history, science, and mathematics departments. While at the institute, the team is encouraged to use the three AVID methods—writing to learn, inquiry, and collaboration—with all students, not just AVID students. The interdisciplinary team is invited to return to the institute in subsequent years to learn how to diffuse the AVID methodologies throughout the school. The summer institute is supplemented by monthly workshops conducted during the subsequent school year, semi-annual site team meetings, and semi-annual site visitations by County Office AVID staff (Swanson, no date).

AVID Center suggests a basic plan for the weekly instructional activities within AVID classrooms. Two school days are designated tutorial days. On these days, students work in small groups with the assistance of a tutor. On the other two days, writing as a tool for learning is emphasized. On these days, students engage in a variety of activities, including essay writing for their academic classes and college applications. One day a week, usually Fridays, are "motivational days." Guest speakers are invited to address the class, and field trips to colleges are scheduled on these days.

Tracking the Untracking Experiment in San Diego
We (Mehan et al., 1996) have been tracking the San Diego untracking effort since 1990, using official school records,

observations in classrooms, and interviews of students, teachers, parents, and school officials. The San Diego City Schools (SDCS) kindly supplied us with the Cumulative School Records (CSRs) of AVID students in the classes of 1990, 1991, and 1992. We used information from the CSRs to determine students' ethnicity and to calculate their academic record in high school (e. g., AVID classes taken, CTBS scores, college preparatory courses taken and completed, etc.).

Of the 1,053 SDCS students grades 9-12, enrolled in AVID, we found 353 students in 14 high schools who had completed three years of AVID during their high school careers when they graduated in 1990, 1991, and 1992. We also identified 288 students who had entered AVID in the same academic year as the "untracked group," but who did not complete three years of the program. Instead, they left after one semester or one year.

In order to determine students' post-graduation activities, we attempted to interview the 353 graduates of the classes of 1990, 1991, and 1992 and the 288 students who started but did not complete AVID. We were able to interview 248 of the program graduates and 146 of the program leavers. We asked both groups of students what they had done since high school graduation, i. e., whether they had enrolled in four- or two-year colleges or were working. In order to place students' college enrollment and work information in context, we asked students about their family background (e. g., parents' education, languages spoken in the home). We also discussed their high school and AVID experiences with them. This information helped us determine whether untracking helps students from low-income and underrepresented backgrounds enroll in college.

In order to measure the socioeconomic background of students, we considered their parents' income and educational attainment. We calculated the parents' median income using census track information from the 1990 census kindly supplied to us by the San Diego Association of Governments (SANDAG). We obtained information about parents' education through our interviews with AVID students.

In order to determine what makes untracking work, we went beyond correlational data and examined classroom practices and organizational processes. To do so, we conducted case studies of 8 of the 17 high schools in the San Diego Unified School District that are participating in this untracking effort. We chose high schools in the San Diego district because AVID started there and because that was the only district in San Diego County that had computerized student records. We chose the eight schools based on their students' ethnic enrollments, their college enrollment rates and, of course, their willingness to participate in the study.

UNTRACKING AND COLLEGE ENROLLMENT
In order to determine the educational consequences of placing low-achieving students in college-prep courses with their high-achieving peers, we will compare the college enrollment of 248 AVID students who graduated in 1990, 1991, and 1992 to the enrollment of 742 students who graduated in 1991 from a number of high schools in the SDCS district, and 7,964,000 students who graduated from U.S. high schools in 1990 and with 146 students who left the program after participating for one year or less. These comparisons will provide us insight into the value of organizing schools to emphasize an academic curriculum as an alternative to compensatory education for underrepresented students. The college enrollment records of students who completed three years of AVID in contrast to those who completed one year will be particularly instructive for determining the effect of the program.

The College Enrollment of AVID Students
This untracking program has been successful in preparing its students for college. Figure 5.1 shows that 48 percent (120 of the 248 students) who completed three years of AVID reported enrolling in four-year colleges, 99 (40 percent) reported enrolling in two-year or junior colleges and the remaining 29 students (12 percent) said they are working or doing other things, such as engaging in church service, traveling, or doing voluntary work.

Of the 120 students attending four-year colleges, 52 (43 percent) are enrolled in colleges within the California State University (CSU) system; 19 (25 percent) are enrolled in colleges in the University of California (UC) system, and the remaining 49 students are enrolled in a variety of private universities in and out of California. Most of the UC and CSU enrollees have stayed close to home; 18 of the 29 (62 percent) UC enrollees attend the University of California, San Diego (UCSD), whereas 42 of the 52 (81 percent) CSU enrollees attend San Diego State University (SDSU).

Figure 5.1.

The College Enrollment of AVID Students

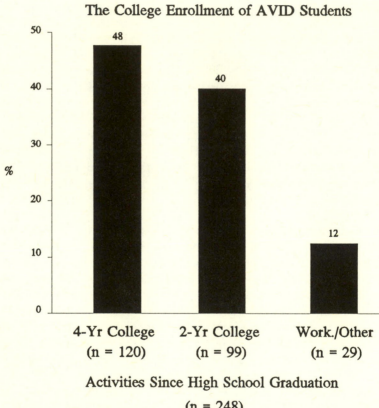

Activities Since High School Graduation
(n = 248)

Figure 5.2 allows us to compare the college enrollment of the 248 students who graduated in 1990, 1991, and 1992 after participating in AVID for three years with three other groups: (1) those students who graduated in 1991 from a number of high schools in the SDCS district, (2) those students who graduated from U.S. high schools in 1990 and (3) AVID students who started in AVID but left within one year. In Figure 5.2 and all subsequent figures, we will refer to students who completed AVID as "AVID 3" and students who left after one year as "AVID 1."

The Enrollment of AVID, SDCS, and U.S. Students in Four-Year Colleges
The AVID four-year college enrollment rate of 48 percent compares favorably to the local average and the national average. Bell (1993) surveyed 742 students who graduated from San Diego high schools in 1991. He found that 37 percent of that class went on to four-year colleges, 34 percent attended two-year colleges, and 29 percent reported working or doing other things. The American Council of Education reported that 39 percent of the 20 million students who graduated from high school in 1990 enrolled in four-year colleges. This means that the four-year college enrollment rate of AVID students is higher than the local and national rate.

The 48 percent four-year college enrollment rate of students who participated in AVID for three years also compares favorably with the four-year college enrollment rate of students who completed one year or less of AVID. Our interviews with the 146 AVID leavers revealed that 34 percent of them enrolled in college within a year of their graduation from high school. The difference in college enrollment rates between these two groups suggests that the AVID untracking program has an effect on students' career choices after they complete high school. The longer they stay in the program, the more likely they will enroll in college.

The 48 percent figure for enrollment in four-year colleges is important because U.S. students from underrepresented groups are not going to college at just the time the number of jobs requiring college education is increasing (NCEE, 1990). In fact, students across the nation are enrolling more often in two-year colleges than they are enrolling in four-year colleges. From 1978 to 1988, two-year colleges increased enrollments by 21 percent whereas four-year colleges increased by only 14 percent (Carter & Wilson, 1991: 4).

Figure 5.2.

The Enrollment of AVID, SDCD, and U.S. Students in Four-Year Colleges

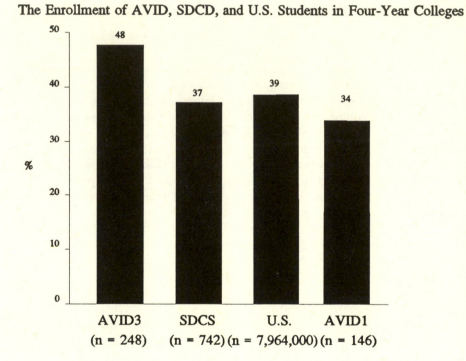

College Enrollment

The College Enrollment of African American Students
Even though more African American students have been enrolling in college since the civil rights era, they are still below the college enrollment figures of white students, as noted earlier. Figure 5.3 shows that 55 percent of African American students who participated in AVID for three years attend four-year colleges; 50 percent of those who participated in AVID for one year attend four-year colleges, while 38 percent of African American students who attended SDCS high schools go on to four-year colleges. The national average (33 percent) is slightly lower than the SDCS average (38 percent). These data indicate that African American AVID students, whether they participate in AVID for one or three years, are enrolling in college at rates that are considerably higher than the local and national averages.

The Enrollment of African American Students in Four-Year Colleges
A large number of African American students across the nation are enrolling in historically black colleges and universities (HBCUs). In 1990, approximately 17 percent of African Americans in college were enrolled in HBCUs (Carter & Wilson, 1991). Based on our interviews with AVID graduates, we are seeing a similar trend among African American students in San Diego: 21 percent of African American graduates from the classes of 1990-1992 enrolled in historically black colleges and universities. Likewise, 26 percent of the African American students who began in AVID but left after one year enrolled in HBCUs the fall after they graduated from high school.

The college enrollment of African American students who participate in AVID is important because the college enrollment gap between whites and African Americans has been fairly constant during the last decade. African Americans have made relatively little progress in achieving parity in college participation in the latter half of the 1980s. In fact, the gap between African American and white college enrollment has widened since the 1970s (Carter & Wilson, 1991: 36-37).

Figure 5.3.

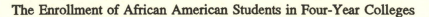

The Enrollment of African American Students in Four-Year Colleges

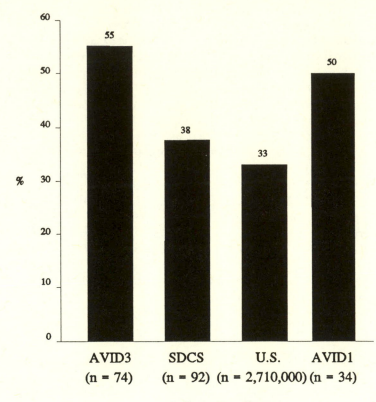

College Enrollment

The College Enrollment of Latino Students

Latinos have made only modest gains in college enrollment in the past decade. Although the overall *number* of Latinos enrolled in the nation's colleges and universities has increased since the 1970s, their college enrollment *rate* may be declining. Between 1988 and 1990, the total number of Latino students enrolled in college rose by 11 percent from 680,000 to 758,000 students (Carter & Wilson, 1991: 43). The rate of enrollment, however, is declining. In 1972, 25.8 percent of the Latinos who graduated from high school went on to college. For two years, 1975 and 1976, this figure increased to 36 percent but declined then to 29 percent in 1990 (Carter & Wilson, 1991: 37). Furthermore, more Latino students attend two-year colleges than four-year colleges. As of 1988 (the last year for which this information is available), 56 percent of Latino students enrolling in college went to two-year colleges (Carter & Wilson, 1991: 26).

By contrast, the Latino students who participated in AVID for three years are enrolling in college in numbers greater than the national and local average: 43 percent of Latino AVID students enroll in four-year colleges, while the SDCS average is 25 percent and the national average is 29 percent. Furthermore, there is a considerable difference in the college enrollment rates of students who participate in AVID for different amounts of time. Those Latino students who participate in AVID for three years enroll in four year colleges at a 43 percent rate, while those who left the program after one year enroll in four-year colleges at a 20 percent rate. This finding is especially impressive because the national Latino college enrollment rate is not increasing. In 1972, 26 percent of the high school graduating class enrolled in college. See Figure 5.4.

Parent's Socioeconomic Status and Students' College Enrollment

Socioeconomic status (SES) is normally measured using some combination of parents' occupation, income, and educational level. Our indicator of parents' income is the family's median household income as calculated from census track data and parents' education from our interviews with AVID graduates.

Figure 5.4.

The Enrollment of Latino Students in Four-Year Colleges

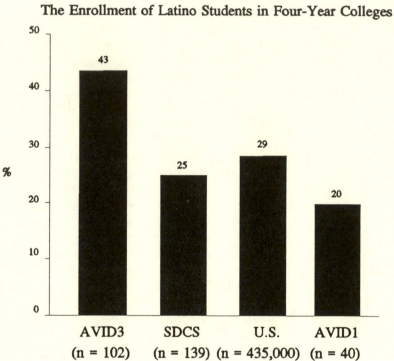

College Enrollment

Figure 5.5 shows the college enrollment of students in the untracking experiment according to the median income of their parents and the years the students spent in the program.

Let us consider the group of students who completed three years of AVID first. If we disregard the eleven students from the $60K+ group, we find that the students who come from the lowest income strata enroll in four-year colleges in greater proportion than students who come from higher income strata; 57 percent of three-year AVID students whose parents earn less than $20,000 enroll in four-year colleges; that is greater than the college enrollment figure of the three-year AVID students in the $20-39,000 and the $40-59,000 range. Now, examining the college enrollment records of students who complete one year of AVID, we find that 31 percent of students from the lowest income group and 35 percent of the students from the $20-39K income group enroll in college, whereas 37 percent of the students in the $40-59K income group enroll in college.

Thus, the college enrollment record of the group of students that leave AVID is highly correlated with their parents' income; the higher the parents' income, the more likely their children are to enroll in college. We do not find this linear correlation among the group of students who have completed three years of AVID. Students from low-income families enroll in college at rates that are higher than students who come from more well-to-do families.

When we compare the college enrollment rates of the two groups of AVID students at each income level, we find that (with the exception of the $60K+ group) the students who have completed three years of AVID enroll in college at a higher rate than the students who have completed one year or less of AVID. The most striking difference appears in the lowest income group. Three-year AVID students who come from this income group enroll in college at almost twice the rate of one-year AVID students (57 percent vs. 31 percent). In the higher-income brackets, the enrollment gap is not quite as dramatic but is still significant. Three-year AVID students who come from families who earn between $20,000 and $39,999 enroll in college 11 percent more often than students who have completed one year of AVID (46 percent vs. 35 percent). Three-year AVID students who come from families who earn between $40,000 and $59,999 enroll in college 12 percent more often than students who have completed one year of AVID (49 percent vs. 37 percent).

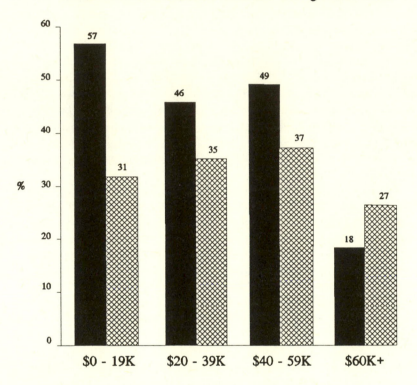

Figure 5.5.

AVID Parents' Income and Students' College Enrollment

Enrollment in 4-Year Colleges

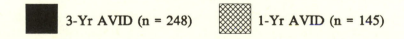 3-Yr AVID (n = 248)   1-Yr AVID (n = 145)

The possibility that this untracking program is suppressing the effects of SES gains support when we examine students' college enrollment in relation to parents' education. Recall that 48 percent of the students who completed three years of AVID enrolled in four-year colleges and 34 percent of the students who completed one year of AVID enrolled in four-year colleges in the fall after they graduated from high school. Figure 5.6 arrays the college enrollment of one-year and three-year AVID students according to the education that their parents obtained.

First, considering three-year AVID students, we find that those students whose parents took college courses or graduated from college do not enroll in college in greater numbers than students whose parents have a high school diploma or less. In fact, students who come from families whose parents are high school graduates enroll in college as often as students who come from families whose parents have had college experience; 51 percent of the former and 51 percent of the latter go to college.

We find a different, in fact linear, relationship within the AVID leaver group. The higher the educational level of one-year AVID parents, the higher the college enrollment rate of their children. Although only 17 percent of the one year AVID students whose parents have less than a high school education and 32 percent of the first-year AVID students whose parents have earned a high school diploma enroll in college, 39 percent of the students whose parents have earned some college credit and 45 percent of the students whose parents have earned a bachelor of arts degree enroll in college.

At each level of their parents' education, students who have participated in AVID for three years have a better college enrollment record than students who participated in AVID for one year. When we consider the group of parents who do not have high school degrees, we find that three-year AVID students enroll in college almost three times more than one-year AVID students (44 percent vs. 17 percent). When we consider the group of parents who have completed high school, we also find that this difference is greater (51 percent vs. 32 percent). The gap in college enrollment is not as great when we consider the group of parents who have some college, yet students with more untracking experience still outstrip students with less untracking experience: 51 percent of the three-year AVID students enroll in college compared to 39 percent of the one-year AVID students. The difference is least among the

Figure 5.6.

Parents' Education and Students' College Enrollment

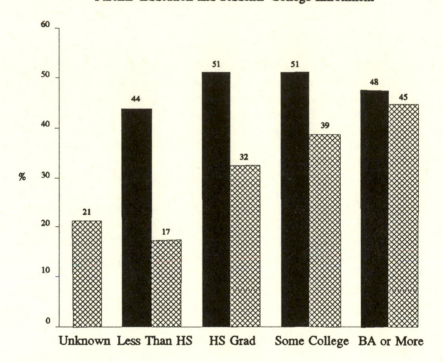

Parents' Educational Level

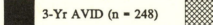 3-Yr AVID (n = 248)   1-Yr AVID (n = 146)

group of students whose parents have completed college: 48 percent to 45 percent.

SUMMARY: UNTRACKING WORKS
Students from underrepresented ethnic and linguistic backgrounds who participated in the San Diego untracking experiment are enrolling in college in numbers that exceed local and national averages. Forty-eight percent of the "untracked" students who graduated in the classes of 1990, 1991, and 1992 enrolled in four-year colleges. This figure compares favorably with the local average of 37 percent and the national average of 39 percent.

The college enrollment rate for students who participated in AVID for three years is also superior to the enrollment rate of students who participated in AVID for one year or less. This difference implies that the untracking program has an effect over time; the longer students stay in the untracking program, the greater its impact on students' college enrollment.

The factors usually associated with SES (e. g., parents' income, parents education) are not responsible for the impressive college enrollment figures of these "untracked" students. Students who come from the lowest income strata enroll in four-year colleges in equal or higher proportion to students who come from higher-income strata. Students who were raised in families in which their parents have less than a college education enroll in four-year colleges more than students who were raised in families in which the parents have a college education.

These data invite us to look more closely at the educational practices of the untracking program in order to understand the reasons for its success. In the following sections, we explore the idea that the academic success of "untracked" students is the result of institutional practices operating within the program.

EXPLICIT SOCIALIZATION INTO IMPLICIT ACADEMIC CULTURE
There are implicit, often unstated, dimensions of instruction that accompany the more obvious, explicit, academic dimensions of instruction. Whether they call it the "hidden curriculum" (Dreeben, 1968; Apple, 1982; Apple & Weis, 1983; Young, 1971; Keddie, 1971) or the "culture of the classroom" (Cazden & Mehan, 1988; Mehan, 1992), commentators suggest that certain ways of talking, thinking, and acting are demanded by the conventions of schooling.

The imperative to transmit a certain body of knowledge from teacher to students, the concern for factually correct information, the use of "known information questions" in verbal instruction, an insistence on text-based knowledge, the high value attached to naming, labeling and categorizing information, especially out of context, are part and parcel of this culture. Like other aspects of culture, the unique features of the classroom are tacit, and therefore must be learned implicitly.

The interaction that occurs in the home maps onto this culture of the classroom. The discourse patterns and socialization practices of upper-income and middle-income families resemble those of the classroom, whereas the discourse patterns and socialization practices of low-income families, especially those from linguistic and ethnic minority backgrounds, do not resemble those of the classroom. Although coherent and systematic, the discourse patterns and socialization practices of low-income families do not match so neatly the often-implicit demands of the classroom culture (Heath, 1982, 1986; Tharp & Gallimore, 1988).

The match between the socialization practices implicitly learned at home and the culture of the classroom appears to give middle-class students advantages over their working-class counterparts. The cultural knowledge or "cultural capital" (Bourdieu & Passeron, 1977; Bourdieu 1986) that middle-income and high-income families pass on to their children maps onto the knowledge expected of them in school, whereas the knowledge passed on by low-income families does not match the knowledge expected of students in school. Because the language used by middle-income parents matches the often implicit demands of the school, their children are being equipped with the very skills and techniques that are rewarded in the classroom and on tests. Likewise, because the language used by low-income parents does not match the discourse of the classroom, their children are not being provided with the background knowledge that is so important in the classroom and on tests.

Networks of relationships or "social capital" (Bourdieu, 1986) enable resources to accrue to people because they belong to and participate in certain groups. This social capital also enables elite families to assist their children. Because they have been to college themselves, well-to-do parents know what is expected of their own college-bound children concerning what courses to take, how to study, and how to take tests. Because they are more likely to have more money and time, middle-income parents adopt strategies for assisting their students that are approved and validated by the school (Lareau, 1989). The relationship between implicit social-ization and academic success has particular relevance for the students in this study. The linguistic and ethnic minority students who have been "untracked" (i. e., placed in academically rigorous college-prep programs) most often come from low-income families. As a result, low-income and minority students have not been immersed in the implicit socialization process that accrues social and cultural capital to the sons and daughters of well-to-do families.

Based on our observations in eight schools and on our interviews with students and teachers, we note that AVID coordinators are engaged in an explicit socialization process in their classrooms that parallels the implicit socialization process that occurs in well-to-do families. Students who have been selected into this program devote one academic period per day, five days a week for the 180-day school year to a specially designed course, often in lieu of an extra curricular activity or another elective course. AVID coordinators explicitly teach aspects of the implicit culture of the classroom and the hidden curriculum of the school. Furthermore, they mediate the relationship between families, high schools and colleges by serving as advocates and sponsors of AVID students.

Teaching Study Skills
AVID students are given explicit instruction in a special method of note-taking that stresses specific techniques for compiling main ideas, abstracting key concepts, and identifying questions which guide analysis. They are required to apply these techniques in notebooks that they keep for their academic courses. Tutors collect and check these notebooks once each week or once every two weeks. Students are graded on the completeness and quality of their notes. When asked what helps them the most, eight students from one high school we studied singled out the importance of learning to organize and manage their time and "learning to take good notes."

Test-taking skills were also taught in all AVID classrooms but were differentially emphasized. At a minimum, students were given practice on vocabulary items likely to be found on the Scholastic Aptitude Test (SAT). When a more extensive approach to test preparation was taken, students were provided explicit instruction in ways to eliminate distracting answers on multiple-choice questions. Students were also taught strategies for approximating answers and probabilities about the success of guessing. One AVID teacher devoted two successive weeks to SAT preparation, including practicing with vocabulary items, administering practice tests, reviewing wrong answers and strategies for taking tests. This teacher reviewed with her students the kinds of analogies typically found on the SAT so they could practice the kinds of problems found on their tests. This teacher also sent her students to an expert math teacher for assistance on math test items. She justified the time she devoted to this topic by explaining that she was teaching her students the same test-taking techniques found in the expensive Princeton Review SAT preparation class.

Teaching the College Entry Process
Although writing, note-taking, test-taking and vocabulary-building strategies were taught routinely in the eight AVID programs we studied from 1991 to 1993, the most conspicuous and intriguing teacher-led activity revolved around the complicated process involved in applying to and enrolling in college. Seniors were given extra coaching on how to write statements of purpose and how to fill out college application and financial aid forms. They were reminded about test and application deadlines. At one school, for instance, students must complete an AVID assignment each week in which they perform writing and/or reading tasks in preparation for the college application experience. The junior class at another school was given a handout, entitled "Choosing Your College," that contains a checklist of information typically found in college catalogs. Students were instructed to fill in the application information for a particular college according to the assigned checklist. This research task was intended to make AVID students more familiar with college catalogs and help them choose an appropriate college.

Students received very specific counseling information about applying to college. The AVID Coordinator at one of the schools we studied facilitated the application process by use of a packet, "Planning and Preparation for College," that is a systematic list of instructions that tells students about each step of the college application process. The process and deadlines were reviewed often. The coordinator's constant vigilance minimized students' opportunities to slip up. Mr. Frankfurter, the AVID Coordinator at Golden Gate High School, has constructed a particularly elaborate socialization regimen that covers all aspects of the college application process. This year-long activity is organized well in advance. Even though application packets are often available to students in counseling offices, Frankfurter personally obtains the application packets from the testing agency and distributes them to the students in his class to insure that his AVID students are registered for the SAT. To assist his students with application fee waivers, he drives to local colleges to pick up the necessary waiver forms. This extra effort has paid off; Frankfurter's AVID students have been able to get application fees waived by as many as four colleges. In addition, he makes special trips to local colleges to pick up large numbers of application packets so that each of his students will have one. To convince his students that finances should not limit their opportunities to attend college, he distributes information on more than 175 scholarships to his students.

Starting in October of each year, Mr. Frankfurter works with seniors as a separate group four days a week on all aspects of the college application process. In the first session during the 1992-93 school year, he presented a timeline to the seniors that marked application deadlines. From that point on, he checked each student's timeline weekly, to insure that students were on time and on task.

In subsequent sessions, the seniors filled out photocopies of CSU, UC, and University of San Diego applications line by line. After the draft applications were completed, Frankfurter checked them for accuracy, and then students completed the actual applications. Wanting to insure that his students had a college option close to home, he advised every student to apply to SDSU, either as a first choice or as a "backup."

Later in October, Frankfurter told the students to start thinking about letters of recommendation. He advised them to ask their junior-year English teacher for a letter of recommendation unless they did not do well in that class. Frankfurter told the seniors they could ask, in addition to their teachers, religious leaders and employers for a recommendation. Frankfurter himself writes over a hundred letters of recommendation each year for his students.

Many of these special sessions with seniors are devoted to helping students complete their personal statements and essays. Frankfurter works with each student, reminding him or her to include significant aspects of their biographies. When students have been pressed for time or lacked the skill to type, Frankfurter has typed final applications for them. Frankfurter's senior students at Golden Gate

High School told us this essay-writing was easy for them after so many years of practice.

While students were completing financial aid requests in January, Frankfurter passed on information about the intricacies of the financial aid process. To speed up the application process, he encouraged students to have their parents file their income tax forms early, so financial information could be included with the students' applications. He also addressed the interpersonal side of the college application process. Acknowledging that some parents may oppose students leaving home, he advised students to start preparing their parents early by talking about going to college around the house.

Even students with excellent grades acknowledged that without AVID, they would have missed application deadlines. Students who were not in AVID reinforced this impression:

> I missed taking the PSAT because I wasn't in AVID and I didn't know about it. One of my AVID friends asked me if I was going to take the test but it was too late to sign up. You don't know about this stuff unless you are in AVID.

Teaching Conflict Resolution Strategies
In addition to scaffolding the college application process, AVID teachers explicitly teach conflict-resolution strategies as part of their curriculum. Working-class students, both "minority" and white, often have different codes for resolving conflict than their teachers. Lisa Gonzalez, one of the four AVID Coordinators at Keeneland High School, extends her coaching to the organization of the phrases which students should employ when talking to their teachers. "Don't ask *if* you can make up an exam," she says. "Ask politely *when* the next make up is. If you miss a class, don't say 'I'll get an excuse,' go to the attendance office, get a copy of the teacher's roll sheet and say 'I'm sorry I missed your class, but here's my excuse.' " The conversational prompts that Gonzalez gives her students emphasize the importance of making polite conversation, not putting teachers on the defensive, and assuming teachers are agreeable people who make honest mistakes.

Gonzalez also utilizes students' knowledge and past experience to teach conflict resolution strategies. When two Latinas told her they were having trouble in their algebra class, Gonzalez did not give them advice. Instead, she asked other AVID students in her class to provide suggestions:

Teacher: What are some of the things they can do?
Student: Study ahead and formulate specific questions.
Student: Go to tutoring after school.
Student: Check out library books on the subject [other math texts].
Student: Talk to someone who understands the teacher.

Gonzalez then praised the class for offering "positive strategies" for doing well in class. A few days later, Gonzalez asked one of the students who had asked for help to tell the class how she resolved her problem. In eliciting this testimony, the AVID coordinator was encouraging the student to reflect on positive achievements for her own and others' benefit.

Using students to coach students in conflict resolution has the added benefit of encouraging students to be autonomous instead of dependent upon adults to identify ways to solve problems. In this way, students learn interactive skills that not only work within the high school but may be helpful in other arenas of their life when they are separated from their AVID teachers.

Teacher Advocacy

Another role AVID teachers adopt is that of student advocate. When interviewed, students at the several schools we studied consistently reported that AVID teachers intervene in the academic maze on behalf of their students. If students are absent, teachers call them in the evening. By talking to their AVID teachers, AVID students obtain missing assignments, and make sure not to be penalized for their absence.

The coordinator at Monrovia High School circulated to all teachers of advanced courses a list with the names and classes of the AVID students. She informed the teachers that the AVID students would be receiving extra help in this subject, but if they were having any problems, she was to be contacted. This strategy shifts the burden of failure away from the student and toward the teacher who must monitor the student's progress.

We observed several episodes that confirmed student opinion about the importance of teacher advocacy. One incident occurred when a new "tardy sweep" policy was implemented at Saratoga High.

One of the AVID students was late to a class. According to the new policy on tardiness, she would be punished by spending the remainder of the period in a detention room. The AVID student would not be allowed to make up missing work, including tests. She was irate. She and her friends complained to Mrs. Lincoln, her AVID Coordinator:

> I'm just trying to get an education. I just want to learn. They are keeping me from learning, just for being a minute late.

Mrs. Lincoln arranged for the vice principal to hear the students' complaints the very next day. Many students affirmed that no one would have listened to them had they not been AVID students and if Mrs. Lincoln had not acted on their behalf. Clearly, this teacher has adopted an advocacy role that extends beyond traditional teaching duties.

Advocacy on behalf of students is not limited to the academic realm; it extends into their personal lives as well. Mrs. Lincoln at Saratoga High School has intervened in suicide attempts, visited sick students, and called parents if she felt that their child was employed too many hours outside of school.

When Holly, a senior at Saratoga, had been missing a great deal of school, Mrs. Lincoln discussed the situation with her. Evidently, Holly had been baby-sitting a neglected young relative. Holly's grades had fallen drastically. Mrs. Lincoln talked to the head counselor to prevent Holly from being expelled. She then helped Holly continue with her application to SDSU, and she saw to it that other professionals could relieve Holly of the baby-sitting responsibility. By the end of the year, Holly's grades had improved; she had been accepted at SDSU, and both Mrs. Lincoln and the head counselor were working with Holly's father to insure that personal barriers would not prevent her from going to college.

Clearly, these teachers' interventions were instrumental in keeping students on the college track. Although students, especially those from low-income families, continue to labor under heavy academic and social pressure, they receive encouragement and support from dedicated AVID teachers. Not all interventions, however, are successful. The resources that an innovative school program such as AVID can muster are limited. Sometimes they are not sufficient to overcome the constraints imposed by the overwhelming practical circumstances in the lives of AVID students.

Jamala is one such student. When we interviewed a group of AVID students at Keeneland High School and asked them who planned to go on to college, everyone in the group responded in the affirmative. When asked if they planned to go to college before they started AVID, most, but not all, replied that they had. Jamala was one of the few students who had not had college plans before AVID; she just recently decided to go. When asked what led her to change her mind, she replied:

> I didn't want to be like the people in my family. Half haven't even graduated from high school. They stick together but they don't go anywhere together. I found out more specifics about college. AVID showed me that I had a choice.

Jamala's AVID teacher confirmed her story.

In her first (freshman) year in AVID, Mr. Johnson recalled that "she fought me all the way." She came back from her sophomore year, however, a changed person. In her third year in Keeneland's AVID program, Jamala was much more positive and motivated. Then her life circumstances changed considerably. Jamala was having trouble in her chemistry class and stopped going. Because Jamala was avoiding school and staying home, her mother, an unemployed high school graduate, suggested that Jamala look after her younger siblings regularly and attend an "alternative" (continuation) school. Jamala decided to do that and left Keeneland. Mr. Johnson put Jamala in contact with the AVID coordinator at the continuation school, and Ms. Gonzalez told him that Jamala still has college plans. It will be more difficult for Jamala to achieve this goal, however, from a continuation school that does not have a comprehensive college-prep curriculum. Although Jamala attributed part of her new ambition to the choices that AVID made her see, her high aspirations were not enough. The scaffolding AVID provided Jamala was not sufficient to sustain her ambitions in the face of a weak academic record coupled with overwhelming financial constraints.

Jamala's story is informative beyond the tragedy of her individual life. The existing social resources invested by AVID–a special class that meets once a day for 180 days, a dedicated teacher who serves as an advocate, college tutors—are not sufficient to propel all students down the college track. To reach Jamala and students like her, even more extensive resources are necessary. To be sure, if AVID deployed more extensive social support resources, then the program could help more low achieving students. We have to realize, however, that such school reform efforts as untracking are not a panacea. Unless the world of work is reorganized to provide more job opportunities with viable career mobility, then changes in the organization of schooling such as this untracking program will not be able to make a significant difference.

Institutional Sponsorship
In addition to mediating the life of students in high school, AVID teachers mediate the college entry process. Visits to colleges were a recurrent feature of AVID programs across all schools we studied or observed on a more casual basis. All programs organized day-long field trips to colleges in the local area, most notably SDSU and UCSD. Almost all programs organized trips to schools which are some distance away, UCLA and USC, for example. More extensive visits were less frequent. Of particular note, the AVID coordinator at Pimlico takes her students to northern California schools and also arranges a lengthy trip to historically black colleges and universities every other year. For many students, these field trips provided their first opportunity to see a college campus. While on college campuses, students visit classes, talk to college students, and, in some cases, visit dorms.

The following comment underlines the importance these trips have for AVID students:

> Field trips were great. I didn't even know what a college looked like until Mrs. Lincoln took us. Its like eating a cookie. It really tempts us to eat another one. You've smelled it and seen it and you want to buy it really bad.

"Career days" are another mediating mechanism visible in AVID programs. Guest speakers are invited to the class to discuss their professions or occupations. These career talks are always geared to those occupations that require a four-year college degree.

In the pages above, we described the elaborate socialization process Alex Frankfurter implemented at Golden Gate High School. His personal involvement in the application process does not end when students complete college application forms, however. He personally mails the applications, sometimes affixing his own stamps if students have forgotten them. He personally delivers the applications to one of the local colleges and goes through each application with the Equal Opportunity Program (EOP) admissions officer there.

In short, AVID teachers first introduce students to the possibility of attending college and then lead them through the college application process. In that respect, AVID coordinators act in ways that are similar to college advisors at elite college prep schools, who visit colleges, make numerous phone calls, compile elaborate dossiers and write well documented letters on behalf of their students (Cookson & Persell, 1985:167-189).

CONCLUSIONS AND POLICY IMPLICATIONS

I have examined the educational consequences of untracking as an alternative to compensatory education and remedial tracking for underachieving high school students. We found that the college enrollment rate for students who participate in the AVID untracking program for three years is higher than the college enrollment rate for students who did not participate. Ethnic and linguistic minority students from low-income backgrounds who have been untracked do as well or better than students from more well-to-do backgrounds.

These data suggest that the AVID untracking program is suppressing the well established effects of parents' income on students' academic achievement. This is an important finding, because the so-called "reproduction" school of thought on social class and educational attainment (e.g., Bowles & Gintis, 1976; Bourdieu & Passeron, 1977; Willis, 1977; MacLeod, 1987; MacLaren, 1989) suggests that students from low-income and poorly educated families are hampered by structural constraints relative to the children from middle-and upper-income families. As a result of these constraints, the sons and daughters of low-income and poorly educated families wind up in the same kinds of jobs as their parents. They do not progress upward through the occupational structure; their lowly positions are maintained, generation after generation.

Our data show that such students are not necessarily trapped by their social circumstances. Students from the lowest income and educational levels are attaining a prestigious and economically important goal, enrollment in college. This means social environments can be rearranged, at least under certain circumstances, in order to facilitate educational opportunities.

Social Supports Contribute to the Success of Untracking
A system of social supports contributes to the success of this untracking effort. Students are taught explicitly about the often implicit hidden curriculum of the school. Teachers serve as mediators between students and both the high school and college educators. Among the most visible social supports in AVID classrooms are test taking, note-taking, and study strategies. By teaching these academic skills, AVID is giving students explicit instruction in the hidden curriculum of the school. That is, AVID teaches explicitly in school what middle-income students learn implicitly at home. In Bourdieu's (1986) terms, AVID gives low-income students some of the cultural capital at school that is similar to the cultural capital that more economically advantaged parents give to their children at home.

Teacher advocacy (which is what an AVID teacher does to help a student in high school) and institutional sponsorship (which is what an AVID teacher does to assist a student move between high school and college) complement this explicit socialization process. The success of the San Diego untracking experiment is due, in large part, to the fact that the academic life of AVID students is supported by dedicated teachers who enter the lives of their students and serve as mediators between them, the high school and the college system. By expanding the definition of their teaching role to include the advocacy and sponsorship of students, AVID coordinators encourage success and help remove impediments to students' academic achievement.

The teachers' practices of advocacy and sponsorship seem to operate in the way that Bourdieu (1986) says *social* capital works, but these practices have a different institutional base. In Bourdieu's framework, social capital is rooted in the institution of the family, indeed the elite family. Although his conceptualization does not preclude the location of social capital in other institutions, the thrust of his formulation privileges the family as the basis of social capital. Teacher advocacy and institutional sponsorship look like the workings of social capital. Yet these processes are rooted in different soil. They have the school, not the family, as their base. In effect, AVID teachers act like the upper-middle-income parents

Lareau (1989) described and the college advisors at elite board schools that Cookson and Persell (1985) described. They monitor their students' work and build bridges between high school students and college admissions officers. The students' teachers, not the students' families, provide the "backing of the collectivity," which Bourdieu (1986) says is emblematic of social capital. The students' teachers, not the students' families, "provide a credential which generates 'credit' in the educational world," which Bourdieu (1986: 248) says marks the deployment of social capital (cf. Lamont & Lareau, 1988: 156).

If schools, not just well-to-do families, can deploy social capital to form productive social networks, then it means that schools can become transformative institutions, not just reproductive institutions. The sons and daughters of less privileged families can gain access to the often invisible networks of relationships that are often reserved for the sons and daughters of more privileged families.

Institutionalizing the Process of Support
As celebrated in the popular press and the popular movie, *Stand and Deliver*, Jaime Escalante single-handedly prepared dozens of Latino and Latina students from the barrio of East Los Angeles to pass the dreaded AP calculus test. To do so, he transformed the low expectations which the students held of themselves. He changed the cultural expectations that the students' parents held for their children's careers. He knocked down the institutional barriers that his colleagues at Garfield High School erected in his path. He overcame the thinly veiled racism signaled by officials at ETS after his first batch of students passed the test with similar test profiles. Thus portrayed, the Jaime Escalante story is a romantic tale of a modern hero. Escalante works incredibly long hours, without extra pay, suffers antagonism from his family, even survives a heart attack to help his beloved students.

While idealizing a romantic hero who works single-handedly to assist "down and out" students may be satisfying to our cultural self-image, the Jaime Escalante story reinforces many of the points I wish to make in this paper. First, many of the mechanisms that operate to assist students gain access to the resources that are highly valued in our society are hidden from view. Second, although students' aspirations and parents' expectations are important for students' success, institutional supports are absolutely essential for students' success. Students must be placed in college-prep courses if they are going to go to college. But academic placement in and of itself is not sufficient. AVID is a successful program because it erects social scaffolds in order to insure that students who have not had previous experience with academically oriented classes perform well in them. The social scaffolding supporting student placement in college-prep courses is as important as the academic placement itself.

A third point concerns educational policy more generally. If students, parents, and educators must rely on the superhuman efforts of zealous teachers in order to reduce the gaps between rich and poor, underachieving and achieving students, then our society is in deep trouble. We must institutionalize the process of support, not rely on the isolated and sometimes random efforts of dedicated teachers to achieve equality.

From Untracking to Detracking
At the present time, AVID selects students with high potential and mid-range grades, places them in academic programs, and then gives them social supports for two or three high school years. Students are placed in college prep classes starting in 9th or 10th grade. The existing system of social supports surrounding AVID students (notably explicit socialization, teacher advocacy, and sponsorship) operates during 180 hours of an elective class each academic year. This academic arrangement with its accompanying social support system is apparently adequate to elevate students with average to high GPAs and CTBS scores to college eligibility. In order to enhance the opportunities of students with average to below average academic records, the academic and social program would have to be deepened and broadened.

The academic program would need to be deepened so that students would spend more time in academic subjects. Instead of the current practice of spending three to five hours a week on laboratory sciences, three to five hours in trigonometry, geometry, or algebra, perhaps two or three times that amount of time would need to be spent with students who enter the program with weak academic records. Deepening the program in this way could be accomplished by extending the school day, the school year, or a combination of both. This recommendation is consistent with Sizer's (1992) idea to lengthen the school calendar from 36 to 42 weeks, and the school day by an hour or two.

Under this proposed arrangement, untracked students would participate in regular lab or math courses and participate in an AVID elective class as is the procedure now. In addition, a second or third session of the academic courses would meet after school, the purpose of which would be to deepen the students' knowledge of the work in their academic courses. Next, the school year would be extended so that students who did not grasp the material within the current system of 180 class meetings would have an extra 30 or 40 class meetings to gain mastery.

The social support system accompanying this academic activity would have to be broadened so that students would receive more preparation in test-taking, study skills, essay writing. Students who enter the program with low grades and low test scores would need more than 180 hours per year of mentoring and tutoring. Perhaps twice that amount would be required. In effect, this is the approach that the highly celebrated Garfield High School teacher, Jaime Escalante, took with his previously low-achieving Latino calculus students. Although he has been rightfully applauded for his charismatic motivational efforts, we have to keep in mind that Escalante also increased exponentially the number of hours, days and weeks that his students spent in the classroom. Instead of spending 180 hours in business or consumer math classes in one academic year, his students spent three times that amount each year in algebra, trig, or calculus courses (Escalante & Dirmann, 1990).

Of course, there must be a qualitative dimension as well as a quantitative dimension to transforming an untracking experiment to a full-scale detracking activity. It would do little good to increase the quantity of instructional time if that instructional time is not well spent. Fortunately, there are a number of promising proposals for improving the quality of classroom instructional practices.

Cooperative learning, the classroom practice of grouping students heterogeneously for the purpose of accomplishing tasks collaboratively, is one such possibility. This practice seems to help low-achieving students improve their classroom performance while helping high-achieving students maintain their classroom performance. Furthermore, cooperative learning seems to work as well for students from linguistic and ethnic minority backgrounds as it does for "majority" students (Slavin et al., 1989). The proposals to build instruction on inquiry, solving authentic problems in natural science, math, and social science, reading genuine texts and writing for meaningful purpose that are contained in the current round of the California frameworks for instruction are other provocative possibilities. Employing students' expertise as a resource for classroom instruction (Au & Jordan, 1980; González et al., 1993; Roseberry et al., 1992) also holds promise for making school a meaningful experience once again for disaffected youth.

Basically, I am proposing a sliding scale of social support surrounding rigorous academic instruction. While all students would continue to be placed in challenging courses, those students who begin AVID with a high academic record will need less support within AVID than students who have a weak academic record at the start of the program. Such an expansion and deepening of an untracking program like AVID would accomplish two goals. One, AVID would serve better the students it already accepts. Those students that AVID accepts now with low GPAs and test scores would be given a bigger boost toward academic success. Two, AVID would change from its present status as a program that assists a small number of select students to move to the top track (while leaving the tracking system intact) to a program that provides assistance to the broader base of the school population while dismantling the tracking system itself. In short, it would shift AVID from an untracking to a detracking effort.

REFERENCES

American Council on Education. 1989. *Minorities in Higher Education*. Washington, DC: ACE Publications Department.

Apple, Michael W. 1982. *Education and Power*. Boston: Routledge & Kegan Paul.

Apple, Michael W., and Lois Weis. 1983. "Ideology and Practice in Education: A Political and Conceptual Introduction." Pp. 3-33 in *Ideology and Practice in Education*, edited by Michael Apple and Lois Weis. Philadelphia: Temple University Press.

Au, Kathryn, and Cathie Jordan. 1980. "Teaching Reading to Hawaiian Children: Finding a Culturally Appropriate Solution." Pp. 139-152 in *Culture and the Bilingual Classroom*, edited by Henry Trueba, Grace P. Guthrie, and Kathryn H. Au. Rowley, MA: Newberry House.

Bell, Peter. 1993. *Graduate Follow-Up Study: San Diego Unified School Districts' Class of 1991 the First Year After Graduation*. San Diego City Schools: School Services Division, Planning, Research and Accountability Team.

Bourdieu, Pierre. 1986. "The Forms of Capital." Pp. 241-258 in *Handbook of Theory and Research for the Sociology of Education*, edited by John G. Richardson. Westport, CT: Greenwood Press.

Bourdieu, Pierre, and Claude Passeron. 1977. *Reproduction in Education, Society and Culture*. London: Sage.

Bowles, Samuel, and Herbert I. Gintis. 1976. *Schooling in Capitalist America*. New York: Basic Books.

Carter, Deborah J., and Reginald Wilson. 1991. *Minorities in Higher Education: Ninth Annual Status Report*. Washington, DC: American Council on Education.

Cazden, Courtney B., and Hugh Mehan. 1988. "Principles from Sociology and Anthropology." Pp. 45-57 in *Knowledge Base for the Beginning Teacher*, edited by Maynard C. Reynolds. Oxford: Pergamon Press.

Cicourel, Aaron V., and Hugh Mehan. 1983. "Universal Development, Stratifying Practices and Status Attainment." *Research in Social Stratification and Mobility* 4: 3-27. Greenwich, CT: JAI.

Comer, James P. 1988. "Educating Poor Minority Children." *Scientific American* 259(5):42-48.

Cookson, Peter W., Jr., and Caroline Hodges Persell. 1985. *Preparing for Power: America's Elite Boarding Schools*. New York: Basic Books.

Dreeben, Robert. 1968. *On What Is Learned in School*. Reading, MA: Addison-Wesley.

Escalante, Jaime, and Jack Dirmann. 1990. *The Jaime Escalante Math Program*. Washington DC: National Education Association.

Gándara, Patricia. 1995. *Over the Ivy Walls: The Educational Mobility of Low-Income Chicanos*. Albany, NY: SUNY Press.

González, Norma, Luis C. Moll, Martha Floyd-Tenery, Anna Rivera, Patricia Rendon, Racquel Gonzales, and Cathy Amanti. 1993. *Teacher Research on Funds of Knowledge: Learning from Households. Educational Practice Report #6*. Santa Cruz: National Center for Cultural Diversity and Second Language Learning.

Heath, Shirley Brice. 1982. "Questioning at Home and at School: A Comparative Study." Pp. 96-101 in *Doing the Ethnography of Schooling*, edited by George Spindler. New York: Holt Rinehart & Winston.

Heath, Shirley Brice. 1986. "Sociocultural Contexts of Language Development." Pp. 143-86 in *Beyond Language*. California State University, Los Angeles: California State University, Los Angeles Education Dissemination and Assessment Center.

Keddie, Nell. 1971. "Classroom Knowledge." Pp. 31-60 in *Knowledge and Control*, edited by Michael F. D. Young. London: Routledge & Kegan Paul.

Lamont, Michelle, and Annette Lareau. 1988. "Cultural Capital: Allusions, Gaps and Glissandos in Recent Theoretical Developments." *Theoretical Sociology* 6(2):153-168.

Lareau, Annette. 1989. *Home Advantage: Social Class and Parental Intervention in Elementary Education*. New York: Falmer Press.

Levin, Henry M. 1987. "Accelerated Schools for Disadvantaged Students." *Educational Leadership* 44(6):19-21.

MacLaren, Peter. 1989. *Life in Schools*. New York: Longman.

MacLeod, Jay. 1987. *Ain't No Makin' It: Leveled Aspirations in a Low-Income Neighborhood*. Boulder, CO: Westview Press.

Mehan, Hugh. 1992. "Understanding Inequality in Schools: The Contribution of Interpretive Studies." *The Sociology of Education* 65(1):1-20.

Mehan, Hugh, Alma J. Hertweck, and J. Lee Meihls. 1985. *Handicapping the Handicapped: Decision Making in Students' Careers*. Stanford: Stanford University Press.

Mehan Hugh, Irene Villanueva, Lea Hubbard, and Angela Lintz. 1996. *Constructing School Success: The Consequences of Untracking Low Achieving Students*. Cambridge: Cambridge University Press.

Mercer, Jane. 1974. *Labeling the Mentally Retarded*. Berkeley: The University of California Press.

National Center for Education and the Economy. 1990. *America's Choice: High Skills or Low Wages*. Washington, DC: NCEE.

Oakes, Jeannie. 1985. *Keeping Track: How Schools Structure Inequality*. New Haven, CT: Yale University Press.

Oakes, Jeannie, Adam Gamoran, and Reba N. Page. 1992. "Curriculum Differentiation: Opportunities, Outcomes and Meanings." Pp. 570-608 in *Handbook of Research on Curriculum*, edited by Philip Jackson. New York: Macmillan.

Oakes, Jeannie, Karen Quartz, Jennifer Gong, Gretchen Guiton, and Martin Lipton. 1993. "Creating Middle Schools: Technical, Normative and Political Considerations." *The Elementary School Journal* 93(5):461-479.

Page, Reba N., and Linda Valli. 1991. *Curriculum Differentiation*. Albany, NY: SUNY Press.

Roseberry, Ann S., Beth Warren, and Faith R. Conant. 1992. *Appropriating Scientific Discourse: Findings from Language Minority Classrooms. Working Paper #1*. Cambridge, MA: TERC.

Rosenbaum, James M. 1978. *Making Inequality*. New York: Wiley Interscience.

Sizer, Theodore R. 1992. *Horace's School: Redesigning the American High School*. New York: Houghton Mifflin.

Slavin, Robert E., Nancy L. Karweit, and Nancy A. Madden. 1989. *Effective Programs for Students at Risk*. Boston: Allyn and Bacon.

Swanson, Mary Catherine. No Date. *AVID: A College Preparatory Program for Underrepresented Students*. San Diego: San Diego County Office of Education.

Tharp, Roland, and Ronald Gallimore. 1988. *Rousing Minds to Life: Teaching, Learning and Schooling in Social Context*. Cambridge: Cambridge University Press.

Wheelock, Anne. 1992. *Crossing the Tracks: How "Untracking" Can Save America's Schools*. New York: The New Press.

Willis, Paul. 1977. *Learning to Labor. How Working Class Kids Get Working Class Jobs*. Westmead, England: Saxon House Press.

Young, Michael F. D. 1971. *Knowledge and Control*: London: Routledge & Kegan Paul.

CHAPTER 6

Changing the Discourse in Schools

Eugene Eubanks, Ralph Parish, and Dianne Smith

In this chapter, we are going to discuss two very simple ideas. First, if American schooling is to be transformed, its participation in the reproduction of long-term unequal social arrangements must be eliminated. Second, the current dominant discourse in schools (how people talk about, think about and plan the work of schools and the questions that get asked regarding reform or change) is a hegemonic cultural discourse. The consequence of this discourse is to maintain existing schooling practices and results. We call this hegemonic discourse, Discourse I.

If the announced purpose of school reform, to educate everyone well, is taken seriously, then a different, more critical discourse (which we call Discourse II) must precede and guide reform (Aronowitz, 1994; Fullan, 1988; Kilmann et al., 1985). It must prepare a cultural ground for change. The most serious question facing substantive school reform is how to create Discourse II in school cultures.

Schools are a major part of society's institutional processes for maintaining a relatively stable system of inequality. They contribute to these results by active acceptance and utilization of a dominant set of values, norms and beliefs, which, while appearing to offer opportunities to all, actually support the success of a privileged minority and hinder the efforts and visions of a majority. Some social scientists call this condition and its sustaining process hegemony, i.e., when a cultural set promulgated by an elite or dominant class comes to be pervasive and taken for granted in a society even when its practice is not in the interests of many others. Because of strong elements of social reproduction and hegemony in American society and its schools over a long period of time, we would assert that schools have not typically been instruments of social change, except when needed to preserve the overall hegemonic social/economic order.

Since John Dewey (1966), many educators have espoused a belief that schools in a democratic society should educate all people well. We suggest that the difficulty in initiating schooling for a democratic society flows from the strength of social reproduction in American schooling. Social reproduction as defined by McLaren (1994) is perpetuation of social relationships within the larger society. Another way to say this is that children are developed to replace their parents and/or family members in the social and economic life of a society. There are, in addition, a series of steps in an effective change process for schools that have been observed and documented. Since most change efforts falter ultimately, there must be something more to making systemic change than simply understanding and using effective change processes.

Efforts in the past four decades to change outcomes of American schooling, so that they no longer correlate highly with race, class, and gender and to provide a higher quality and level of education for everyone, have, at best, been modestly effective. That assessment is probably a kind one. How do we explain this poor record of reform? Are the programs and processes that have been offered as "school improvement solutions" poor ones? Perhaps, but let us briefly examine this history. The federal government and the private sector heavily invested in promoting school curriculum reform, beginning with the National Defense Education Act in the late 1950's. In the 1960s, curriculum reform and the retraining of teachers (for modern mathematics, linguistics, and whole language, and inquiry approaches to teaching science and social science) were massive reform efforts. When this proved to have little effect by the 1970s, research and development approaches to reform were tried through such means as the Elementary Secondary Education Act, Regional Educational Laboratories and Centers, National Science Foundation Consortiums, and funding by many non-profit foundations. National dissemination systems emerged in the 1970s to allow local school districts to have access to the newest and best educational research and development. Newly developed innovations were believed to be excellent and have potential for substantially changing the outcomes of America's schools. Many, if not most, of these new programs were superior to existing ones and could have been effective in educating everyone well. There is no lack of well-known and effective solutions. If we have effective solutions and if we know, as some suggest, effective organizational change processes, why is it so difficult to produce substantial and lasting change in schools?

We are going to suggest two possible reasons. One is that a focus upon processes of change assumed that following certain steps would promote change. The second is that substantive issues are seldom identified as the purpose of change. Focus upon the change process produces questions like: Is it top down?; Is it bottom up?; Is it renewing?; Is it vertical as well as horizontal?; Is it more or less linear or sequential? These questions are the wrong focus. Such questions generally maintain an organization's ability to reproduce itself. Some top-down changes work very well but not most. Some bottom-up changes work very well but not as often as claimed. Yet trying to follow or implement such linear change processes has seldom led to substantial change in educational settings. There are also examples of interactive and renewal approaches to change that work very well. But more often than not such efforts rarely become truly interactive and renewing, let alone establish meaningful change. Some recent school interventions like Re: Learning, Comer Schools, Accelerated Schools, and Total Quality Management (TQM) have made use of what can be identified as a general model of renewal. The renewal process makes use of collaboration, shared decision making, and a much wider involvement of people at site-based change. Comer (1988) has reported that the schools in Hartford, where he began work in the 1960s, have begun to achieve substantive improvement. He also indicates that other sites have not been able to replicate this same outcome. The evidence from the Accelerated School implementation indicates that somewhere around the third or fourth year, most schools begin to discontinue their efforts. Sarason (1990) describes these outcomes as predictable and common.

We think the "something more" consists of the second of the two factors we identified above. The purpose or reason, the substance of the thing, that is discussed as the reason for attempting to change must not be superficial. It makes a difference what is identified as needing change! Practitioners often understand and implement the mechanics of the process but not the implications and consequences of a new idea. Training and workshops are often identified as being for improved practice. This does not carry a message of changing something significant but rather of improving what is already occurring. From a beginning in teacher education pre-service programs throughout "on-the-job" learning and including staff development and school improvement efforts in school districts, teachers are trained to believe in process and methods. Techniques, methods, and new curriculum content are the stuff of improvement efforts. Learning and the effect of classroom relationships and conditions seldom if ever become a focus of improvement, unless it is a new discipline program to aid control. Teachers are seldom if ever given the opportunity to do active learning and engage in reflective discourse about the effects of their work.

Even when an attempt to identify and discuss substantive issues occurs, there are serious barriers. Existing cultural patterns, ways of thinking and accepted practice tend to conceal significant problems and contradictions. Symptoms often get identified and treated as causes and the problems persist. For example, children do not turn in their homework assignments, which drives many teachers to distraction. The homework problem will get identified as something within the student and/or home conditions. Different policies will then be employed that reward or punish doing or not doing homework. What will seldom be considered is the idea that the relationships and conditions of learning in the school and classroom are major contributors to why children do not do homework. Such things are not considered because teachers and principals are coming to school every day "doing their work" in ways that are acceptable within the culture of schooling. Thus it cannot be anything they are doing.

Giroux (1991), Aronowitz (1994), McLaren (1994), Foucault (1977), and others including Deal and Kennedy (1982) and Fullan (1988) suggest that getting at the substance of systemic or cultural change requires demystifying the hegemonic cultures. Elites not only rule through informal consent, incentives, or even the use of force but rather often through taken-for-granted, accepted social conventions or practices that define and constitute what is "natural," "normal," and the "way things are" or "should be." Hegemony, then, preconditions a social discourse that allows the powerful and those who use the discourse to blame outsiders and subordinates for their own oppression and "failings." It can also lead to those groups blaming themselves for their fates. Finally, it provides explanations and solutions for dealing with deviations from the natural or normal.

In order to begin to identify substantive issues involved in systemic change, it is necessary to use a critical theory approach that enables the deconstruction or demystification of the underlying assumptions and values that drive an existing school culture. Systemic change must be understood to be related to what is troubling us, i.e., the hegemony. The use of existing cultural ways promotes symptomatic issues like attendance, dropouts, discipline, low test scores, and low grades. Often in cultural organizations like schools, we exchange one cultural way for another that maintains outcomes that sort by race, class, and gender. (The new discipline policy has much the same effect as the old discipline policy.) We simply follow "the change process" and implement something adapted to the old cultural ways (how we do things here). A fundamental belief in process is part of school cultures. If we followed the process and nothing changed, then the explanation must be in the thing being implemented. It did not work. This cultural way is a major factor in allowing schools to have the appearance of responding to change without having to change anything substantive.

In another example, many local schools are conducting inservice efforts on topics like assertive discipline, discipline with dignity, positive discipline, gaining control of the learning, to mention only a few. They all ignore the substantive issue and instead view the issue as one of finding ways of controlling children. The substantive issue is the question: What are we doing in this school that alienates many of our children so that they create problems and are disruptive? For example, it is not uncommon in urban profile elementary schools to find that minority males may represent 60 percent or more of the discipline problems, failing grades and poor attendance. These young men may represent only 30 percent or less of a school population. How do we account for this disproportionate outcome? Yet, in the vast majority of cases introspection or reflection about underlying problems in the school are not considered as relevant to this as a "school effect." The problem will universally be identified as in the students and/or their families.

Similarly, children in urban type schools are viewed as "needing more structure" because they are "from disadvantaged conditions" or "from single parent families" or "working families" or "more dangerous." The problem is viewed as part of something in the children and/or their existence outside of school. Therefore, controlling or "teaching them discipline" is viewed as a solution and a precondition for learning. Such approaches have the effect of maintaining the existing cultural ways in schools and assuring that the children continue to be sorted to replace their parents in the social order.

We suggest that the effect a change will have depends upon the discourse that sustains and accompanies a change effort. Are substantial issues raised as the essential discourse for change? Is there a Discourse I or II attending the change effort? When teachers and others in school sites are confronted with efforts to change, what are their ways of deciding what is happening and how they must respond? Does the discourse engage in a dialogue about important relationships and conditions in the school settings, i.e., the hegemony? Is there a discourse of hope, of despair or of how "they" will not leave us alone, i.e., cultural oppression? Is the cultural discourse about how the students and the administrators are not competent, and, therefore, teachers are confronted with an impossible task, blaming the victim? Do the people have a Discourse I or a Discourse II colloquy?

Words like "staff development," "inservice," and "school improvement" are terms that have meaning in the existing school cultures. They have invariably come to mean that people in schools can go through a process that appears to be change oriented but, in fact, has not resulted in any substantial improvement of student learning. These processes are cultural ways to maintain the status quo without appearing to be unresponsive to outside demands for improvement (Parish & Arends, 1983). These standard processes have become a primary part of a Discourse I in schools.

Discourse II conversations tend to be about uncomfortable, unequal, ineffective, prejudicial conditions and relationships in a school. Discourse II processes create demystified schooling eventually. It is not that some of the more conventional terms could not be about substantive change. It is that they already have these other meanings and thus are difficult to consider in a different light. Is the discourse about conventional and traditional teaching and organizing or does it relate to creating a transformed school that is about learning, not only for students but for everyone there? Is the result that outcomes no longer correlate with social class, race or gender? This can be answered by asking, do outcomes continue to favor certain people and groups?

Discourse II schools create an organizational setting that is continually changing and developing because the members are continually learning. In a Discourse II school, ambiguity and change are part of a purposeful structure. The direction for change is clear. It is intended to produce schools where every student develops intellectually to high levels and the performance gap related to race, class and gender narrows until school effects are no longer correlated with those factors. How schools get there is varied and part of the human dynamics. Teachers and principals can figure it out, given time and a path to follow. This is what Discourse II becomes.

What we want to consider here is, can Discourse II schools be created? What is the substance of Discourse II and how do we get such a transformational agenda in schools? How do we get practitioners in school cultures who accept existing cultural ways to deconstruct and demystify their beliefs about their work? How do we create a Discourse II dialogue without creating anger, defensiveness, blame, guilt, and denial?

We search for answers to this question as we work in schools. In this search we have come to realize that there may only be paths to discover, not answers. The values and beliefs of existing school cultures lead to insistence upon answers. "Searching for answers," in fact, may be the first casualty of demystification. "Just tell us what to do," is a status quo value. We wish to share with you our discourse around this question.

In the twenty-first century, even now, knowledge and creation of meaning become essential for whatever life choices people wish to make. To deny a person the fullest intellectual and personal development is to deny a fundamental human right. Certainly, in our social context it denies property, liberty, and probably eventually life. Everyone will not want the same things or same paths, but to have a choice requires intellectual development beyond that to what we now provide for a select 20 percent. We are convinced that almost all of our population across all races has the intellectual capacity to reach that type of development. They have spoken a human language since the age of 3-4. That is the hardest thing they will ever have to learn. It is all they need to get smart.

In the past, the better educated you were, the more options you had or the greater chance to, at least, be in some manner in charge of your own life—to be free. That is why Western cultures have historically assured the best schooling for the privileged and limited the schooling of others as a cultural priority. It is one of cultures' ways of preserving social reproduction. That is one reason why, in this period of change, political/economic solutions like privatizing, vouchering, and other marketing strategies are advocated by conservatives for Year 2000 goals. The resources of a family determine access to quality and preparation. These "reform" measures have the effect of maintaining schooling advantages for the privileged, in the name of choice, freedom, standards, and the American Way. These are all part of our old cultural ways. Old cultural ways endure even when their continuation threatens the very culture they are trying to preserve.

A helpful note is that cultural ways are not absolute. Such ways were part of the rhetoric of the Robber Barons of the 1880s and the 1980s as well. But, there were also persons of wealth, power, and privilege in the 1880s and also in the 1980s who recognized the hegemony for what it was and sought to dismantle it (Josephson, 1962). An intelligent view of the twenty-first century would reveal that it is important to abandon some old cultural ways in order to make new ones. It is necessary to create a new "debate" and a Discourse II. It is possible to understand a good deal of our current political turmoil as emanating from a public debate, or lack of, over these very issues. If one argues for the reduction of civil government in providing for the health, education, and welfare, does that require more civil responsibility on the part of the private sector? Are the cultural ways of American capitalism geared to such a condition?

In mercantile and industrial capitalism there were opportunities for persons to acquire meaningful work and financial rewards without extensive formal academic preparation in order to have a decent life (Hodgkinson, 1986a, 1986b). Education was a way to aid this development. Experience and on the job development were also ways to achieve some social/economic security, although much more difficult, often more time consuming and often less rewarding than formal education. It was not so important in America that the privileged received superior educations, because most believed everyone could still have an adequate standard of living. However, many are beginning to understand that to assign someone to an apprenticeship in an information-based culture has the likely effect of assigning someone to a limited/lesser life (Katznelson, 1981). America, more than any other nation, may have encouraged a higher amount of upward social mobility, but the dominance of class and especially of race still reigns in America. Those who work in schools are still enmeshed in the reproduction of a highly stratified society, whether they understand it or not. A story from Ralph Parish illustrates what we mean by the historical hegemony. Although, accounting for different generations, each of us has a similar story, with a different war.

I remember Percy, who was in my 5th and 6th grade urban school classrooms. This was during WWII. He was always a little strange, it seemed to many of us. He dressed in bib overalls (only country people or lowly working people wore them). Percy did not always appear very clean and did not talk exactly like the rest of us. Yet, I had come to like him. He had a good sense of humor and if you took the time to know him he was often fun to be around. He was very quiet and never took an active role in class or school things. In my recollection, he had never been identified as good at anything we did in school. He usually only came to school three or four days a week, except in winter. Then, in the spring of our 6th grade year, he just disappeared. He, plainly, wasn't at school anymore. After a couple of weeks, I asked our teacher about Percy. She said to me, "He won't be in our class anymore." "Why not?" was my response. She informed me that he had had his twelfth birthday. This concerned me because my twelfth birthday was coming up in less than a month. When I pushed for more information, she only said that his family had decided that it was time for him to go to work with his father. I already knew that Percy's father was a "junkman."

At the time it seemed to me that Percy was rewarded and was already being treated like an adult. He worked every day and had no school. Wouldn't that be great! I asked my parents about such a possibility for me, about going to work in a store, like our family did. They responded with a conventional dialogue concerning education and school and that I "was going to amount to something." Those dreaded words. The point here is Percy. Years later when I finally understood what really happened with Percy, I tried to find Percy to see how life turned out for him. I went to the place where his father had his junk yard. It was gone and so was the old weatherworn house next to the junk yard, Percy's home. I learned later that he had gone into the Army and had been killed in Korea. We know now that there are legions of Percys in America, as there are also smaller legions of us.

Both of us started on our life paths from birth. By the time either of us was old enough or wise enough to understand that most of the choices that controlled our lives were not made by us, it was too late, especially for Percy. Percy was smart and could learn anything. "Just don't like school stuff," he said once. That was OK, I was somewhat embarrassed that I liked school anyway. "You sure do like reading," he had told me. "How come you do so much of it?" he wanted to know. I described my feelings about the adventures you could have through reading. All the stuff you could know that others didn't know, how good it felt just to know things. He looked at me in a funny way and shook his head. However, I noticed after that, he started carrying library books around more. One day I caught him reading when it was not reading time. It was Jack London, one of my favorites. I had told him one day just before he left, "You're just like someone out of Jack London."

Now I understand that while I thought it might have been great to go to work and not have to do school work, the one who had to live that reality did not feel that way. His path was not filled with a lot of hope, good news, or joy. America's cultural ways owned him. There was no adult nor any system like school that provided him with a different construction of meaning. His path was filled mostly with, "looking for ways out," without much hope of finding any, unless he got lucky. He was trapped in the "working boys" culture described so well by Lois Weis (1990). His trap was the accident of birth. Who Percy was or could have become never became anyone's consideration, most of all not to Percy. Not even at school, where it could have been and should have been. Current authors who discuss critical theory argue that schooling should actually be a process that demystifies the cultural reproductive role of schools (Giroux, 1991; Aronowitz, 1994; Freire, 1970; Apple, 1993). These scholars assert that schools should be about assisting all students to be developed to the point where they are free to understand and make their own life choices.

The cultural path left open to me had some good news, hope, and joy available but a prescribed amount of each. I was to be a manager of something. It is what the men in our family did. It took me well into my first year of teaching before I saw that schools were a part of this sorting of people (Bowles & Gintis, 1986; Anyon, 1980; Kozol, 1991; Oakes, 1986). We teachers are conditioned to be instruments of this sorting of children according to their "appropriate" condition. Nobody tells us this when we begin to learn about teaching. No one tells us as we begin our teaching careers. To the contrary, we either discover it ourselves and search for ways to understand the "why" and "how" of it, or we continue in the accepted way.

Urban schools are full of Percys, regardless of their race or gender. We blame each other, we blame "downtown," but mostly we blame the children and their families. We blame everyone and everywhere except where the problem probably largely lies—in a social/economic-cultural system that requires and "needs" to create persons of poverty to preserve a well-protected system of social privilege (Fine, 1990). Adam Smith (1776) said that in order to create persons of wealth to advance civilization, it is necessary to create persons of poverty. Six hundred to one was his ratio. In America today the ratio may be a little higher.

Those who work in urban schools will tell you all the staff are doing their work. Yet certain children are being pushed out; others do not do well, and many schools are full of stress and anger. Teachers and principals become resentful and defeated. The world of "urban type" schools, whether they are in the suburbs, inner city, or areas of rural poverty, is full of announced good intentions and poor outcomes. Most of all they are full of denial. "Not my fault. Not our fault. It's their fault" (Aquila & Parish, 1989).

Let us describe a statement recently made to us by an urban teacher. She is white, over 40, has more than twenty years teaching experience, and is very angry and insistent that we hear and appreciate her understanding and presentation of why teachers in her urban school were not effective with many of their students:

They can't expect us to do it with classes over 30 and over 150 overall. They come from unstable, dysfunctional, and non-supportive families. They expect us to teach this curriculum, and most of them can't read and aren't smart enough to learn. The administration tells us that everyone can and will learn, but they haven't a clue about how to do it, even if it were true. It's a politically correct statement. Authentic schools is a phrase our principal learned at a recent conference. He tells us that this is a new relationship in schools. Most of us find it insulting to imply that we are somehow not authentic teachers and persons and it's our fault that schools aren't. (As she delivered this group report, heads were nodding all over the room.)

This teacher and her colleagues at this meeting were in an urban school located in a suburban community. It had once, in the memory of a majority of the teachers, been an all-white community and school. Over 95 percent of the teaching staff are still white, and 90 percent of the administrative staff are white. Thirty percent of the students are now nonwhite. Twenty-six percent of all students are on free lunch. Twenty years ago there were less than 5 percent on free lunch and only two families of African Americans. In this suburban-URBAN school, as in most urban schools, the fundamental issue of race, racism, and classism could not only not be discussed but must also be denied as a factor in schools. There have developed, in these urban school cultures, code words and phrases to express their racism, classism and anger. Chris Argyris (1982) calls this the "undiscussables in organizations." Edgar Schein (1985) discusses them as hidden cultural ways in an organization. They prevent organizational cultures from changing or identifying problems that block them from accomplishing their stated purposes and becoming more authentic organizations. The code words allow for denial, or, at least, set the parameters of action. However, everyone understands what is being said. The denial is for outsiders and their own self-esteem.

It is not only the professional staff who participate in this organizational culture, so do the others who live in, around, and with urban schools. In our metropolitan area almost all of the school districts have some urban schools in them. School boards and school board elections regularly make use of the code words about preserving "standards." They regularly, in the name of some acceptable cultural value, develop policies that result in continued sorting by race, class, and gender. School boards, administrators, and teachers can thus deny any official-intentional racial practices. They practice them informally on a daily basis in terms of who they hire, who they promote, who gets suspended, who gets educated well or less well, and often who gets resources.

Some examples of these racially based cultural code words we hear regularly are: "We're a school in transition. Things have changed, students just aren't what they used to be. You just can't teach as much as you used to. We have so many single parent families. We have drugs and crack babies now that teachers didn't have to deal with before. The disintegration of the family structure makes it harder for children to learn. Children are having children." The words not only reflect class, gender, and racial hegemony in schooling but also the helplessness many urban educators feel about their ability to do anything about the conditions in which they find themselves. They desegregate school populations and then resegregate the students in buildings through programs, curriculum, and schedules. Schools sort students through teaching methods, schedules, school rules, administrators, and teachers. The right kids still get sorted or "tracked" down the right paths, including out the door.

It is not just majority Euro-ethnic teachers who use these code words and follow cultural ways. These code words are sometimes said by some non-Euro-ethnic principals and teachers, who have become white middle class by adoption and preference. It is not a new story in America's racial history. An urban school leader recently told us, "Some of the most biased teachers in my school are middle class non-white teachers who have moved to the suburbs and teach in the inner city." She continued, "It is how they show they belong." We must somehow find ways to help our educators confront this system of schooling that continues and maintains the hegemony and sorting (hooks, 1992a; Shor and Freire, 1987; Parish et al., 1989). When all the rhetoric regarding school reform and restructuring is said and done, it is this hegemonic culture of schooling that must be transformed.

Discourse II must be about transformational issues (Bennis, 1984). The work of those in schools must become learning: this applies to teachers, principals, students, and others who come to the school as volunteers and helpers. Schools must develop into and promote what we and others have called "learning organization cultures." Learning organizations are those that provide intellectual and character development and a desire to become lifelong learners for all. There are schools where the discrepancies in development and learning are eliminated by the time students graduate from high school. Anything less leaves America behind in a world where intellect is the medium of exchange and power.

There is available knowledge that will allow us to move towards developing these learning organization cultures (Sergiovanni, 1991). As a society, all we lack is the will to do so. By this, we mean that those with power have not decided to share it. If history is any judge, they probably will not voluntarily do so. Some are concerned that if we create a nation of smart people, hegemonic culture will no longer be accepted. Those who support/promote American cultural ways do not trust just anyone to be smart enough to create a better, more equitable society. Those who rule fear the creation of a new set of losers out of the old winners. It is a fundamental cultural hegemonic belief of capitalism and racism that if those who have little get better, then those who have much will get less. It is the Adam Smith model. Everything we have learned about change so far tells us that until high intellectual development for all becomes the common cultural purpose/discourse of schooling, the reforms that can change schooling will never be implemented. This is the "stuff" of Discourse II.

What we must also recognize is that "hegemonic cultural ways" work in hidden and oblique ways to maintain themselves. The ways of school reform and change that most of us know about and practice are basically those ways we have learned from our teaching and school cultures. These are the hidden ways that maintain Discourse I ideas: the code words that promise but do not deliver change. In Missouri, we have identified seventy-five academic benchmark standards that will enable us to compete economically with Europe and Japan. World class standards is the language. This is essentially a Discourse I paradigm. The only thing being changed is the number of benchmarks. There will probably be no meaningful Discourse II reform in such a schooling agenda.

The challenge before us is how to go about changing the work of schools. How do we change so that the work and convenience of the adults, i.e., Discourse I, takes second place to learning, for everyone? How do we help those in schools cut through cultural myths without making them feel defensive, guilty, or at fault?

Administrators with whom we work invariably come back to talk to us about this issue. Their conversation often begins something like this: "Well, what we studied and talked about regarding sorting is true. We hear it and see it every day. What we want to know again is how do we change it? We get so frustrated. How do I change the discourse in my school?" One recently said, "Most of our discourse uses adversarial ways to identify personal blame when things don't go well." They often continue, "Some (teachers) still want to call me boss and have me decide things for them. If I ask them what do they think, they respond in various ways, 'that's not my job.' They do all sorts of things that demand that I be in charge and then complain because they are not consulted. In other words, the discourse is about adult work and work relationships, not essentially about the learning and how it is going." (While this note is taken directly from one conversation, there have been over twenty similar conversations.)

As our conversations continue and as we explore together what has to occur, a look of unease begins to appears in their faces. Eventually, we and they agree that Discourse II is what has to occur and that somehow the Discourse I picture of reality must be broken. Then these administrators almost universally say, "But this is going to take a long time. The teachers where I work do not want to be free, except free to do whatever they want in their room. What can I do Monday?" When we say "start," there is a long silence. Then they most often say something like, "They'd never let me." The belief among most practicing school leaders is that they may not have that much time. Five to ten years is the minimum time required to get started down the learning path. This is a long time for leadership positions in today's schools, especially if we are asking them to challenge and dismantle strongly held schooling ways. "Not having time" is part of the sorting way of Discourse I. If I (we) never have time to reflect, to consider, to question, then what prevails is how we do it now.

The length of time in leadership roles is decreasing in America's schools. If people have to keep starting over, they never get very far. Changing leadership regularly is one way to keep starting over. Part of the dynamics that maintains the sorting machine is that urban type schools are often not allowed any continuity when they do get good leadership. The mean term of service for urban superintendents is two and a half to three years. Organizations do not get very far when they are continually required to start over all the time.

It is necessary to deconstruct (Foucault, 1977; hooks, 1992b) these sorting ways so that educators can no longer accept the existing system of schooling. We are convinced that once educators understand they are part of maintaining the hegemonic culture, they will reject such behavior. We believe it violates the basic reasons most of them became teachers and principals. We must learn to ask different questions and to question everything we do in schools from a perspective of effects and consequences. There needs to be a focus upon creating learning conditions and relationships that do not sort and also provide high levels of intellectual development for every student.

So we argue very strongly that any real effort to make substantive (systemic) change must begin with a Discourse II dialogue in schools, one that blames no one and deconstructs what is really going on (Smith, 1994). It must have leadership that asks smart questions and leadership that creates discourse so there is sufficient dissatisfaction with what is, among not only the staff, but the community and students as well. Once that Discourse begins they can all move forward together to implement changes that will transform their school.

Discourse II paths are full of land mines and ambushes. It takes courage, intelligence, guile, determination, sensitivity, patience, caring, and time. We do not fully understand how to develop, prepare, cajole, or entice the type of people to lead and carry out a Discourse II agenda, especially in urban schools, but we are looking and trying to find these ways because we are convinced that anything else is just Discourse I window dressing.

This is our issue and dilemma: Where are the people who are willing and committed to engage in the struggle? The ones who will find joy in Discourse II paths to Discourse II schools. That is, people who will claim Discourse I as their terrain of contestation. Given the contest, Discourse II becomes an overriding project of possibility and hope for change. If, as Alice Walker (1992) suggests, resistance is the secret of joy, then we seek the joyous people.

REFERENCES

Anyon, Jean. 1980. "Social Class and the Hidden Curriculum of Work." *Journal of Education* 162(1):67-92.

Apple, Michael. 1993. *Official Knowledge: Democratic Schooling in a Conservative Age.* New York: Routledge Press.

Aquila, Frank, and Ralph Parish. 1989. "Clash of Cultures: Instruction Technology and the Craft of Teaching." *Journal of Research and Development in Education* 22(2):49-56.

Argyris, Chris. 1982. *Reasoning Learning and Action: Individual and Organization.* San Francisco: Jossey-Bass Publishers.

Aronowitz, Stanley. 1994. *Dead Artists, Live Theories, and Other Cultural Problems.* NewYork: Routledge Press.

Bennis, Warren. 1984. "Transformation Power and Leadership." Pp. 64-71 in *Leadership and Organizational Culture*, edited by Thomas J. Sergiovanni and John E. Corbally. Urbana, IL: University of Illinois Press.

Bowles, Samuel, and Hebert Gintis. 1986. *Democracy and Capitalism: Property, Community and the Contradictions of Modern Social Thought.* New York: Basic Books, Inc., Publishers.

Comer, James P. 1988, November. "Educating Poor Minority Children." *Scientific American* 259(5):42-48.

Deal, Terrence E., and Alan Kennedy. 1982. *Corporate Cultures.* Reading, MA: Addison-Wesley.

Dewey, John. 1966. *Democracy and Education.* New York: Macmillan. (Reprint of 1926 original).

Fine, Michele. 1990. *Framing Dropouts.* New York: Columbia University Press.

Foucault, Michel. 1977. *Power and Knowledge.* Translated by C. Gordon, L. Marshall, and K. Sopes. New York: Pantheon Press.

Freire, Paulo. 1970. *Pedagogy of the Oppressed.* New York: Continuum.

Fullan, Michael. 1988. *Change Process in Secondary Schools: Towards a More Fundamental Agenda.* Toronto: University of Toronto.

Giroux, Henry. 1991. *Border Crossings: Cultural Workers and the Politics of Education.* New York: Routledge Press.

Hodgkinson, Harold. 1986a. "Today's Numbers, Tomorrow's Nation." *Education Week,* May 16:14-15.

Hodgkinson, Harold. 1986b. "The Patterns in Our Social Fabric Are Changing." *Education Week,* May 16:16-18.

hooks, bell. 1992a. *Yearning*. Boston: South End Press.

hooks, bell. 1992b. *Black Looks: Race and Representation*. Boston: South End Press.

Josephson, Matthew. 1962. *The Robber Barons*. New York: Harcourt, Brace and World.

Katznelson, Ira. 1981. *City Trenches: Urban Politics and the Patterning of Class in the United States*. New York: Pantheon.

Kilmann, Ralph H., Mary J. Saxton, Roy Serpa, & Associates. 1985. *Gaining Control of the Corporate Culture*. San Francisco: Jossey-Bass.

Kozol, Jonathan. 1991. *Savage Inequalities*. New York: Crown Publications.

McLaren, Peter. 1994. *Life in Schools*. (2nd Ed.). White Plains, NY: Longman Press.

Oakes, Jeannie. 1986. *Keeping Track: How Schools Structure Inequality*. New Haven, CT: Yale University.

Parish, Ralph, Frank Aquila, Eugene Eubanks, and Sandra Walker. 1989. "Knock at Any School." *Phi Delta Kappan* 70(5):386-394.

Parish, Ralph, and Arends, Richard. 1983. "Why Innovative Programs are Discontinued." *Educational Leadership* 40(4):62-65.

Sarason, Seymour B. 1990. *The Predictable Failure of Educational Reform: Can We Change Course Before It's Too Late?* San Francisco: Jossey-Bass.

Schein, Edgar. 1985. *Organizational Culture and Leadership: A Dynamic View*. San Francisco: Jossey-Bass.

Sergiovanni, Thomas J. 1991. *The Principalship: A Reflective Practice Perspective* (2nd Ed.). Needham Heights, MA: Allyn & Bacon.

Shor, Ira, and Paulo Freire. 1987. *A Pedagogy for Liberation*. New York: Bergin & Garvey.

Smith, Adam. 1982. *The Wealth of Nations*. Reprint of Books I&II (1776). Andrew S. Skinner Ed. Penguin Classic Publications, Penguin Press, New York.

Smith, Dorothy. 1994. "Why Do We Have to Read About Girls Living in Australia and London?: Reflections from a Womanist Theorist on Critical Education." Pp. 328-335 in *The Education Feminism Reader*, edited by Linda Stone. New York: Routledge Press.

Walker, Alice. 1992. *Possessing the Secret of Joy*. New York: Harcourt Brace Jovanovich.

Weis, Lois. 1990. *Working Class Without Work*. New York: Routledge Press.

CHAPTER 7

Making Multicultural Education Policy: The Transformation of Intentions

Margaret Placier, Peter M. Hall, and Barbara Jo Davis

"Multicultural education" is most often treated as a classroom and school-level activity, but it is also a topic of policy-making. Grant and Millar (1992) have urged policy analysts to conduct research on multicultural policies, to examine when they promote equity for all students and when they fall short of this goal. Similar recommendations emerged from an OERI meeting on the Policy Uses of Sociology (Persell et al., 1993). However, to date there are few studies of multicultural education policy. The case study in this chapter makes a needed contribution to the knowledge base in this area.

Cornbleth and Waugh (1993) further call for a certain *kind* of multicultural policy study, paying more "systematic attention to the politics of policy-in-the-making" in contrasting settings with different dynamics. The term "policy" connotes a concrete object or text, the product or *outcome* of a process. In this study we offer an alternative perspective grounded in the symbolic interactionist paradigm, in which policy *is* a process (Hall, 1987, 1992, 1995). From this perspective, policy research is an attempt to capture significant events in a continuous flow of collective activity that begins before and extends past the point at which a policy text (report, legislation) is produced. For example, our case study of a district-level multicultural policy process shows how a racial conflict became the catalyst for district multicultural policy-making. The case "begins" with the conflict and "ends" with the adoption of policy recommendations, but the process began long before the conflict and continues today, with the implementation of the recommendations.

Our perspective also assumes that policy is conditioned by the particular organizational culture and structure in which it unfolds, that policy-making is context specific. However, micro-level descriptions of particular policy processes need not be atheoretical (Hall, 1995). There are ample opportunities for theory-building in the analysis and comparison of cases. While our case study portrays a process that can best be understood within the historical and cultural context of a specific school district, it also exemplified ways of thinking about multicultural education that theorists such as Sleeter and Grant (1994) or Banks and Banks (1995) have identified and other researchers have observed in other contexts (Borman et al., 1992; Cornbleth & Waugh, 1995; Foster, 1990).

SCHOOL DISTRICT MULTICULTURAL EDUCATION POLICY

In the United States, multicultural education policy has not been a "top-down" process. Federal leadership in this area has been relatively weak. Desegregation Centers have disseminated information on multicultural education to districts involved in federally mandated desegregation, but other federal policies for the education of culturally different students since the 1960s have reinforced the "cultural deficit" model that is the bane of multicultural theorists. States control most aspects of schooling, including curriculum standards and teacher preparation/licensing, and states have responded variously (if at all) to the multicultural education movement (Gollnick, 1995). State-level policy processes are manifestations of the values and characteristic policy mechanisms of a specific state (Marshall et al., 1989); therefore, state policies addressed toward the "same" problem are often quite different (Placier, 1993).

For example, in case studies of New York and California, Cornbleth and Waugh (1995) found that in both states advocates of multicultural education had made strides toward curriculum reform, until they encountered political resistance in the late 1980s-early 1990s. In New York, these reactions stalled but did not entirely halt the adoption of a curriculum based on "multiple perspectives." In California, a more organized and media-savvy opposition dramatically redirected the state curriculum away from "multiple perspectives" toward an assimilationist "we're all immigrants" position. These state controversies made national news and galvanized conservative political networks in other states to resist reforms that they perceive as undermining national unity. The message was out: State multicultural education policies could not go "too far" in challenging traditional treatments of American culture and history in schools. While Gollnick (1995) reports some state-level movement, at the time of her survey only 21 states had at least "minimal" multicultural education policies.

When state initiatives are weak, ambiguous or absent, actors in school districts, in response to local beliefs and conditions, construct "multicultural education" in different ways. Nevertheless, two general rationales for district-level multicultural education policy can be identified: 1) reducing racial or cross-cultural conflict, and 2) improving success rates of culturally different students.

Reducing Racial or Cross-Cultural Conflict
Especially since desegregation, school administrators have been concerned about inter-racial relationships among students, teachers, and parents. Educators are not well prepared to deal with the tensions they encounter as school populations become more diverse; and without adequate preparation, schools can become flashpoints for cross-cultural conflict (Harvey, 1987; Lynch, 1993; O'Neil, 1993). For example, a 1990 Harris poll found that more high school students would join in or silently support racial confrontation than would condemn or try to stop it (O'Neil, 1993). School districts tend to respond to conflict through limited crisis management rather than proactive, long-range planning (Tomlinson, 1990). After a conflict, there may be more attention to improving understanding and communication, but interest diminishes over time. Critics of this human relations approach to multicultural education policy argue that addressing racial conflicts requires more than encouraging "cultural sensitivity"; it requires teaching active resistance to racism (Bagley, 1991; Foster, 1990; McCarthy, 1990; Sleeter & Grant, 1994; Troyna & Carrington, 1990; Troyna & Williams, 1986). But political expediency, based in the reality of the need for acceptance of policy by a white majority, often leads to the less threatening human relations approach (Banks, 1992; Lynch, 1989; Olneck, 1990; Sleeter, 1995; Tomlinson, 1990).

Improving Success Rates of Culturally Different Students

A second rationale for multicultural education policy is to change educational structures and practices that perpetuate lower achievement among culturally different students. Mehan et al. (1995) summarize the research showing that high academic expectations along with social supports, changes in classroom organization and discourse, and incorporation of students' cultural knowledge as resources for learning can improve achievement. District policies can provide resources and assistance for such school- and classroom-level changes. Vincent (1992) further argues that educators must recognize the structural or institutional aspects of racism. For example, there is ample evidence in many districts of disproportionate expulsion, suspension and dropout rates among culturally different students (Harris, 1992) and over-representation in special education and remedial classrooms accompanied by under-representation in advanced placement classes, gifted and talented programs, and extracurricular activities. In some communities, complaints about such disparate opportunities have been catalysts for multicultural policy-making. This policy direction poses a more serious challenge to "business as usual" in school districts than the human relations approach, because it requires a rethinking of long-standing assumptions and practices (Sleeter & Grant, 1994).

Two previous case studies of district multicultural education policy illustrate these points. Researchers Borman et al. (1992) were hired to assess a school district's "racial environment" after inter-racial fighting erupted at the high school. African American parents and community organizations saw this not as an isolated "incident" but as a symptom of ongoing, broader problems in district-community and teacher-student interactions. They reported their concerns to state officials, who responded with a grant to study the problem. Surveys, observations, interviews, and focus group meetings showed that whites and African Americans had very different images of the district. To bridge this gap, the researchers recommended "comprehensive" integration of multicultural education throughout district programs and curricula. However, they were not optimistic that their recommendations would be implemented for the following reasons: whites' avoidance of "race" and adherence to an assimilationist ideology; educators' preference for limited, piecemeal approaches; school personnel's denial and defensiveness in the face of evidence of problems; and ambiguous administrative support for the study and its recommendations.

Foster's (1990) study of multicultural education policy in one Local Education Authority (school district) in England found that in the 1970s the LEA had moved from an assimilationist to a human relations position. Faced with the apparent failure of the latter approach to ameliorate low achievement and disruptive behavior among Afro/Caribbean students, in the early 1980s LEA administrators re-identified the problem as racism. In 1982 the Chief Education Officer (superintendent) directed all headteachers (principals) to report racial incidents and all schools to develop anti-racist policies. However, in this case district multicultural policy was not strictly a "top-down" process. At least one school was consistently ahead of LEA policies because of a group of progressive teachers and political pressure from minority parents. The LEA's policies were not specific enough to give clear direction to teachers and school administrators who were *not* committed to or informed about anti-racist multicultural education. Foster concludes that effective multicultural policies should be based on evidence of actual school conditions/practices and their effects on minority students, not vague anti-racist rhetoric.

THEORETICAL PERSPECTIVE ON THE POLICY PROCESS
Both studies just described define district "policy" as a set of recommendations or administrative directives. As previously noted, "policy" as we consider it in this study is more than a text; it is a process. Typical policy discourse also bifurcates the process into stages called "policy-making" and "policy-implementation." This implies that policy is a thing made in one place or time and then transmitted elsewhere to be practiced. Rather, in a symbolic interactionist framework policy is constituted when multiple actors, representing multiple intentions, interests, and roles, interact under conditions of environmental uncertainty and ambiguity (Estes & Edmonds, 1981). Policy is a "transformation of intentions" in which content, practices, and consequences are generated in the dynamics (Hall, 1992, 1995). (See Hall, 1995, for a more thorough explanation of this framework.)

Intentions

Policies are vehicles for the realization of intentions. They express aims and purposes intended to shape the behavior of actors in the future and at other sites. Multiple actors with different and perhaps divergent intentions enter the process at different points and negotiate with one another to construct policy. Actors utilize power, the ability to mobilize resources to achieve goals, in attempts to further the policy process and/or their own intentions. The more divergent the intentions, the more the process becomes a "double entendre" in which some actors seek to subvert and resist others' intentions. Because actors have limited information and foresight and are engaged in dynamic interactions under unpredictable and changing conditions, the process can also have *un*intended consequences.

Conditions and Linkages Across Site and Time

The policy process occurs temporally through developmental phases and spatially across linked sites (e.g., state-district-school). Policy initiators, dependent on those who follow to fulfill their original intentions, set conditions which both limit and facilitate later action. Conditional effects vary according to the strength of linkages between phases/sites. In each context, actors must deal with each other, environmental conditions, and policy ambiguity/incompleteness. They may clarify, amend, or even subvert the initial intentions and content of the policy. Therefore, points at which one set of actors must delegate tasks or decisions to another set of actors are key points in the policy process. If previous decisions do not set clear conditions for delegates or if linkages are weak, delegates have more autonomy. Nevertheless, even strong linkages are not automatic and must be enacted to have effects.

Contingency and Conflict vs. Conventions

The policy process provides numerous opportunities for contingency and conflict. Institutional conventions, taken-for-granted ways of understanding, communicating, and doing for accomplishing collective activity are hedges against contingency and conflict. Conventions make cooperation and coordination simpler, quicker, and more efficient, but they also constrain alternatives and may privilege some interests over others (Becker, 1982). Moreover, conventions may be counter-productive in certain cases or become *passé* under changing conditions. Policy analysts must identify the conventions in a particular policy-making context in order to recognize when they are invoked and how much they constrain or facilitate the process.

Organizational Structure and Culture

Because policy is influenced by the organizational culture and structure, those who dominate the organization are frequently able to shape the context in which subordinates act, a form of meta-power (Baumgartner et al., 1976). Actors with better access to resources have an advantage in controlling or dominating the process. The organizational culture of policy-making and its conventions serve as resources for organizational leaders (Clegg, 1989; Sewell, 1992). The distribution of other resources, e.g. information or authority, tends to support the established order. However, organizational leaders must delegate responsibility in order to achieve their aims, and delegation implies some degree of discretion and interpretation. Thus, despite the advantages of organizational leaders, contingency, conflict, and resistance are a distinct possibility in policy production.

METHODS

The case study presented here represents a "slice of time" from an ongoing school district policy process. The primary method of data collection was participant observation at meetings of groups established by the district to develop and implement multicultural education policy in the wake of a racial conflict. One of the authors (Hall) was chair of the Curriculum Subcommittee of a larger Committee on Multicultural Issues convened to develop policy recommendations for the school board over the course of two summer months. Another author (Placier) was a nonparticipant observer during meetings of the committee, subcommittee and school board, and a member of the Multicultural Task Force established to implement the committee's recommendations.

The researchers kept detailed field notes of meetings and discussions and collected a file of documents distributed to members of these groups. Additional data came from two newspapers that regularly covered the process and published letters, editorials, and commentaries both promoting and opposing multicultural reforms.

Finally, the third author (Davis) interviewed a sample of participants from the original committee as well as school board members. The interviews, which followed a semi-structured protocol, were designed to elicit a better understanding of their interests and intentions and whether they perceived these interests and intentions as having been fulfilled through the policy process. Analysis of the interview data is ongoing; the case study presented here is based for the most part on analysis of observations and documents. Data were analyzed to identify phases of the policy process, key relationships, and interactions among the actors and how various actors, within the limits of their prescribed roles in the process, mobilized to advance their interests.

CASE STUDY: MAKING MULTICULTURAL POLICY IN WESTWOOD

As Cornbleth and Waugh (1995) argue, studies of multicultural policy-making should look at how the "particular locality influences investigation, interpretation and action" (p. 29). Our case study is set in Westwood, a city of 70,000 with an economy dominated by higher education, health care, insurance, and light industry. The school district has received national and state awards for high academic achievement, and the administration's most strenuous efforts have gone toward maintaining this reputation of "excellence." At the time of the study the steadily growing student population of 14,500 was 80 percent white, 15 percent African American, 4 percent Asian, and 1 percent other. The percentage of ethnic minority teachers and administrators is very low. A state university brings increasing numbers of international and middle-class African American students into the schools and also has complex effects on the politics and culture of the school district. The school board at the time of the study had seven members, six white and one African American. The African American, a university professor, had recently taken a position with a national organization in another city and did not participate in these events.

At the time of our study, the same superintendent had led the Westwood district for 17 years and set the tone for the district culture. He generally acted in a low-key, behind-the-scenes style, rarely taking a strong public stand on controversial issues. He structured how issues reached the board through control of the agenda and presentation of information. Open public comment and debate at board meetings was limited, and the administration also tried to minimize negative press coverage. Occasionally the board and/or administration appointed committees with community participants to study problems and make recommendations, but memberships, structures, agendas, and timelines were carefully managed, and the administration put the final "spin" on all recommendations.

"Racial issues" were not new to the district's policy agenda. A few years after the 1954 *Brown* decision, the district closed secondary programs at the black K-12 school and transferred students to formerly white schools. Low black participation in extracurricular activities became an issue. In 1969 black high school students protested selection of an all-white cheerleading squad. Negotiations with school administrators led to integration of the squad, as well as the creation of new extracurricular groups and courses to improve black-white relations. The segregated elementary program was finally disbanded in 1967, following a year-long community debate. Black students and teachers were dispersed to other schools amid some white resistance. Soon came reports from teachers of "discipline problems" with black students, and from black parents of their children's mistreatment by school people. The district created a new position: Home-School Communicators, African Americans intended to serve as liaisons between schools and African American parents.

In the early 1990s the district implemented Outcomes Based Education, and some adopted outcomes were related to multicultural education. For example, students were expected to "describe and address the challenges of a multi-cultural society and world," "exhibit an awareness and understanding of diverse cultural, linguistic and ethnic heritages," "display respect and sensitivity when interacting with others in diverse community settings," and "demonstrate understanding of past and present cultures." All curricula were reportedly being re-examined for consistency with these outcomes. However, principals and teachers had a relatively high degree of autonomy in deciding how to reach them. Principals and/or teachers in some schools, particularly elementary schools with African American and immigrant students, had initiated multicultural activities on their own. Other schools, particularly in affluent neighborhoods, were almost entirely white. We were told repeatedly that because such schools did not "have much diversity," multiculturalism was not a priority for them. Another expressed district norm was that teachers could not be "forced" or "required" to do anything. The district had an extensive staff development program, but until the events in this study, multicultural education had not been a frequent topic. Even then, the staff development program presented teachers with a menu of *voluntary* choices.

The district has few external incentives for implementing multicultural education. The state has not been active in promoting multicultural education as official policy (Gollnick, 1995). A state School Improvement Program requires district reviews by a visiting team every five years. One standard for the review reads: "Multicultural and gender-fair concepts and practice are infused in curriculum, instructional programs and all other school activities." This is fairly strong language, but the state so far has not sanctioned noncomplying districts.

In summary, the following aspects of the history, structure and culture of the district would have important effects on the making of multicultural education policy: the influence of the university, a history of racial tension and unresolved post-integration issues, low numbers of minority school personnel, the administration's preference for avoiding open controversy, and school/teacher autonomy. In addition, based on the commitment expressed in the district's adopted "outcomes" and the ongoing curriculum review as well as the efforts of particular schools and teachers, there was a perception among some district personnel that the district had already made great progress toward multicultural education. This perception was in direct contrast to the perception among community critics, particularly some African Americans, that the district was doing nothing to address their concerns.

Phase I: Establishing the Committee on Multicultural Issues
The press and most participants attributed formation of the Committee on Multicultural Issues to one event: a speech by a university Black Studies expert at a high school Black History Month assembly. Invited to speak on "contributions of African Americans," the speaker said that he overheard some white students complaining about the assembly. He decided to deliver a critique of racism in schools. Some white students took offense, while some

African American students voiced agreement. Scuffles broke out, reported as anywhere from a "riot" to minor shoves. Some school staff responded defensively to the critique as an attack on *their* school. Counselors spent hours calming students down. The speaker received telephone death threats. The media gave the incident extensive coverage, and district people quoted in the press tried to downplay its seriousness and emphasize that it would not undermine progress in race relations.

At the next board meeting in March, one member proposed formation of a Committee on Race Relations, to which a majority agreed. After all, some members pointed out, "cultural sensitivity" was one of their adopted outcomes. The same board member who proposed the committee wrote the initial version of its "charge" and circulated it for comment. As some board members emphasized, this process established the committee as a *board*, not an administration, initiative. However, the board delegated responsibility for managing the committee's formation and operation to the administration.

The superintendent placed an associate superintendent, an African American woman who had worked in Westwood for over 30 years beginning at the segregated school, in charge of the committee. She was in a cross-pressured position, representing potentially conflicting interests and expectations. African Americans would expect her support, while the administration would expect smooth, conflict-free management. She announced in the media that anyone interested in committee membership should call her office. She also formulated a list of members to be recruited, primarily those who had worked on district committees before and/or were well known in the community. A large number were African Americans. The associate superintendent said that she tried to balance the membership to include district staff and community members, racial and cultural groups, men and women. When the board saw the initial list, however, some wanted to nominate people they saw as excluded from consideration. For example, one advocated successfully for an Islamic African American man known as an activist and school critic. As a result of such negotiation, the final list of 43 members was not approved until June.

In the meantime the name of the committee was changed to the Committee on Multicultural Issues. The original focus on race was shifted to a more diffuse focus on multiple cultures. The associate superintendent said that the change was intentional, to prevent the committee from falling into the past "blame game" of complaints about racism. This time, she wanted a more positive, action-oriented approach.

When the associate superintendent (now acting as committee chair) convened the members on June 30, she informed them that they had only until mid-August to complete their process. An outside consultant available to the district without charge through a federally funded agency in Chicago would advise them. The consultant, a Hispanic woman, had visited Westwood before at the request of the English as a Second Language coordinator, who had given her high recommendations.

Next the committee heard two speeches presenting different definitions of the problem they would be addressing. First the board president delivered the committee's "charge," touching on both human relations and equity themes. She invoked her own cultural background (an American Indian grandmother), Thomas Jefferson's ideals of equality and liberty, and Frederick Douglass' faith in education as the road to freedom. The board, she said, wanted all students to achieve up to their "potential." The charge was: 1) to determine programs already in place to do that; 2) to decide if there were any deficiencies in current practices, if programs needed to be enhanced, changed, or eliminated; and 3) to recommend new options. She acknowledged that some in the community might ask: Should we be doing this? *Learning* of course came first, she said, but learning could be undermined by low self-esteem, victimization and lack of discipline. The board wanted students to learn mutual understanding and respect for diversity.

Next the outside consultant presented her definition of the problem. A Ph.D. candidate in political science who had studied with African American historian Manning Marable, she took an academic, critical, social reconstructionist approach that went beyond anything the district had previously considered. She emphasized the political purposes of schooling and the need for "authentic" reform. She criticized shallow "add-on" or "tourist" approaches to multicultural reform and spoke of her disappointment with educators' resistance to change, giving specific examples from her visits to schools. She said that multicultural education should focus on equity, work against racism, and question taken-for-granted assumptions.

These two speeches presented the committee with contrasting definitions of the problem and of "multicultural education" as the solution. The board president, the district insider, placed multicultural education in the framework of a liberal, meritocratic ideology of individual rights and equal opportunity, coupled with human relations. She stressed the psychological and social conditions necessary to fulfill each individual student's potential. The consultant, the outsider, took a critical, anti-racist stance more challenging to the district's positive self-image. However, because of a sudden change in her job this would be the consultant's only opportunity to meet with the committee.

The chair next announced that committee meetings would be open. People other than official members could participate, and the group could seek outside advice. Then she divided the committee into four subcommittees, whose membership had already been decided. The subcommittees were: Curriculum, Cultural Awareness and Tolerance, Minority Hiring, and Extracurricular Activities. These four categories showed how the board and administration had constructed "multicultural education." The first two topics encompassed two major areas of multicultural reform: curriculum infusion and human relations/prejudice reduction (Banks, 1993; Sleeter & Grant, 1994). The other two addressed issues that had been topics of concern to African Americans in Westwood since desegregation. The associate superintendent distributed copies of the specific charges for each subcommittee. The charges were daunting, perhaps impossible, to accomplish in a very limited time. For example, the Curriculum subcommittee was to evaluate the district's entire curriculum for inclusion of cultural groups and to identify programs that promoted academic excellence and prevented dropping out among minority students.

The associate superintendent said that she tried to balance subcommittee membership based on identities, knowledge, and interests. The subcommittees had 8-12 members, each including 2-4 district staff, a move that some community participants questioned in terms of control and independence. The subcommittee chairs were pre-appointed by the administration, and some participants also questioned that decision in terms of democratic process. The first two chairs were male university professors, one white American and one Middle Eastern, who had previously provided service to the district and were seen as having expertise; the other two chairs were African American women, one a high school assistant principal and the other a doctoral candidate in educational administration who had worked for the district as a parent volunteer.

Summary and Interpretation of Phase I. In this phase elements of the theoretical framework were strikingly evident. The process was an interplay of different intentions, negotiations between board and district, openness versus control, and conventions versus contingency and ambiguity. The board majority's intentions were to exercise independent leadership and legitimate authority, to communicate to the public that they took racial conflict seriously and invited public criticism, and to act on one of their adopted goals. However, they delegated logistical responsibility to district administrators, who intended to balance this open responsiveness with their established conventions for controlling the structure, leadership, membership and timeline of community committees as well as their desire to avoid "unproductive" conflict. The membership for the most part reflected an existing network of collective activity, including linkages between the university and district. However, opening membership to call-in volunteers and the board's negotiation to include more outsider voices created the possibility of more contingency and conflict than the administration might have preferred. The inexplicably short timeline seemed to deny the depth of the problem to be addressed. Another time constraint was that in the summer many members would be absent and district staff would not be as available to provide information.

A major source of ambiguity was that the charges to the committee presented no explicit definition of "multicultural education," and the members heard conflicting definitions from the board president and the outside consultant. "Race relations" might have entailed generating ideas to improve "human relations" among students, teachers, and parents. What did "multicultural education" mean? The relationship between the high school conflict and "cultural awareness and tolerance" seemed fairly obvious. Why the other three subcommittees? What problems were they addressing? The members were expected, apparently, to work this out for themselves.

Phase II: Committee and Subcommittee Meetings
The committee as a whole met only twice. Decisions were made in the subcommittees, which met once a week for 6 weeks. Division into subcommittees meant that only the associate superintendent, who circulated among the groups and met with subcommittee chairs, could track the entire process. Two board members also observed some meetings. Another observer was a newspaper reporter, who was vigilant for signs of dissatisfaction with the district. His stories weighed in on the side of community participation and included quotes from the most critical committee members. Subcommittees also had invited and uninvited guests from both district and community.

The two more narrowly-defined subcommittees (Minority Hiring and Extracurricular Activities) seem to have proceeded with little tension, focusing on identifying current district practices and making recommendations for improvement rather than probing for the district's "deficiencies." Some participants did complain that the Minority Hiring subcommittee was too district directed; for example, membership of the district personnel director seemed to preclude criticism of his office's performance. This subcommittee primarily recommended expansion of existing minority recruitment practices. The Extracurricular Activities chair used group process techniques to elicit a long list of suggestions for expanding minority student participation, along with one major, costly recommendation to make them more feasible—providing after-school transportation.

The other two subcommittees were chaired by university professors who were more independent of the district administration and had broader and more ambiguous topics to address. The following account focuses on the Curriculum subcommittee.

At the first meeting, the Curriculum subcommittee chair noted that although the subcommittee's charge defined "curriculum" as content and special programs, he defined "curriculum" very broadly to include equal access to knowledge and democratic participation of all students. Looking at the district from this perspective would take a long time, he said, and he expected that the subcommittee's recommendations would be preliminary. Other members voiced concerns as diverse as the district's "outcomes," teacher racism and lack of cultural knowledge, libraries, institutionalized racism, and lack of "sensitivity." One member asked, "Do we agree with the charge?," indicating that he would question the subcommittee's predefined purposes. An African American community member and a white teacher debated briefly whether racism in schools was "institutionalized" or merely a series of "isolated incidents." It was obvious from the start that different members had different intentions, relationships to the schools, and interpretations of the subcommittee's purposes.

In subsequent meetings, the Curriculum chair attempted to move the subcommittee toward a common (admittedly his) definition of the problem, while at the same time incorporating the members' disparate points of view. One member called him a "benevolent dictator," pushing the process along and gently challenging the group to expand their interpretation of the charge. As a sociologist of education, he defined "curriculum" to include all structural and policy patterns (tracking, disciplinary procedures, special education placement) that could have negative effects on minority students, and said that he intended to request data from the district administration that might substantiate those effects. He distributed documents that reinforced his position, e.g., James Banks' (1994) five-dimensional model of multicultural education.

Four community members attended meetings much more consistently than others and therefore exercised more influence over the process. The subcommittee's actions were shaped in major ways by three African American men, only one of whom was officially appointed. They took full advantage of the openness and ambiguity of the process to further their intentions. The first African American member, a postal worker, was appointed after he called a board member about the high school conflict. As a Westwood student, he had experienced so much discouragement from teachers that he had given up his college dreams. On the other hand, he had attended the high school where the conflict took place and felt that "race relations" among *students* then were positive. He wondered what had made the situation worse over the years. He and his wife, parents of two students, shared readings about multicultural and Afrocentric education with the committee. He strongly supported diverse curriculum content, but he also wanted more vocational training for African American students as a route to economic mobility.

A Ph.D. candidate in English and Black Studies, husband of a specialist in the district and father of two students, arrived as a "walk-in" volunteer. After committee membership had been determined, he asked the associate superintendent if he could attend. She approved his attendance but did not officially add him to the committee roster. He had a strong commitment to infusion of content on African American history and literature and also wanted to dismantle the ideology of "cultural deprivation," which he believed permeated Westwood educators' thinking. His often-stated intention was to recommend that all district teachers be *required* to attend professional development sessions on those themes.

Also attending this subcommittee was the previously mentioned Islamic community activist. He was appointed to Minority Hiring, but he switched to Curriculum on the first night, challenging the chair's control. He emphasized democratic participation, conflict resolution, and inclusion of content important to Islamic students. Through his political activism and role as a community radio talk show host, he knew how to use the media to express his dissatisfaction with the district. He also invited parents and students to attend the meetings and was adamant about wanting to extend the committee's role and timeline in order to include more community input.

The remaining active community member, a businesswoman originally from India, had been invited to join the committee because she was effective in promoting multicultural education at her children's junior high school. She emphasized better understanding of cultural and religious differences and more study of non-European cultures, which, from her observations of her children's assignments, was inadequate. She was quieter than the men in the group, but when she did speak she came out strongly in favor of curriculum infusion.

The district representatives on this subcommittee did *not* seem to constrain its activities. Both were absent from several meetings due to other scheduled activities. One, a white male social studies teacher, spoke about his diligent efforts to expand the curriculum beyond textbooks. He listened to community members with respectful interest and was open to the idea of curriculum infusion. He did keep returning to the point that schools, teachers, and texts cannot do everything, that *parents* must be involved and responsible.

The central office representative, a white male assistant superintendent, for the most part took on the roles of observer and information source. He arranged two meetings with district personnel to explain what was already being done to address the problem.

At these meetings, district people stressed that programs already in progress were facilitating multicultural education. While they tried to demonstrate their intentions to change, some subcommittee members had the impression that they intended to *resist* change. District personnel argued that there were constraints on change, such as state requirements, teacher and school autonomy, limited staff development and teaching time, low student interest in specialized courses, and the cost of new materials. Community members at times interpreted these references to practical or external constraints as excuse-making.

When the subcommittee turned to its second task, identifying programs to promote academic excellence or prevent dropouts among minority students, district staff told them that existing or upcoming programs were already addressing these problems. On the other hand, an African American Home-School Communicator said that she did see problems with low teacher expectations and disproportionate special education placement of African American students. However, beyond the information provided in this meeting, the Curriculum chair was unable to obtain data from the district about the effects of structures and policies such as tracking and suspension on minority students. An administrator said that the district did not keep records by race and did not have the capacity to conduct research on these questions. Therefore, the district hindered efforts to expand the subcommittee's charge in a more structural direction.

Meanwhile, on the Cultural Awareness and Tolerance subcommittee, the chair said that he intended to facilitate as much open participation as possible. The subcommittee's charge was to identify, evaluate, and make recommended improvements for components of the district curriculum and staff development programs designed to teach tolerance, appreciation, and acceptance of racial and cultural diversity and programs meant to facilitate positive communication and cooperation among teachers, students, and parents from different cultural backgrounds. It soon became clear to the chair, however, that while his intention was to promote understanding of all cultural groups, the intentions of some members were to focus only on "black" issues. From his perspective these members *narrowed* the subcommittee's charge, from "multicultural" to "race." Some members had experienced negative interactions with school people, and for them the district's "deficiencies" in race relations seemed evident. Like some members of the Curriculum subcommittee, they were impatient with reports of what the district was "already doing." Several favored gathering more information on community perceptions of the schools through a survey, but the restricted time did not allow for such an ambitious project. Their complaints were picked up by the newspaper reporter, to support his portrayal of the district as an undemocratic bureaucracy. Of all the subcommittees, the associate superintendent saw this one as the most negative and out of control. The subcommittee chair by the end seemed to have lost patience with the process.

At the last night of subcommittee meetings, the associate superintendent visited each group and for the first time unexpectedly presented them with a definition of multicultural education: "Understanding and appreciating differences, as it relates to race, gender, national origin, exceptionality, religion and age" (a human relations definition). She also asked each subcommittee to submit only 2-3 major recommendations for the board. But by this point, each group had generated so many ideas that to reduce their lists to 2-3 points would lose much of the substance of their discussions. The associate superintendent did not specify a process for arriving at a final list of recommendations. In retrospect, some members could not remember how they made the decision; it just "happened." The associate superintendent told one subcommittee that only officially appointed members should participate in the final decision, which would have ruled out walk-in members and those who switched committees. However, this belated reassertion of administrative control had little effect.

The Curriculum chair presented his own list of recommendations, based on his structural analysis of the problem along with ideas that had emerged in their discussions. He included his position that the district should collect and analyze data on the effects of structural patterns. The Ph.D. candidate contributed a list, and a university administrator who had been absent from the meetings sent the chair a list by mail. That is, only the "academics" in the group submitted written lists. After a discussion about all of the lists, and whether anyone had objections or additions to them, the chair said he would synthesize them into a final report. The community activist argued that they still did not have sufficient information to make recommendations and the meetings should continue. However, as a lone dissenter, he was unable to halt the process.

The Cultural Awareness and Tolerance chair was unavoidably absent from the meeting to decide on final recommendations. Facilitated by an African American woman who worked as a specialist in the district and was not an "official" member, the group agreed on a list of general categories. The woman took that list home, where she and her husband, the Ph.D. candidate on the Curriculum Subcommittee, filled in the details of the final recommendations. As a result of their initiative, two subcommittees' recommendations were very similar.

Summary and Interpretation of Phase II. The same interplay of factors made the process in this phase more open and unpredictable than the administration might have preferred. Control of logistics, time, and information as resources reinforced the administration's authority. District staff for the most part presented a positive view of existing practices and protected their autonomy by explaining why some of the subcommittees' ideas would not be feasible. The associate superintendent served as a center of communication and information, monitoring subcommittee processes through the chairs and reporting to the administration. Although too late, she attempted to impose a human relations definition of "multicultural education" and to limit the number of recommendations.

On the other hand, subcommittee members who actively participated took advantage of the openness and ambiguity to advance their intentions as far as possible. Some exercised their agency by switching subcommittees, attending more than one subcommittee, strategizing outside of meetings, and using the media to criticize district control. An unspecified decision-making process meant that virtually all submitted recommendations were included in the subcommittee reports rather than the limited number the associate superintendent requested. Some recommendations also went far beyond the limits of the human relations definition of multicultural education the administration proposed.

Phase III: "See the Future Together" and Recommendations to the Board

There was no final meeting of the entire committee to reach agreement on consolidated recommendations. Instead, the committee met with the board to present individual subcommittee reports. In her opening remarks, the associate superintendent said that although the committee had not found solutions, they had "set up a vehicle to find a solution." After this meeting she would collect all recommendations, meet with the chairs and outside consultant, and develop a final report eliminating "redundancies" that would come to the board for action. The subcommittee chairs then presented their reports, which were essentially long lists of recommendations with varying degrees of organization and synthesis. All recommended establishing an ongoing group to carry their work forward. None seemed to feel entirely finished or resolved, but neither did any question district authority to cut off their deliberations. Similarities in the subcommittee recommendations, especially Curriculum and Cultural Awareness and Tolerance, were obvious. They both recommended the hiring of a district-level multicultural education coordinator, and the fact that this recommendation came from two "separate" committees gave it added weight.

The consultant by this time was unavailable to work on the final report. Her absence left the associate superintendent in a difficult position, cross-pressured by the community and the administration. In her synthesis of subcommittee reports into a shorter draft report, she excluded some specific recommendations. She explained that she had concentrated on the most substantial recommendations; for example, her first priority was to win approval for the multicultural coordinator position, which would make someone directly *responsible* for implementing the remaining recommendations. When she sent the first draft to committee members for comment, those whose specific recommendations had been deleted called or wrote to demand that their ideas be restored. The newspaper reporter implied in a story that the associate superintendent was censoring the committee's work. For the most part, the associate superintendent restored the deleted recommendations, but some committee members were still suspicious of her intentions.

The final draft of the report was presented to the subcommittee chairs in October and scheduled for presentation to the board in November. The chairs asked that their original reports be attached to the back, to avoid any further question of censorship. In the meantime, the Committee on Multicultural Issues was dissolved and could no longer take action. The associate superintendent proceeded with the first meeting of a Multicultural Task Force made up almost entirely of district personnel, with a few university representatives.

The associate superintendent eventually pared the subcommittee recommendations down to a 6-page report titled "See the Future Together." The first three sections outlined a three-level structure: 1) a district multicultural coordinator assigned to "carry out" the board's policy, concentrating on inservice training and curriculum changes; 2) a district task force of school personnel and community members to "insure that the board's multicultural education policy is implemented uniformly throughout the district"; and 3) building-level multicultural committees including teachers and parents to "assess the presence of multicultural education in the school program and develop ways to expand and infuse the program where necessary." Next followed sections of recommendations on minority hiring, staff development, curriculum, culture and tolerance, extracurricular activities, and parent/community involvement taken from the subcommittee reports. Considering how little time the committee had had to work, it was a relatively comprehensive report. In November, the associate superintendent presented it to the board, read the consolidated list of recommendations, and told the board that the committee members requested they also read their original subcommittee reports "very carefully." Then, in a surprising move, she said she would make her *own* recommendations to the board. She said that "we" (the administration) had prioritized six "major" recommendations: 1) budgeting for a multicultural coordinator and support for a district multicultural task force; 2) expanding the minority intern program; 3) multicultural curriculum materials for each school; 4) staff development for teachers and administrators; 5) appointing someone to work with the city on transportation for extracurricular participation; 6) planning co-curricular activities for new middle schools. These recommendations would require board action, she said, because they had "funding attached." The remaining recommendations could be delegated to building-level committees.

A board member moved to accept the report, including all of the attached reports, and the floor was opened for public comment. The only speaker was the Curriculum subcommittee member who had protested the closure of the process, who reiterated his concerns that the report was too broad, that it downplayed or excluded specific recommendations important to him, and that the committee had not had enough time to fulfill its charge. The board voted to accept the report. Then they discussed what voting on the administration's short list of recommendations would mean, because costs were not specified. The superintendent made his first *public* contribution to multicultural policy-making, saying that the board could vote on the "general direction" of the recommendations, and he would bring information on costs and feasibility to their next meeting. The board followed suit.

At the December board meeting the superintendent presented recommendations for "selected" funded reforms, the ones the administration had "prioritized." This list was further reduced from the one the associate superintendent had presented—negotiate with the city on transportation for extracurricular activities, pursue *external* funds for staff development activities, allocate $5-10,000 for new curriculum materials, and expand the minority intern program. He reported that the Multicultural Task Force was already underway, at no expense. Finally, he wanted to hire the chair of the Extracurricular Activities subcommittee as a half-time Multicultural Coordinator to work under the supervision of the associate superintendent for the remainder of the year, with the position to be reassessed at that time. The coordinator would chair the Multicultural Task Force. He said that the board would be "very pleased" with what "we" (the administration) could accomplish with "few resources." With the board's approval of these recommendations, multicultural education policy-making was back in the district's court.

Summary and Interpretation of Phase III. In this phase, control of multicultural education policy returned to the administration, after several months of unpredictable and (for the administration) uncomfortable community participation, media scrutiny, and ambiguity. The associate superintendent took over formulation and presentation of the written report to the board. She dissolved the committee despite the strong misgivings of some members and initiated a Multicultural Education Task Force involving almost entirely district employees, signalling that the time for direct community involvement had ended. The superintendent assumed a public role only when finances became a factor, but his and the associate superintendent's "we" statements implied that administrators had reached consensus behind the scenes on which of the committee's recommendations they were willing to advocate for funding. The committee was also not consulted about the closed hiring process for the multicultural coordinator. The door that had been opened to community participation was closed, and it was back to business-as-usual between the board and administration.

This phase marked a return to conventional modes of district governance, with the administration again controlling the agenda, mediating between the public and the board. Although protests brought the restoration of all recommendations to the "See the Future Together" report, the administration's selection of only *certain* recommendations as fundable priorities for board action froze the other recommendations as *mere* recommendations for schools to consider. Further, the associate superintendent claimed that the "leftover" recommendations could be delegated to building-level committees, but some required district-level action, especially the Curriculum chair's recommendation that the district collect data on structural inequities. Given school/teacher autonomy and misgivings among district staff about the difficulty of certain changes, the fate of many of the committee's recommendations was uncertain. In the end, new financial investment in multicultural education was low (the coordinator's half-time salary for 6 months and $5-10,000 for materials). The district had a "comprehensive multicultural policy" on paper but with minimal expense and disruption.

Still, the board had set a precedent for inviting community participation in problem solving, including African American community members who were critical of the district and had a stake in substantive rather than symbolic solutions. The most assertive committee members had taken advantage of a brief opening in district control to push multicultural education further, perhaps, than the district administration had intended. A district-level multicultural education coordinator, even part-time, is a rarity in this state.

CONCLUSION
The case study further demonstrates the usefulness of a symbolic interactionist theoretical framework for understanding educational policy as a process, not a product. This process was a complex interplay of conventional and unpredictable elements. It was a "transformation of intentions" in which content, practices and consequences were generated in the dynamics (Hall, 1992, 1995). The following discussion applies the framework to the case to demonstrate how different actors mobilized power/resources or took advantage of ambiguity to fulfill their intentions, how linkages between the board, administration and the committee influenced the process, how administrative conventions served as hedges against contingency and conflict, and how actors who dominated the organization were able to shape the context and shape the outcomes of the committee process.

The Black History Month speaker's sudden decision to change his rhetoric revealed some negative undercurrents beneath the district's positive image. Liberal white board members intended to face the "race issue" head-on, but their delegation of committee oversight to the district administration meant that this historically volatile issue would be contained within the administration's conventional ways of thinking and acting. The administration carefully selected subcommittee members and chairs and limited the time frame, extent, and intrusiveness of the process and the formal authority of the committee. The board even had to negotiate with the administration over membership on a board committee. The associate superintendent would be cross-pressured between the intentions of African American community members to push for major changes and the intentions of the administration to limit change based on feasibility and cost (both financial and political). Negotiations among these divergent intentions continued through the writing of the "See the Future Together" report, which in the end did include all of the members' recommendations.

The relative openness and independence of the committees' participation and deliberation, absence of formal rules for decision-making, exercise of individual agency, and members' use of the media, all of these sources of ambiguity and contingency ran counter to district power. The associate superintendent replaced "race relations" with "multicultural," ironically (given raging conflicts over multiculturalism in other settings) considered to be less controversial. This broader umbrella allowed the committee to consider issues beyond human relations. The two subcommittee chairs from outside the district had the most ambiguous topics to address and the most critical members and, from the district administration's standpoint, allowed their committees to "get out of hand." The Curriculum chair's intention was to pressure the district to face the consequences of its traditional structure and culture for minority students. The three African American men on this committee presented strong arguments, backed by experience, religious commitment, and academic expertise in Black Studies that challenged the district overtly. Nevertheless, once the committee process was arbitrarily ended, administrative professionals took back control, reasserting their conventions for mediating between the community and the board and setting the parameters for feasible change. The associate superintendent and superintendent used their power to see that district *resources* were allocated only to recommendations they prioritized. In the end no provisions were adopted for evaluating the effectiveness of the proposed changes, for holding the district accountable for carrying out the committee members' intentions. A further source of ambiguity in this particular policy process was the unclear definition of "multicultural education." "Multicultural education" is a contested term, with multiple meanings (Sleeter & Grant, 1994). Other writers have noted that lack of consensus on the meaning of "multicultural education" creates conflict and uncertainty in the policy process (Banks, 1992; Crumpton, 1992; Gaff, 1992; Gibson, 1984; Glazer, 1993; Gordon, 1992; Ogilvie, 1983; Young, 1991). The associate superintendent chose "multicultural" because it seemed more positive than "race relations," less likely to invoke unresolved conflicts from the past, and inclusive of groups other than African Americans. Meanings of the term in this context were implicit in the four subcommittee topics. But beyond this, the meanings of "multicultural education" were pragmatically constructed. The Curriculum subcommittee chair did distribute Banks' (1994) five-dimensional model of multicultural education (content integration, prejudice reduction, knowledge construction, equity pedagogy, and empowering school culture/structure), but it did not structure their decisions as it might have if there had been more time for reflection and discussion. The external consultant was not available to lend an overarching framework to the committee's work.

Instead, the outcome of the committee process was a policy document that presented mostly recommended add-ons or expansions of existing programs, not the genuine rethinking of the district's practices that many multicultural education theorists advocate. The administration did not "prioritize" the Curriculum subcommittee chair's recommendation for a self-study of institutional policies and practices that might be detrimental to minority students. There was no mandate or funding for professional development on working successfully with minority students and parents that community members claimed was desperately needed, just a statement of intention to raise "external funds" for this purpose. On the other hand, as Cornbleth and Waugh (1995) make evident, when multicultural policy-makers *do* threaten deeply held assumptions and practices they are vulnerable to conservative reactions. Avoidance of "radical" rhetoric about structural inequality or racism may be politically realistic in order to avoid such reactions (Sleeter, 1995). This district's add-on approach to multicultural education evoked very little backlash from the community. A board member noted that whether intended or not, news portrayals of the committee as too "conservative" may have prevented conservative reactions from surfacing in Westwood.

In comparison with the district described in Borman et al. (1992), this district administration demonstrated a much higher commitment to change. The school board responded to a crisis on its own initiative rather than in response to state intervention. Yet like the administration in Borman et al., this administration also did not want to dwell on collecting evidence of "wrong-doing" but to move fairly quickly to concrete, do-able recommendations. Administrative support for the school board's initiative was also ambiguous although not as overtly resistant as in Borman et al.'s case. The politically astute superintendent made no public statements in support of multicultural education; his only statements presented himself as carrying out the will of the board. With the high level of school and teacher autonomy evident in this district, most of the "recommendations" seemed destined to remain voluntary, optional suggestions, not mandates for change. However, the board did open the door to direct participation by African American community members, rather than hiring researchers to survey their "opinions" as in Borman et al.'s (1992) case. Although cut off prematurely, the subcommittee discussions were a small start in the direction of the "dialogue of differences" that Cornbleth and Waugh (1995) recommend as a key part of multicultural reform. The associate superintendent, although in a cross-pressured position, did advocate for many of the committee's recommendations. The hiring of a multicultural coordinator, even if the position was part-time and marginalized, bolstered the legitimacy of multicultural education in the district. The reinforcement of minority teacher recruitment in the face of growing white resentment of affirmative action made a political statement. Although not approaching the "comprehensive" ideal Borman et al. advocated, multicultural education became more firmly institutionalized in this district.

As a result of his LEA study, Foster (1990) argued that effective multicultural policies should be based on evidence of actual school conditions/practices and their effects on minority students, not vague anti-racist rhetoric.

> It is extremely difficult to formulate sensible, specific and clearly directed policy if we have little idea of what is actually happening in schools or wider educational systems (p. 190).

The subcommittees in this case were not given sufficient time to collect specific evidence of the extent of racial intolerance, lower achievement, or structural patterns with deleterious effects on culturally different students, and the administration did not express any intention to follow this course. The committee was encouraged to move ahead quickly to concrete, practical recommendations rather than delving for "deficiencies." This allowed the administration to continue to downplay the exceptions to the district's "excellent" performance. Foster also found that in the absence of clear district-level messages about multicultural education and what it means in practice, schools where administrators and teachers already have knowledge of and a commitment to multicultural education will be much more successful. In Westwood, there was already a pattern of variability in knowledge and commitment among schools and teachers. According to the "See the Future Together" report, the district Multicultural Task Force was to see that district policies were "uniformly implemented" throughout the district, but given the norm of school/teacher autonomy, the weak commitment to extensive professional development, and the lack of provisions for policy evaluation, we expected that schools and classrooms would continue to vary widely.

In our retrospective interviews we found that participants were divided in their interpretations of "what happened" in the policy process. Some were relatively satisfied, while others were still extremely distrustful of the district's intentions. One board member sent a memo to committee members shortly after adoption of the report questioning why their recommendations had not directly mentioned *racism*. Had they addressed the original intentions of the board, to reduce racial conflict? Another board member, however, pointed out that the adopted policy was very progressive. Of course, they did not solve all of the district's race problems, but no one could suggest that this was a step backward. District follow-through would tell the story. Yet as some critical community participants questioned, with no provisions for monitoring or evaluating the fulfillment of the recommendations, how would they ever know if their intentions had been fulfilled? At the end of our analysis of this "slice of time" in the policy process, we were not as pessimistic as Borman et al. (1992), but we surmised that the Westwood district administration had once again devised a way to defuse and contain public criticism and to limit the district's multicultural policies to changes that preserved the district's positive image among the more influential white, middle-class, and affluent residents of Westwood.

This case study, along with Foster (1990) and Borman et al. (1992), leads to several policy implications. The aim of multicultural education policy-making, according to multicultural education theorists, is to transform schools in fundamental ways in order to make them instruments of social justice. The efforts of schools and school districts continue to disappoint the theorists. The persuasiveness of theorists is limited at this point among people who require empirical support for their claims, because there are as yet few studies demonstrating the effectiveness of multicultural education reforms. There is a desperate need for such studies, given the growing strength of ideological arguments against multicultural education. Advocates need to show that multicultural strategies make a difference in cross-cultural relationships in schools and/or the achievement of culturally different students.

The definition of "effectiveness" will vary according to one's definition of the problem. If the problem is defined as negative "race relations" in schools, how would researchers know if such relations had improved? If the problem is defined as a structure that systematically provides unequal educational opportunities to minority students, how would researchers know if a district had equalized opportunities? And even if equal access to programs has been provided, does this take into account "curriculum, staffing, instruction and other schooling factors that are critical to equitable education" (Grant & Millar, 1992, p. 15)? The demands of two of the subcommittees in this case for more baseline data on the extent of these problems seem very reasonable from this perspective, while the district administration's insistence that they move on to practical recommendations was short sighted. As Foster (1990) argues, policy-makers should base policy on a deep knowledge of actual conditions in communities and schools. On the other hand, Borman et al. (1992) did gather considerable data on the extent of the "race relations" problem, but the district administration would not acknowledge its validity or importance and was unwilling to implement solutions that matched the seriousness of African Americans' concerns. The district administration in our study also did not want to make the effort to collect evidence of structural inequities, seeing that as a "negative" approach. While dwelling on problems and assigning blame may not be productive, neither is crafting solutions with little knowledge of the problems they are supposed to solve. In addition, rather than fearing and attempting to limit conflict, school district administrators should work to create more forums for "dialogue among differences" (Cornbleth & Waugh, 1995) like the all-too-brief one described in this case study, if they want to arrive at solutions that represent the entire school community.

Like Cornbleth and Waugh (1993) we recommend that policy researchers conduct more qualitative studies of multicultural education policy-in-the-making in order to better understand how and by whom "multicultural education" is being locally constructed. Why do school district activities in most cases seem to fall so short of the "comprehensive" models recommended by theorists? What do we know about school districts that come closer to the theorists' models? Are there cases in which multicultural policies have been in place long enough to judge their effects, keeping in mind Grant and Millar's (1992) warning that effects must be defined more broadly than achievement scores? There is much more work to be done in this policy arena.

REFERENCES

Bagley, C.A. 1991. *The Marginalization of Racism: A Study of a Local Education Authority Project on Multicultural Education*. The British Library Document Supply Centre Boston Spa, Witherby, West Yorkshire, UK (Dissertation Abstracts # AAC DX 94407). Open University.

Banks, James A. 1992. "African American Scholarship and the Evolution of Multicultural Education." *Journal of Negro Education* 61(3):273-300.

Banks, James A. 1993. "Multicultural Education: Development, Dimensions and Challenges." *Phi Delta Kappan* 75(1):22-28.

Banks, James A. 1994. *Multiethnic Education: Theory and Practice*. 3rd Ed. New York: Allyn & Bacon.

Banks, James A., and Cherry A. M. Banks (Editors). 1995. *Handbook of Research on Multicultural Education*. New York: Simon & Schuster Macmillan.

Baumgartner, Thomas, Walter Buckley, Tom Burns, and Peter Schuster. 1976. "Meta-power and the Structuring of Social Hierarchy." Pp. 215-288 in *Social Structures and Their Transformations*, edited by Tom Burns and Walter Buckley. Beverly Hills, CA: Sage.

Becker, Howard S. 1982. *Art Worlds*. Berkeley CA: University of California Press.

Borman, Katherine M., Patricia Timm, Zakia Al-amin, and Markay Winston. 1992. "Using Multiple Strategies to Assess Multicultural Education in a School District." Pp. 71-88 in *Research and Multicultural Education: From the Margins to the Mainstream*, edited by Carl Grant. London: Falmer.

Clegg, Stewart. 1989. *Frameworks of Power*. London: Sage.

Cornbleth, Catherine, and Dexter Waugh. 1993. "The Great Speckled Bird: Education Policy-in-the-Making." *Educational Researcher* 22(7):31-37.

Cornbleth, Catherine, and Dexter Waugh. 1995. *The Great Speckled Bird: Multicultural Politics and Education Policymaking*. New York: St. Martin's Press.

Crumpton, Robert. 1992. "Policy Analysis of State Multicultural Education Programs." Pp. 240-49 in *Research and Multicultural Education: From the Margins to the Mainstream*, edited by Carl A. Grant. Washington, DC: Falmer Press.

Estes, Caroll, and Beverly Edmonds. 1981. "Symbolic Interaction and Social Policy Analysis." *Symbolic Interaction* 4(1):75-86.

Foster, Peter. 1990. *Policy and Practices in Multicultural and Anti-Racist Education*. London: Routledge Press.

Gaff, Jerry G. 1992, Jan/Feb. "Beyond Politics: The Educational Issues Inherent in Multicultural Education." *Change* 31-35.

Gibson, Margaret H. 1984. "Approaches to Multicultural Education in the United States: Some Concepts and Assumptions." *Anthropology and Education Quarterly* 15:94-119.

Glazer, Nathan. 1993. "Where Is Multiculturalism Leading Us?" *Phi Delta Kappan* 75(4):319-23.

Gollnick, Donna M. 1995. "National and State Initiatives for Multicultural Education." Pp. 44-64 in *Handbook of Research on Multicultural Education*, edited by James A. Banks and Cherry A.M. Banks. New York: Simon & Schuster Macmillan.

Gordon, Edmund W. 1992. "Conceptions of Afrocentrism and Multiculturalism in Education: A General Overview." *Journal of Negro Education* 61(3):235-36.

Grant, Carl, and Susan Millar. 1992. "Research and Multicultural Education: Barriers, Needs and Boundaries." Pp. 7-18 in *Research and Multicultural Education*, edited by Carl Grant. London: Falmer.

Hall, Peter M. 1987. "Interactionism and the Study of Social Organization." *The Sociological Quarterly* 28(1):1-22.

Hall, Peter M. 1992. "Transformational Processes and Structural Linkages: A Meso-Domain Analysis of Missouri Career Ladder Policy." Paper presented at the annual meeting of the American Educational Research Association, San Francisco.

Hall, Peter M. 1995. "The Consequences of Qualitative Analysis for Sociological Theory: Beyond the Micro Level." *The Sociological Quarterly* 36(2):397-423 .

Harris, Michael D. 1992. "Afrocentrism and Curriculum: Concepts, Issues, and Prospects." *Journal of Negro Education* 61(3):301-316.

Harvey, James. 1987. "Ethnicity and Gender in Australian Education." Paper presented at the annual meeting of American Educational Research Association, Washington, DC. (Eric Document Reproduction Services #ED 282951).

Lynch, James. 1989. "Cultural Pluralism, Structural Pluralism and the United Kingdom." Paper presented at a joint seminar of the Commission for Racial Equality and the Runnymede Trust. (Eric Document Reproduction Services #ED 315479).

Lynch, James. 1993. "Youth, Interethnic Relations and Education in Europe." Paper presented at the Carnegie Corp. Consultation, New York, NY, May. (Eric Document Reproduction Services #ED 361412).

Marshall, Catherine, Douglas Mitchell, and Frederick Wirt. 1989. *Culture and Educational Policy in the American States*. New York: Falmer.

McCarthy, Cameron. 1990. *Race and Curriculum: Social Inequality and the Theories and Politics of Difference in Contemporary Research on Schooling*. London: Falmer Press.

Mehan, Hugh, Angela Lintz, Dina Okamoto, and John S. Wills. 1995. "Ethnographic Studies of Multicultural Education in Classrooms and Schools." Pp. 129-144 in *Handbook of Research on Multicultural Education*, edited by James A. Banks and Cherry A.M. Banks. New York: Simon & Schuster Macmillan.

Ogilvie, A. Barreto. 1983. *The Multicultural Education QAT* (Quick Assessment Test). Olympia, WA: Washington Office of the State Superintendent of Public Instruction, Office for Multicultural and Equity Education. (Eric Document Reproduction Services #ED 240216).

Olneck, Michael R. 1990. "The Recurring Dream: Symbolism and Ideology in Intercultural and Multicultural Education." *American Journal of Education* 98(4):147-74.

O'Neil, John. 1993. "A New Generation Confronts Racism." *Educational Leadership* 50(8):60-63.

Persell, Caroline H., Kevin J. Dougherty, and Harold Wenglinsky. (1993, Oct.). *Equity and Diversity in American Education.* Report from Round Table #1 of the OERI Conference on Equity and Excellence in Education: The Policy Uses of Sociology. Unpublished manuscript. Washington, DC.

Placier, Margaret. 1993. "The Semantics of State Policymaking: The Case of 'At Risk.'" *Educational Evaluation and Policy Analysis* 15(4):380-395.

Sewell, William H. Jr. 1992. "A Theory of Structure: Duality, Agency and Transformation." *American Journal of Sociology* 98(1):1-29.

Sleeter, Christine E. 1995. "An Analysis of the Critiques of Multicultural Education." Pp. 81-94 in *Handbook of Research on Multicultural Education*, edited by James A. Banks and Cherry A.M. Banks. New York: Simon & Schuster Macmillan.

Sleeter, Christine E., and Carl A. Grant. 1994. *Making Choices for Multicultural Education.* 2nd Ed. New York: Macmillan.

Tomlinson, Sally. 1990. *Multicultural Education in White Schools.* London: B.R. Batsford Ltd.

Troyna, Barry, and Bruce Carrington. 1990. *Education, Racism and Reform.* London: Routledge Press.

Troyna, Barry, and Jenny Williams. 1986. *Racism, Education and the State.* London: Croom Helm.

Vincent, Nelson C. 1992. "The Philosophy and Politics of Multicultural Education and Anti-Racist Education: An Analysis of Current Literature." Paper presented at the annual meeting of the National Association for Multicultural Education, Orlando FL. (Eric Document Reproduction Services #ED 346022).

Young, Russell L. 1991. *A Paradigm for Examining Multicultural Education.* Paper presented at the annual meeting of the American Educational Research Association, Chicago IL. (Eric Document Reproduction Services #ED 334320).

CHAPTER 8

The Integration of Restructuring and Multicultural Education as a Policy for Equity and Diversity

Peter M. Hall

Previous chapters have demonstrated the recurrence of many factors and practices that reinforce and perpetuate racial and ethnic inequality in schools in the United States. They also presented and suggested some alternatives that would counter those effects. Bart Landry criticizes tracking as a response to diversity and in the projection of increasing diversity calls for implementation of multicultural pedagogy and curriculum and the training of teachers to respond to multicultural populations. Aaron Thompson and Reid Luhman point to the failure of higher educational institutions in facilitating educational attainment of African Americans and the need for those institutions to improve their recruitment and retention practices. Hugh Mehan believes schools can be transformative in moving from untracking to detracking but they must find ways to institutionalize support structures and processes as well as to expand the populations served by those programs. Mehan thinks that more time needs to be focused on academic subjects by extending the school day or year or both. Time can be also used more effectively through cooperative learning, inquiry-based instruction, authentic curriculum and use of student experience as a classroom resource. Luis Moll and Norma González clearly concur on the value of student experience. It is part of their agenda for future research. Their current work strongly demonstrates the funds of knowledge in family households that have classroom utility. Beyond content, they show the benefits of collaboration between university researchers and educational practitioners. Particularly important is the need for the researchers to become aware of the difficulties of producing changes in schools. Moll and González argue effectively for the development of teacher study groups and providing the time for that activity in the school day. They also note the importance of high academic demands for all students. Finally they suggest preservice teachers should be taught how to study households and communities. Eugene Eubanks, Ralph Parish, and Dianne Smith believe that significant change cannot occur in schools unless the staffs engage in a critical discussion about the meaning of race, ethnicity, class and gender; the ability of all children to learn; the manner in which "school as usual" contributes to inequality; the assumption of collective responsibility; and the ongoing never-ending process of organizational learning and change. Changing the organizational discourse is the mandatory beginning. Margaret Placier, Peter Hall, and Barbara Davis, while supportive of multicultural education, observe the absence of research on the topic and call for more. In addition, they are supportive of efforts to openly address suppressed issues in school districts. They favor "dialogues among differences" and are critical of institutional structures that avoid critical issues and marginalize opposition.

These authors, in sum, recommend an end to tracking, changes in curriculum and pedagogy, provision of more time to teachers and students, teacher collaboration and reflection, multicultural education, high expectations for all students, family-school relationships, and initiation of a "learning organization" culture and critical discourse. The literature in the field would strongly support these recommendations. For example, increasing scholarship is emerging on untracked schools (Pool & Page, 1995). Changes in curriculum and pedagogy as well as assessment in order to produce critical thinking are receiving widespread support (Newmann, 1991). Numerous authors have commented on the need to eliminate constraints on time. Teacher collaboration and reflection has been a common theme in the improvement of schools (Rosenholtz, 1989). The importance of family-school relationships is underlined by its addition as a national goal. High expectations and standards have been in the conversation for at least a decade (Powell et al., 1985). The emphasis on changing school culture and adopting a learning organization orientation has been a key aspect of professional development activities (Senge, 1990).

In this chapter I argue that those valuable suggestions and necessary changes will be most effective if they are integrated into a coordinated, concerted, coherent approach that fuses school restructuring, multicultural education, and systemic reform to achieve the goals of producing equity for all children and generating positive valuation of diversity. The factors that sustain inequality and prejudice in schools are not simply the product of individuals or separate programmatic elements that can be reformed. They are a function of a pervasive organizational system in which structures, cultures, and processes feed back upon themselves and reproduce the systemic outcomes. It is that system that must be transformed.

Elementary and secondary schools, however, cannot generate social equity alone. Indeed, the efforts and effects of schools would be strengthened significantly by societal and institutional actions and policies that increase the likelihood that all children possess comparable status and cultural capital upon entering school. In periods of economic growth, likened to a tide lifting all boats, it is easier to gain support for such programs. This is increasingly made problematic now in an economy experiencing instability, downsizing, and increasing inequality. However, it is imperative that nationwide initiatives occur which stimulate equitable economic growth with adequate employment opportunities that are meaningful and rewarding and provide job training or retraining programs wherever necessary. Not only would that generate greater security for domestic institutions, it would provide concrete expectations for youth about the value of education for the future. Particular efforts are required to improve the viability of inner-city communities and the reduction of residential segregation, not only as matters of justice and empowerment, but also to facilitate a more integrated society. This is all the more crucial if lagging support for desegregation programs continues. Economic constraints and political polarization often focus on and exacerbate racial and ethnic relations. It is evident that continuing efforts need to be made at all levels of the society to confront and refute racism, discrimination, and prejudice through national leadership, political empowerment, conflict mediation, and education. Institutions of higher education, as observed by Thompson and Luhman, need to address diversity and focus upon recruitment and retention of students at all degree levels as well as on their staffs. The educational mission of these institutions should also include multicultural education because the study of race and ethnicity by all students is necessary as part of the societal effort to understand the benefits of diversity.

Public schools, however, cannot wait for society to change. They must respond to those who enter their doors. There are some general improvements that can be made to help provide some basic assistance in their efforts. Evidence cited in this volume points to the benefits of and need for an educational work force at all levels that reflects the diversity of classrooms and communities. This suggests the need for improved recruitment and provision of attendant incentives and rewards for more minority educators. Teaching must be made an attractive option. Students from all backgrounds can benefit from this development. At the same time both preservice teacher development and ongoing staff/professional development must provide educators with perspectives, knowledge, and skills for teaching students from diverse backgrounds, dealing with racial and ethnic issues, and preparation to work in restructured schools. These are major challenges for colleges of education and school systems.

Schools in the United States, as a rule, do not receive enough resources to fulfill the expectations of society. It is evident they do not educate *all* children to their highest potential. One major reason for this fact is the tremendous resource disparity between schools and the manner in which state governments have contributed to this inequity (Kozol, 1991). Schools that serve poor neighborhoods within districts, poorer districts, and poorer states receive much smaller expenditures per student than do their more affluent counterparts. This is not only unjust and discriminatory but also shortsighted because there is evidence that increased financial support has direct positive effects on student achievement, which is also translated into increased earning power (Hedges et al., 1994; American Sociological Association, 1994; Berliner & Biddle, 1995). Not only are increased expenditures necessary, they need to be directed in a more equitable manner to reverse the disparity. These resources can provide the technology, class sizes, and stable, professional staffs required for the twenty-first century world. In addition, it can be argued that priorities ought to be given to the poorest schools to overcome their old structures, overcrowding, and multiple problems.

Analysts of public policy and social programs have frequently commented on the fragmentation of government services in the United States and their consequent ineffectiveness. Evidence of one recognition that institutional efforts need to be coordinated, integrated and delivered in a holistic manner is the movement to link schools and social services (Adler & Gardner, 1994). Thus at a local school, families, children, and community residents could receive a range of services—health, mental health, social welfare, job development, child development and care, recreation as well as education. These service providers seek to overcome their fragmented efforts and to respond with a total approach that is focused on prevention, community development, family preservation, and collective empowerment. This approach requires systemwide change, planning, flexibility, new ways of working together and empowerment of "street level" workers. The movement has arisen in particular in inner cities with populations confronting multiple problems. Such an approach clearly makes sense here but it obviously has benefits for all communities. There are numerous problems in making such action effective because of diverse organizational cultures, insulating bureaucracies, and extensive rule manuals. There is also insufficient research on the process or its effectiveness (Smylie & Crowson, 1996). Nevertheless, it is a model to be encouraged, facilitated, and studied more extensively.

It is possible to change the qualities and knowledge that individual educators bring to the classroom. However, unless the conditions and structures of schools change, these individuals will be ineffective and eventually leave or lower commitment and expectations (Kanter, 1977). It is possible to implement a series of reforms, e.g., untracking, cooperative learning, site-based decision making, and parent involvement. Changing one element at a time, however, produces unintended consequences and implies changes in others. Unless those changes are viewed systemically in relation to other forms and processes, the results are likely to be minimal, short-lived, and isolated. While it is critical to increase and reapportion the resources directed to schools, unless those resources are part of a systemic plan and coordinated in their utilization, the results will be ineffective.

The circumstances are now even more demanding because schools are expected to generate qualitatively higher levels of learning, sometimes referred to as critical thinking. This higher order thinking has been typically associated with gifted students but now is a goal for all students. The world of the twenty-first century will need graduates with abilities to face significant change, complexity, and ambiguity and skills in problem solving, critical analysis and interpretative sensemaking. These skills will be necessary, not just for college-bound students, to prepare all citizens, workers, and family members for their future responsibilities. National and international issues will require a citizenry prepared to sustain and revitalize a democratic society through community service and civic participation. Future economic opportunities are expected to require more teamwork, cooperative experience, and communication skills with people from diverse backgrounds. Given the challenges we face and the consequences of lost capacity due to discrimination and inequality, the potentials of all citizens must be developed. Schools as presently constituted cannot do that. Traditional structures, cultures, and practices that emphasize basic skills, lecture technology, passive students, fact-based curriculum, and objective tests do not foster critical thinking. The development of conditions that facilitate that thinking cannot be created in hierarchical, insulated, and routinized schools located in centralized, bureaucratic districts. A holistic transformation is absolutely crucial.

There is some research which not only demonstrates the overall positive effects of restructuring but its specific implication for reducing inequality. Valerie Lee and colleagues (Lee & Smith, 1994; Lee et al., 1995) have shown that high schools with higher degrees of restructuring produced greater gains in student achievement in core academic areas over a four-year period, using data on over 11,000 students from 820 schools nationwide. They also found greater student engagement in restructuring schools. In addition, the research showed that the achievement levels were more equitably distributed between socioeconomic categories, i.e., the differences between achievement by high-SES students and low-SES students was less in restructuring schools than non-restructuring schools. Lee and her colleagues argue that the major reasons for these findings are attributable to: 1) a common academic curriculum (no differentiated or tracked curricula), 2) high academic press (high standards/expectations for all students), 3) authentic instruction (critical thinking, active learning), and 4) communal school organization (collective staff responsibility for all students). Their overall conclusion is that in order to be more effective with students, particularly those from minority and low-income backgrounds, high schools need to be smaller and restructured in more personalized communities that are focused on learning.

While there are many definitions and forms of restructuring, the following is presented to illustrate the holistic, systemic nature of a restructured school (Hall & McGinty, forthcoming). I begin with the assumption that all students will be expected to develop critical analytical facilities. Developing these abilities requires changes in student-teacher relationships and the curriculum. Students must become engaged in the learning process and take an active stance toward it. Students will begin to define the problems and participate in individual and collaborative complex tasks that will culminate in meaningful practical and intellectual accomplishments. In these activities, students will show they can organize, synthesize, interpret, explain and evaluate information in relation to problems. In addition, using ideas, perspectives and theories they will apply them to specific cases, elaborate and extend them to different conditions, and be able to establish relationships and make sense of complexity (Newmann & Wehlage, 1995). In this context, the student can be seen as producer, actor, and player. Teachers then shift their orientation away from lecturer, tester, and monitor toward coach, mentor, and tutor. They focus upon indirectly facilitating learning by creating the conditions for active learning. More of their effort is spent in diagnosing students, structuring groupings and activities, and evaluating strategies. Curriculum then would be changed from a superficial, fragmented series of subjects and facts to one that is integrated for depth, coherence, problem orientation, and concept development. Thus there would be more interdisciplinary efforts, greater attention to significant periods or topics, more time for themes and projects, and more connections to experiences and interests of students.

Restructuring suggests that many of the features of schools would have to change to accommodate a new curriculum and teacher-student relationships. Time use would be more flexible to allow student progress at more natural rates and completion of larger problem-based projects. Scheduling would reflect an integrated curriculum and modular themes with larger blocks of time than the standard 50-minute daily class period. Student groupings would be altered for interdisciplinary work, cooperative learning, the elimination of tracking, and personalization. To counter problems of large size, small learning communities of students and teacher teams would be organized.

The effective implementation of these arrangements depends on a common culture, time for teacher collaboration, decentralized decision making, and shared governance. The development of a common culture (vision, goals, expectations) serves to unify, motivate, and mobilize restructuring efforts. Staff must have time to develop, assess, and revise curriculum, team teaching, and student groupings. They require opportunities for professional development, team building, and problem solving. Current knowledge suggests that decision making is most effective when it occurs at the actual practice site and when all stakeholders are empowered to participate. Thus, school level democratic decision making and governance are favored over centralized top-down structures (district level and/or school principal). Restructuring programs also recognize the central roles of family and community in schooling and include those constituencies in shared governance and school programs.

Restructuring dramatically alters fundamental assumptions about what schools can do, e.g., expect and facilitate new forms of learning at high levels for all children. It radically transforms the organization of schools because it recognizes the systematic interconnected nature of its components, i.e., only changing parts creates contradictions, conflict, and failure. Restructuring is perceived as an ongoing process with no set end point since schools must continually deal with changing external and internal conditions to which they develop new solutions. They become, as Eubanks et al. discuss, "learning organizations." Given the diversity of communities and the inextricable linkage to schools, there is no one standard model of schooling or process of restructuring. Rather restructuring seeks to enable participants to build new forms, roles, and processes that meet collective goals.

Restructuring accomplishes coordination and integration not by bureaucratic standardization but through the development of a common culture. Commitment and participation are generated by a redistribution of opportunity and resources, not demanded by hierarchical power. Isolation and alienation are overcome through collaboration and community-building processes. Restructuring acknowledges that much of teacher's work is non-routine and facilitates professional discretion rather than limiting it by bureaucratic rules.

Why and how can restructuring schools challenge inequality and facilitate equity for children from all backgrounds? Since restructuring involves interrelated, interactive, and reinforcing patterns and processes, the two-dimensional page and linear format do not provide the most appropriate mode to demonstrate its workings. Nevertheless, it is possible to present some of the rationale. At its base, two elements are present. These schools truly provide equal opportunities to learn and the high expectations and standards that support the learning. The common academic curriculum with the absence of tracking or ability grouping means that all children have access to the same knowledge and that teachers have the resources to develop student learning programs that are responsive to cultural backgrounds and individual variations. Because classrooms are student centered and students are encouraged to be active learners, they are all more engaged and challenged by the hands-on processes. Because students take responsibility for their own learning, they are facilitated in using their own individual and community resources as well as their own problems and issues. Because teachers have time for collaboration and reflexivity, they are able to pursue community research and bring back resources and knowledge that they can mesh with an integrated articulated curriculum that has coherence, depth, and relevance. This points to units, themes, interdisciplinary courses, and individual and group projects that lend themselves to authentic assessment and to research, demonstrations, exhibitions, and performances that permit combinations of connections to student interests and the aims of critical thinking. Teachers can also use the flexibility restructuring allows to organize students in different learning and interactive relationships to maintain engagement and high energy and avoid the stagnant boredom of passive routine. Finally because of personalization, teachers learn about their students as individuals and their classes as distinctive collectivities and are able to adjust approaches, have individual and group discussions about problems and issues, and build strong relationships and collective identification.

Schools are more than simply aggregates of classrooms. Long-term successes in classrooms are due to the overall structure and culture that connects and coordinates classrooms and generates a sense of consensus, direction, and community. Equity is achieved, in part, by its explicit place in the cultural mission and vision and the collective agreement on the norms and practices that promote it. It is also generated by a commitment to a democratic discourse that openly discusses critical, often suppressed, issues and searches for encompassing options. The decentralization afforded by site-based decision making and shared governance induces a contextualization of school practices. Participants can develop curriculum, instruction, and assessment that fit well with community resources and concerns. Collegial collaboration facilitates the integration and articulation of program across the whole school. The openness to the community and families with stakeholder empowerment, involvement, and partnerships not only mobilizes resources but also creates the opportunity for unified support for school activities. It provides a vehicle to challenge barriers, stereotypes and misinformation, suspicion, and opposition. The commitment to collective responsibility and generation of community and common identity is productive because it represents a consciousness that adults, educators, and family can make a difference in learning, that they know that all others share the consciousness and beliefs, and that they therefore can work together with mutual awareness to achieve the desired goals. Such a commitment also represents the view, common in today's discourse, that "it takes a village to raise a child," meaning that all children, not simply those under their immediate care, deserve their attention and energy. This serves to overcome the anonymity and impersonalization of many school settings. The students then feel known, believe they belong to the community, and consequently are committed, motivated to perform, and rewarded by it.

I have suggested the necessity of integrating multicultural education with restructuring. The previous discussion should have made clear the similarities between the two and the bases for connection. While restructuring will accomplish some of the same goals, I want to argue that the significance of race and ethnicity for American society (among other social categories) requires that it is explicitly given attention. There is common ground because proponents of multicultural education and improved race and ethnic relations in schools acknowledge the systemic character of schools and the necessity of holistic change through an empowering site-level organization, governance process, and culture (Banks, 1993; Jackson, 1995). Equity pedagogy issues are addressed when educators reject tracking and ability grouping, adopt high expectations and a common academic core, emphasize critical thinking, and then use multiple methods and forms based upon knowledge of student backgrounds that allow students to use multiple interests, resources, perspectives, and strategies to learn and demonstrate learning. It seems obvious that concerns about equity in student performance would expand the utilization of the multicultural context to provide knowledge, illustrate generic intellectual categories, and to stimulate thinking. Curriculum should provide all students with "mirrors" so that they find themselves in it and use that for motivation to learn.

On the other hand, curriculum should also be a "window" which provides an opening both to the common humanity and the different perspectives of others. Multicultural education is not only for minorities. It is for all students and is necessary to provide the conditions for understanding the history, consequences, and philosophy of human diversity. Prejudice reduction/improved relations in schools, which would strengthen the schools and the nation as well as facilitate equity, cannot occur only by provision of materials. It requires authoritative support, leadership, and proactive strategies to develop equal-status situations and continuous cross-group learning opportunities in addition to intervention and conflict mediation when necessary.

The knowledge construction process is congruent with the assumptions and development of critical analytical thinking. Both are based upon practical, contextual, active hands-on learning that flows from students finding and defining problems and proposing resolutions. Both are based upon questioning, exploring, reflecting, analyzing, conjecturing, imagining, innovating, and synthesizing. Both are based upon more than an examination of internal logic or empiricism about conventional, known problems. Both explore the significance of perspective for understanding, the power of authority and convention, and the importance of historical context for truth. Both should examine different systems of validating truth, the processes of producing history and science, and the meaning of knowledge. But here explicitly, the role of race and ethnicity in human history, and their changing meanings and consequences need to be explicitly and integrally subjects for discussion and research. Given the rest of this volume, that only makes sense.

It is not enough to know what restructured schools should look like and why that transformational process provides solutions to problems. Given the complexity and uncertainty of restructuring, it would be helpful to have a sense of how to produce systemic change. Eubanks et al., echoing many others, have warned us that it will take time, effort, and commitment. While there is no one format for restructuring or a blueprint to implement, some research has provided indications about practices and ideas that make the intended effects more likely outcomes of the process.

Patricia Wasley et al. (1995) offer some propositions based upon longitudinal observation of how some restructuring schools, members of the Coalition of Essential Schools, moved from initial change and partial staff support to whole school change with broad support. The authors observe that the propositions are not separate but mutually reinforcing and the more they are present, the greater the change will be. The propositions are paraphrased as follows:

1) Schools not only need to collectively develop a consensual vision of their intended future school but benefit most from continuously revisiting the vision to determine whether change efforts are working or will work and to re-establish consensus about the meaning of the vision;

2) Schools that see the interconnectedness of their efforts and have a coherent sense of the changes are better equipped to achieve their goals;

3) Schools that are able to deal with difficult and often controversial issues are more likely to continue to involve the whole community;

4) Schools that are able to receive and act on good external critical feedback regularly make more progress than those that proceed autonomously;

5) Schools whose faculty develop skills in rigorous self-analysis focused on student gains have a critical tool that broadens and deepens their efforts;

6) Schools that are able to focus simultaneously on multiple aspects of restructuring; curriculum, pedagogy, assessment, and school culture, are more likely to make significant progress.

Patricia Wohlstetter and Susan Mohrman (1994) present some supporting principles and practices for producing this restructuring. School schedules should be redesigned to encourage staff interaction during the school day. In this change process, principals should be managers and facilitators of the change and experienced teachers should take the lead in areas of curriculum, pedagogy, and assessment. All staff should be involved in the process through the use of multiple teacher-led decision teams that span the horizontal and vertical dimensions of the school in order to generate high levels of interaction and the sharing of information. Finally, all the participants should have opportunities to learn the skills necessary for teamwork, collective problem solving, and conflict resolution. These works provide some initial ideas about successful transformation, but there is an abundance of evidence of numerous starts with limited or little success. There is a need for much attention to this process of restructuring now.

By implication, most of this discussion has focused on high schools and perhaps leaves the impression that individual school change is all that is required. That would be an erroneous conclusion. There are multiple restructuring efforts occurring at all levels. Many elementary schools have been utilizing cooperating learning, active hands-on learning, multiage grouping, and authentic assessment. Many are also involved in the Accelerated Schools (Levin, 1987), School Development (Comer, 1988), or Success for All (Slavin et al., 1992) programs. In addition, the middle school model strongly supported by the Carnegie Foundation (1989) contains all the elements of a restructured school with a focus on reducing inequity. Too often the schools that are changing see themselves as "going it alone." What is needed is an articulation and coordination of these efforts at the district, state, and national levels. On the one hand, local educators need to see that their programs are congruent and that they continue the progress begun at earlier grades. District-level actors need to involve all schools in the decentralized change process, emphasize their commitment to comprehensive and diverse change, and engage in goal-setting, systemic planning, and oversight. They would need to allocate and expedite resources equitably, provide direction, establish accountability mechanisms, and facilitate change through technical assistance. State-level priorities have to shift from regulation and monitoring to stimulating local innovation. States need to coordinate their reform programs to generate restructuring in increased scale within and across districts. States also need to focus upon providing capacity-building and technical assistance to districts and schools. The federal level also needs to continue supporting these systemic changes and most importantly to ensure the provision of equal opportunities to learn for all students. Finally, the various national restructuring programs need to continue their efforts at pooling their ideas and working together (e.g., Atlas Communities). The synergy generated there has enormous potential for schools in America.

Many of the authors of previous chapters have issued calls for additional research. This is necessary because many of the questions, problems, or proposed changes have not been studied adequately or new questions have emerged from the research. It is also true that many reforms are enacted and implemented without sufficient research to justify that action. Unfortunately, it is even more common that program implementation occurs without the design or funding of research to study the process and its effects. As a rule, priorities and allocations for educational research have not been high (Berliner & Biddle, 1995). There is a critical need to encourage, develop, and support research that examines the consequences of, for example, detracking, equity pedagogies, school-family partnerships, and restructuring over time and across different contexts. It is also crucial that research be supported that examines systemic relationships, change of processes, contextual complexity, and participant interactions.

Some might think the call for more research is self-serving. But there is a reality that provides the argument for additional research. Time does not stand still. History brings change and different social conditions. Human activity alters economies and environments. And the meanings of race and ethnicity change in relation to social conditions, governments, political actions, and social definitions. Our views of race and ethnicity as well as schools have been shaped by, but are different from, those of 1965 because of the dynamic character of the intervening years and our interpretations of them. Science and knowledge are conditional. Thus we need to continue analyzing closely, empirically, and conceptually the connections between schooling, race, and ethnicity and institutional, societal, and global contexts and their manifestation in the educational process.

REFERENCES

Adler, Louise, and Sid Gardner (Eds.). 1994. *The Politics of Linking Schools and Social Services*. Washington, DC: Falmer.

American Sociological Association. 1994. *Fact Sheet: Resources and Education Outcomes*. Washington, DC: ASA.

Banks, James. 1993. "Multicultural Education: Historical Development, Dimensions, and Practice." *Review of Research in Education* 19:3-49.

Berliner, David, and Bruce Biddle. 1995. *The Manufactured Crisis: Myths, Fraud, and the Attack on America's Public Schools*. Reading, MA: Addison-Wesley.

Carnegie Council on Adolescent Development. 1989. *Turning Points: Preparing American Youth for the 21st Century*. Washington, DC: Carnegie Council on Adolescent Development.

Comer, James P. 1988. "Educating Poor Minority Children." *Scientific American* 259(5):42-48.

Hall, Peter M., and Patrick McGinty. Forthcoming. "Restructuring." *Education and Society: An Encyclopedia*. New York: Garland.

Hedges, Larry, Richard Laine, and Rob Greenwald. 1994. "Does Money Matter? A Meta-Analysis of Studies of the Effects of Differential School Inputs on Student Outcomes." *Educational Researcher* 23(3):5-14.

Jackson, Anthony. 1995. "Toward a Common Destiny: An Agenda for Further Research." Pp. 435-453 in *Toward a Common Destiny*, edited by Willis Hawley and Anthony Jackson. San Francisco: Jossey-Bass.

Kanter, Rosabeth. 1977. *Men and Women of the Corporation*. New York: Basic.

Kozol, Jonathan. 1991. *Savage Inequalities*. New York: Crown.

Lee, Valerie, and Julia Smith. 1994. "High School Restructuring and Student Achievement: A New Study Finds Strong Links." *Issues in Restructuring Schools* 7:1-11. Madison, WI: Center on Organization and Restructuring of Schools.

Lee, Valerie, Julia Smith, and Robert Croninger. 1995. "Another Look at High School Restructuring." *Issues in Restructuring Schools* 9:1-10. Madison, WI: Center on Organization and Restructuring of Schools.

Levin, Henry M. 1987. "Accelerated Schools for Disadvantaged Students." *Educational Leadership* 44(6):19-21.

Newmann, Fred. 1991. "Linking Restructuring to Authentic Student Achievement." *Phi Delta Kappan* 72(6):458-463.

Newmann, Fred, and Gary Wehlage. 1995. *Successful School Restructuring*. Madison, WI: Center on Organization and Restructuring of Schools.

Pool, Harbison, and Jane Page (Eds.). 1995. *Beyond Tracking: Finding Success in Inclusive Schools*. Bloomington, IN: Phi Delta Kappa Educational Foundation.

Powell, Arthur, Eleanor Farrar, and David Cohen. 1985. *The Shopping Mall High School: Winners and Losers in the Educational Marketplace*. Boston: Houghton Mifflin.

Rosenholtz, Susan. 1989. *Teachers' Workplace: The Social Organization of Schools*. New York: Longman.

Senge, Peter. 1990. *The Fifth Discipline: The Art and Practice of the Learning Organization*. New York: Doubleday.

Slavin, Robert, Nancy Madden, Nancy Karweit, Lawrence Dolan, and Barbara Wasik. 1992. *Success for All: A Relentless Approach to Prevention and Early Intervention in Elementary Schools*. Arlington, VA: Educational Research Service.

Smylie, Mark, and Robert Crowson. 1996. "Working Within the Scripts: Building Institutional Infrastructure for Children's Service Coordination in Schools." *Educational Policy* 10(1):3-21.

Wasley, Patricia, Robert Hampel, and Richard Clark. 1995. "Stepping Up to Whole School Change." Paper presented at Coalition of Essential Schools Fall Forum, New York.

Wohlstetter, Patricia, and Susan Mohrman. 1994. "School-Based Management: Promise and Process." *CPRE Finance Briefs* 5:1-8. New Brunswick, NJ: Center for Policy Research in Education.

Author Index

Adler, Louise, 206, 216
Al-amin, Zakia, 170, 172, 195-199
Alexander, Karl, 21, 36, 39, 68, 88
Allen, Walter R., 69, 71, 88
Allport, Gordon, 20, 36
Amanti, Cathy, 90-93, 98-101, 104, 105, 112, 113, 148, 149
American Council on Education, 115, 148, 149
American Sociological Association, 206, 216
Andrade, Rosi, 113
Anyon, Jean, 161, 167
Apple, Michael, 133, 148, 161, 167
Aquila, Frank, 161, 164, 167-169
Arends, Richard, 156, 168
Argyris, Chris, 162, 167
Aronowitz, Stanley, 151, 154, 161, 167
Au, Kathryn, 148

Baca Zinn, Maxine, 65, 86
Bagley, C. A., 171, 199
Bane, Mary J., 66, 86
Banks, Cherry, 170, 199-201

Banks, James, 31, 32, 36-38, 40, 170, 171, 181, 184, 194, 195, 199, 200, 201, 212, 216
Baumgartner, Thomas, 175, 199
Baumrind, Diana, 30, 36
Becker, Howard S., 174, 199
Bell, Peter, 123, 148
Bennis, Warren, 164, 167
Berliner, David C., 206, 215, 216
Biddle, Bruce J., 206, 215, 216
Billingsley, Andrew, 11, 36
Bissex, Glenda L., 92, 113
Blau, Peter M., 65, 86
Blau, Zena S., 69, 86
Blauner, Robert, 4, 36
Bloom, Alan, 51, 61
Borman, Katherine M., 170, 172, 195-199
Bourdieu, Pierre, 134, 143-145, 148
Bowles, Samuel, 57, 61, 143, 148, 161, 167
Braddock, Jomills, 18, 36
Brookover, Wilbur, 70, 87
Brown, Diane R., 63, 69, 87
Buckley, Walter, 175, 199

Burns, Tom, 175, 199

Campbell, Ernest, 16, 36
Carnegie Council on
  Adolescent Development,
  214, 216
Carrington, Bruce, 171, 201
Carter, Deborah J., 115, 123,
  125, 127, 149
Cauce, Ana, 28, 37
Cazden, Courtney B., 133,
  149
Chachkin, Norman, 24, 36
Cicourel, Aaron V., 116, 149
Clark, Maxine L., 70, 87
Clark, Richard, 213, 217
Clegg, Stewart, 175, 199
Cochran-Smith, Marilyn, 92,
  113
Cohen, David, 26, 40, 204,
  217
Cohen, Elizabeth, 20, 36, 40
Coleman, James, 16, 36, 105-
  108, 113
Comer, James P., 116, 149,
  153, 167, 214, 216
Conant, Faith R., 148, 150
Cook, Martha, 21, 36
Cookson, Peter W. Jr., 143,
  145, 149
Cooley, Charles, 60, 61
Cornbleth, Catherine, 31, 36,
  169, 170, 195, 196, 198,
  199
Crain, Robert, 18, 19, 38, 40
Croninger, Robert, 208, 216
Cross, William Jr., 17, 20, 25-
  28, 31, 36, 39

Crowson, Robert, 207, 217
Crumpton, Robert, 194, 199
Cuban, Larry, 30, 36

Dauber, Susan, 22, 36, 37
Davidson, Ann, 25, 27, 28, 39
Deal, Terrence E., 154, 158,
  163, 167
DeMott, Benjamin, 70, 87
Dempsey, Van, 19, 37
Denton, Nancy, 9, 10, 38, 56,
  61
Dewey, John, 152, 167
Dirmann, Jack, 147, 149
Dolan, Lawrence, 214, 217
Dougherty, Kevin, 14, 21, 37,
  39, 169, 201
Dreeben, Robert, 21, 37, 133,
  149
Drew, David, 15, 37
Duncan, Otis D., 65, 86

Eckland, Bruce K., 68, 88
Eder, Donna, 21, 37
Edmonds, Beverly, 173, 199
England, Robert, 18, 30, 39
Entwisle, Doris, 21, 39
Epps, Edgar G., 72, 87
Epstein, Joyce, 16, 22, 23, 36,
  37
Escalante, Jaime, 145, 147,
  149
Estes, Caroll, 173, 199
Eubanks, Eugene E., 164,
  168

Farley, Reynolds, 10, 37

Farrar, Eleanor, 26, 40, 204, 217
Farrell, Edwin, 27, 37
Feagin, Joseph R., 70, 87
Ferreiro, Emilia, 89, 113
Fine, Michele, 161, 167
Floyd, Martha, 98, 99, 104, 113
Floyd-Tenery, Martha, 90, 91, 93, 104, 105, 148, 149
Fordham, Signithia, 26, 27, 37, 70, 87
Foster, Michele, 30, 37
Foster, Peter, 170, 171, 173, 196-199
Foucault, Michel, 154, 166, 167
Frederickson, George, 55, 61
Freire, Paulo, 161, 164, 167, 169
Frey, William, 10, 37
Fullan, Michael, 151, 154, 167

Gaff, Jerry G., 194, 200
Gallimore, Ronald, 110, 113, 134, 150
Gamoran, Adam, 21, 37, 116, 150
Gándara, Patricia, 116, 149
García, Georgia, 23, 24, 37
Gardner, Sid, 206, 216
Garibaldi, Antoine, 71, 87
Gates, Henry Louis, 4, 37
Gay, Geneva, 70, 87
Gibson, Margaret H., 194, 200

Gilbert, Shirl E., 70, 87
Gintis, Herbert, 57, 61, 143, 148, 161, 167
Giroux, Henry, 154, 161, 167
Glazer, Nathan, 194, 200
Gollnick, Donna M., 170, 171, 178, 200
Gong, Jennifer, 116, 117, 150
Gonzales, Nancy, 28, 37
Gonzales, Racquel, 90, 91, 93, 104, 105, 113, 148, 149
González, Norma, 89-93, 98-104, 105, 114, 148, 149
Goodson, Ivor, 92, 113
Gordon, Edmund W., 194, 200
Gordon, Milton, 52, 53, 61
Graham, Sandra, 16, 37
Grant, Carl A., 169-172, 181, 194, 198-201
Greenberg, James B., 90, 91, 94, 99, 105, 112, 114
Greenwald, Rob, 206, 216
Guiton, Gretchen, 116, 117, 150
Gutman, Herbert, 56, 61

Hacker, Andrew, 4, 8, 9, 37
Hall, Peter M., 169, 170, 173, 175, 193, 200, 204, 208, 216
Hallinger, Phillip, 22, 37
Hampel, Robert, 213, 217
Hare, Bruce, 69, 70, 87
Harris, Michael D., 171, 172, 200
Harvey, James, 171, 200

Heath, Shirley Brice, 28, 29, 38, 134, 149
Hedges, Larry, 206, 216
Hensley, Marla, 99, 113
Herrnstein, Richard, 5, 38
Hertweck, Alma, 116, 149
Hobson, Carol, 16, 36
Hodgkinson, Harold, 159, 168
Hoffer, Thomas, 105, 106, 108, 113
Hollins, Etta, 29, 38
Hood, Denice W., 70-72, 87
hooks, bell, 164, 166, 168
Howard, Gary, 55, 61
Hubbard, Lea, 119, 149

Irvine, Jacqueline, 19, 22, 23, 28-30, 38

Jackson, Anthony, 212, 216
Jarrett, Robin, 11, 38
Jaynes, Gerald, 8, 9, 11, 12, 14, 22, 38, 56, 61
Johnson, Sylvia T., 69, 87
Jordan, Cathie, 148
Josephson, Matthew, 158, 168

Kamin, Leon, 23, 38
Kanter, Rosabeth, 207, 216
Karweit, Nancy L., 116, 147, 150, 214, 217
Kasinitz, Philip, 50, 61
Katznelson, Ira, 159, 168
Kazal-Thresher, Deborah, 18, 38
Keddie, Nell, 133, 149

Kennedy, Alan, 154, 167
Kilmann, Ralph H., 151, 168
Kluegel, James, 12, 38
Kornblum, William, 6, 38
Kosmin, Barry, 49, 61
Kozol, Jonathan, 161, 168, 206, 216

Lachman, Seymour, 49, 61
Ladner, Joyce, 11, 38
Ladson-Billings, Gloria, 30, 38
Laine, Richard, 206, 216
Lamont, Michelle, 145, 149
Landry, Bart, 8, 9, 12, 33, 34, 38
Lareau, Annette, 135, 145, 149
Lee, Valerie, 208, 216
Levin, Henry M., 116, 149, 214, 216
Lintz, Angela, 119, 149, 172, 200
Lipton, Martin, 116, 117, 150
Longshore, Douglas, 18, 20, 38
Lynch, James, 171, 200
Lytle, Susan, 92, 113

MacLaren, Peter, 143, 149
MacLeod, Jay, 16, 38, 143, 149
Madden, Nancy A., 116, 147, 150, 214, 217
Mahard, Rita, 18, 38
Marshall, Catherine, 170, 200
Massey, Douglas, 9, 10, 38, 56, 61

McAdoo, John L., 66, 87
McCarthy, Cameron, 171, 200
McDill, Edward, 21, 36
McGinty, Patrick, 208, 216
McLaren, Peter, 152, 154, 168
McLaughlin, Milbrey, 28, 38
McPartland, James, 16, 36
Mehan, Hugh, 13, 21, 29, 30, 34, 35, 39, 116, 119, 133, 149, 172, 200
Meier, Kenneth, 18, 30, 39
Meihls, J. Lee, 116, 149
Mercer, Jane, 116, 150
Mickelson, Roslyn, 16, 17, 39
Millar, Susan, 169, 198-200
Mitchell, Douglas, 170, 200
Mohrman, Susan, 214, 217
Moll, Luis C., 89-94, 98-101, 105, 113, 114, 148, 149
Mood, Alexander, 16, 36
Moynihan, Daniel, 65, 87
Murphy, Joseph, 22, 37
Murray, Charles, 5, 38
Myrdal, Gunnar, 3, 9, 39

Nagel, Joane, 7, 39
National Center for Education and the Economy, 123, 150
National Center for Education Statistics, 16, 39, 64, 87
Natriello, Gary, 21, 39
Neckerman, Katherine, 66, 88
Neff, Deborah, 90, 91, 99, 101, 113
Newmann, Fred, 204, 209, 216
Noblit, George, 19, 37
Novak, Michael, 41, 61

Oakes, Jeannie, 21, 39, 57, 58, 61, 116, 117, 150, 161, 168
Ogbu, John U., 16, 26, 27, 37, 39, 70, 87
Ogilvie, A. Barreto, 194, 200
Okamoto, Dina, 172, 200
Okamura, Jonathan, 7, 39
Olneck, Michael R., 171, 201
Omi, Michael, 6, 7, 39
O'Neil, John, 171, 201
Orfield, Gary, 17, 39

Page, Jane, 204, 217
Page, Reba N., 116, 150
Pallas, Aaron, 21, 39
Parish, Ralph, 156, 161, 164, 167, 168
Pascarella, Ernest T., 71, 87
Passeron, Claude, 134, 143, 148
Pearson, R. David, 23, 24, 37
Persell, Caroline Hodges, 14, 21, 39, 143, 145, 149, 169, 201
Peshkin, Alan, 7, 26, 27, 39
Pettigrew, Thomas, 20, 39
Phelan, Patricia, 25, 27, 28, 39
Piestrup, Ann, 29, 39
Placier, Margaret, 170, 175, 201

Pool, Harbison, 204, 217
Porter, James N., 69, 87
Powell, Arthur, 26, 40, 204, 217
Prager, Jeffrey, 18, 20, 38

Quartz, Karen, 116, 117, 150

Rendon, Patricia, 90, 91, 93, 104, 105, 113, 148, 149
Riehl, Carolyn, 21, 39
Rivera, Anna, 90, 91, 93, 104, 105, 113, 148, 149
Rivkin, Steven, 17, 40
Roseberry, Ann S., 148, 150
Rosen, Bernard, 16, 40
Rosenbaum, James M., 116, 150
Rosenholtz, Susan, 204, 217
Royster, Deidre A., 68-70, 72, 85, 88

Sarason, Seymour B., 108, 110, 114, 153, 166
Saxton, Mary J., 151, 168
Schein, Edgar, 162, 168
Schneider, Jeffrey M., 70, 87
Schofield, Janet, 18, 20, 21, 40
Schuster, Peter, 175, 199
Senge, Peter, 204, 217
Sergiovanni, Thomas J., 164, 168
Serpa, Roy, 151, 168
Sewell, William H., 175, 201
Shor, Ira, 164, 169
Sizer, Theodore R., 116, 150
Slaughter, Diane T., 72, 87

Slavin, Robert E., 116, 147, 150, 214, 217
Sleeter, Christine E., 170-172, 181, 194, 195, 201
Smith, Adam, 161, 164, 168
Smith, Dorothy, 166, 168
Smith, Eleanor J., 66, 88
Smith, Eliot, 12, 35, 38
Smith, Julia, 208, 216
Smith, Paul M., 66, 88
Smylie, Mark, 207, 217
Solorzano, Daniel G., 69, 88
Spindler, George, 102, 114
Spindler, Louise, 102, 114
Stack, Carol, 11, 40
Stampp, Kenneth, 55, 61
Staples, Robert, 66, 88
Steinberg, Stephen, 54, 55, 59, 62
Stewart, Joseph Jr., 18, 30, 39
Stluka, M. Francis, 21, 39
Swanson, Mary Catherine, 117-119, 150

Tapia, Javier, 98, 112, 114
Tharp, Roland, 134, 150
Thernstrom, Stephen, 66, 88
Thomas, Gail E., 14, 15, 39, 40, 68, 88
Thompson, Aaron, 70, 88
Time Magazine, 41, 45, 50-53, 60, 62
Timm, Patricia, 170, 172, 195-199
Tomlinson, Sally, 171, 201
Troyna, Barry, 171, 201

United States Bureau of
the Census, 63, 67, 75,
86, 88
United States Government
Accounting Office, 23, 40

Valli, Linda, 116, 150
Vélez-Ibáñez, Carlos G., 90,
91, 112, 114
Villanueva, Irene, 119, 149
Vincent, Nelson C., 103,
172, 201

Walker, Alice, 167, 169
Walker, Sandra, 164, 168
Warren, Beth, 148, 150
Wasik, Barbara, 214, 217
Wasley, Patricia, 213, 217
Wasserman, Herbert, 69, 88
Watts, David, 69, 88
Watts, Karen M., 69,88
Waugh, Dexter, 31, 36, 169,
170, 176, 195, 196, 198,
199
Wax, Murray, 20, 40
Wehlage, Gary, 209, 216
Weinfeld, Frederic, 16, 36
Weis, Lois, 133, 148, 160,
168
Weitzman, Lenore, 66, 88
Wells, Amy, 18, 19, 40
Wenglinsky, Harold, 14, 21,
39, 169, 201
West, Cornel, 4, 10, 40
Wexler, Philip, 27, 40
Wheelock, Anne, 116, 150
White, Karl R., 68-70, 86-88
Whitmore, Kathy, 98, 114

Wilkinson, Doris, 66, 88
Williams, Jenny, 171, 201
Williams, Robin Jr., 8, 9, 11,
12, 14, 22, 38, 56, 61
Willis, Paul, 143, 150
Wills, John S., 172, 200
Wilson, Karen, 69, 71, 88
Wilson, Reginald, 115, 123,
125, 127, 149
Wilson, William, 68, 88
Wilson-Sadberry, Karen, 68-
70, 72, 85, 88
Winant, Howard, 6, 7, 39
Winfield, Linda F., 68-70,
72, 85, 88
Winston, Markay, 170, 172,
195-199
Wirt, Frederick, 170, 200
Wohlstetter, Patricia, 214,
217
Wright, Lawrence, 5, 40

York, Darlene, 4, 22, 28-31,
36-40
York, Robert, 16, 36
Young, Michael F. D., 133,
149, 150
Young, Russell L., 194, 201
Yu, Hank, 25, 27, 28, 39

Zipp, John, 9, 40

Subject Index

Ability grouping, 21, 32, 116, 210, 212. *See also* Tracking

African Americans, 3-5, 16, 22 (Includes blacks, black Americans)
  economic inequality, 8-10, 66
  educational achievement and performance, 15, 16, 23
  educational attainment, 13-15, 34, 63-65, 68-73, 83- 85, 115, 117, 125-127, 203
  families, 11, 65, 69
  residential segregation, 9, 10
  teachers, 22, 30
  U. S. population, 5, 41, 45-48, 72-73
  white beliefs about, 12, 55, 56, 59

Assessment, 15, 24, 25, 87, 204, 211, 214. *See also* Testing

Assimilation, 26, 50, 51, 53, 171, 173
  structural, 18

Classrooms, 29, 30, 32, 50, 60, 172
  AVID classroom, 118, 119, 133-39

Collaboration
  student, 30, 119, 139
  teacher-researcher, 91, 92, 109, 203
  teacher-teacher, 109, 153, 204, 209-211

Cooperative learning, 20, 25, 32, 116, 147, 203, 207, 209

Coordinated education and social services, 206, 207

Cultural deficit model, 65, 98, 170, 185

Cultural differences, 13, 27-29, 172

Culture
  academic, 133-139
  American, 12, 55, 56
  black, 19, 26, 30
  black-white differences, 27
  concept, 89, 90, 100, 101
  learning organization, 164-166
  school, 154-156, 162, 163, 204, 209-212, 214

Curriculum, 24, 116, 152,
      209, 214
   academic, 35, 71, 106,
      117, 141, 208, 210
   and critical thinking, 204,
      208, 209, 211
   definition, 183, 184
   hidden, 133-135
   origins of secondary, 57-
      59

Detracking, 117, 146-148.
   See also Tracking and
   Untracking

Educational attainment
   AVID program and
   college enrollment, 121-
      133
   comparisons between
   blacks and whites, 13-
      15, 63-64, 83-86, 125
   differentiation K-12 and
   post secondary, 73, 83, 85
   explanations and research,
      65-73
   and family characteristics,
      73, 75-83, 127-133
   Latino college enrollment,
      127
   operationalization, 74, 75
   regional variation, 80-84
Educational performance, 26,
      115, 212
   black students and black
   teachers, 30
   Catholic school effects,
      106, 107

   comparisons between
   black and white students,
      15, 16, 18
   desegregation effects, 18
   financial resource effects,
      206
   parent effects, 69, 143
   restructuring effects, 208
   testing effects, 23, 68
   tracking and ability group
   effects, 21
Equality
   educational, 31, 32, 146,
      169, 205, 208, 210-212
   of opportunity, 5, 13, 65,
      67, 181
   principle, 3, 12, 180
Ethnic Americans, 26, 34, 42,
      45, 58, 60, 61. *See also*
      Whites
Ethnic minority, 30, 50, 53,
      60, 61, 115-117, 134,
      135, 147, 176
Ethnicity, 28, 41, 54, 120
   meaning, 5-7, 26, 32, 33,
      204
   situational, 7, 28
Expectations
   educators for students, 18,
      21-23, 25, 26, 30, 145,
      172, 186, 204,207-209,
      212
   students own academic,
      16, 17, 19, 27, 70, 145

Family (Includes parents)
   black, 11, 16, 65-67
   and educational

attainment, 64, 68, 73, 77, 80-85, 143
involvement in school, 23, 34, 99, 204
single parent household, 23, 66, 69
and social capital, 105-107, 134
student home world, 25, 26, 28, 100, 101, 104, 141
teacher expectations of, 23, 24, 30, 35, 98, 156, 162, 163
teacher relationships, 23, 92, 98, 99, 140, 141, 145

Hegemony, 151, 154-156, 158, 159, 163, 164
Higher education institutions, 14, 71, 85, 203, 205
Hispanic. *See* Latino

Immigration, 42-46, 50-52, 58-60
Instruction, 24, 31, 50, 91, 147, 148, 205, 214
and critical thinking, 204, 208, 209, 211, 213
equity pedagogy, 29, 30, 32, 212, 215
and tracking, 21, 59, 116

Latina. *See* Latino
Latino, 5, 7, 26, 45, 53, 54, 91 (Includes Hispanic, Latina, Mexican-American)

Catholic school effects, 106
college enrollment, 115, 127
educator attributions 22, 116
student social worlds, 25
student success, 145, 147
testing effects, 23
Learning Styles, 28,29, 38

Minorities, 4, 13, 14, 16, 19, 24, 26, 31, 32, 34, 41, 212
Multicultural education, 31, 32, 59-61, 170
case studies, 169,170, 172, 173, 195-198
critique of traditional, 89, 100
definition, 31, 187, 194, 195
district policy process, 178-199
perspectives, 171-173, 180-182, 198
and restructuring, 205, 212, 213
Multicultural society, 41, 45, 49-51, 53
Multiculturalism, 13, 28, 33, 45, 51, 53, 59, 178, 194

Pedagogy. *See* Instruction
Policy
conceptualization, 169, 173-175

district level process, 182,
    188, 191, 193, 197
purposes for multicultural,
    171-173
Poverty, 9-12, 17, 22, 59, 65,
    66, 69 104, 161
Prejudice, 10, 12, 19, 181,
    195, 205, 212
Preservice teachers, 61, 112,
    154, 204, 206
Professional development,
    25, 152-156, 178, 185,
    186, 190, 195, 197, 204,
    206

Race, 16, 20, 55, 56, 58
    contested meaning, 3-8,
        33, 179, 187, 213, 216
    cultural deficit and in-
        feriority, 59, 65, 162, 170,
        185
    culture, 16, 19, 20, 26, 28-
        30, 69, 85, 163
    educational inequality, 13-
        16, 63, 64, 73, 83, 86,
        163
    identity, 4, 18, 25-28, 70
    inequality and stratifica-
        tion, 13-16, 63, 64, 73,
        83, 86, 163
    and schooling practices,
        21-23, 68, 172, 177, 186
Racism, 55, 56, 145, 162, 178
    anti-racism, 171, 173, 181,
        195, 205
    beliefs about, 13, 22, 27,
        180, 183, 184, 197
    structural and cultural

relationships, 8, 12, 13,
    164, 172
Residential segregation, 8, 9,
    11, 13, 17, 56, 205

School culture, 155, 156, 195,
    204, 214
School desegregation, 3, 4,
    17-20, 63, 163, 170,
    171, 177, 205
School reform, 142, 151, 152,
    164
School resegregation, 18, 163
School restructuring, 32, 116,
    153, 205, 208-215
Schools
    Accelerated, 116, 153, 214
    Catholic, 105-107
    Coalition of Essential
        Schools (Sizer), 116, 213,
        214
    Comer, 116, 153, 214
    comprehensive high
        school, 25
    continuation, 141
    with diversity, 60
    early 20th century high
        school, 57-59
    effective, 22
    middle, 61, 214
    restructured high school,
        208
    urban type, 24, 27, 156,
        161-163, 166, 206
Social capital, 35, 105-108,
    134, 144, 145
Social class (Includes socio-
    economic status [SES])

black middle class, 8-10, 176
and college enrollment, 127-133
cultural capital, 134, 144, 145, 205
differences, 12, 20, 31, 65, 68, 127, 134, 143, 206
and discourse patterns, 35, 134, 157, 204
as SES, 68, 69
school relationships, 23, 190, 204, 205, 210, 215
white middle class, 18, 22, 25, 59, 197
white middle class teachers and black students, 22, 29
working class, 26, 60, 94-96, 98, 110, 138, 140, 159-161
Social networks, 19, 34, 91, 93, 98, 105-107, 145
Social reproduction, 143, 151, 152, 159, 161
Stereotypes, 12, 19, 23, 34, 55, 56, 60, 89, 211
Students
academic self-concept, 16
as active learners, 208, 209, 211-213
conflict resolution codes, 138
experiences as classroom resource, 89, 90, 99-101, 138, 172, 211
identity/self, 7, 25, 26, 27, 60, 70

peer group, 25-27, 61, 68, 70, 71, 85
school orientation, 70, 71
self-esteem, 18, 20, 21, 70, 180
social worlds, 25-28, 111
teacher relationships, 29, 30, 71, 139, 140, 142, 144, 208, 211
Teachers
behavior, 21, 29, 136, 138, 184, 209, 211
black, 19, 30
collaboration and reflection, 103, 104, 204, 209-211
constraints, 110, 154
decision teams, 214
expectations, 21-24, 26, 185, 186
household relationships, 98, 107, 108
reactions to student households, 98-101, 104, 105
researcher relationship, 91, 92, 109
as researchers, 90-93, 101-104
and school culture, 163, 165
as student advocate, 139-142, 144
student relationships, 29, 30, 71, 139, 140, 142, 144, 208, 211
study groups, 108, 109

Testing, 34, 71, 116, 135-137.
    See also Assessment
Time
    constraint as resource,
        165, 166, 182, 188, 190,
        192, 196
    school change process, 35,
        165, 213
    school utilization, 21, 24,
        146, 147, 203, 209
    student utilization, 135,
        137, 209
    teacher, 102, 108, 110,
        204, 211
Tracking, 18, 34, 59. *See also*
    Ability grouping, De-
    tracking and Untracking
    consequences, 21, 32, 116,
        184
    opposition, 32, 59, 204,
        209, 210, 212
    placements, 23, 72

Untracking, 115, 117-119,
    133, 142-144, 146-148.
    See also Detracking and
    Tracking

Whites (Includes Anglos,
    European Americans,
    Euro-ethnic) *See also*
    Ethnic Americans
    attitudes, 10, 12, 13, 56,
        162, 163
    cultural differences with
        blacks, 26, 28
    desegregation effects, 18

discovery of ethnic roots,
    41
economic inequality, 8-10,
    66, 67
educational attainment,
    13-15, 63,64, 68-70, 115
educational performance,
    15, 16, 23
perspective on race, 4
slavery effects, 55
as social construction, 5, 6
U. S. population, 45, 47,
    48
white teachers and black
    students, 22, 29, 162

Contributors

Barbara Jo Davis
Doctoral Student,
Educational Leadership
and Policy Analysis
University of Missouri
Columbia, Missouri

Eugene Eubanks
Professor of Education
and Urban Affairs
University of Missouri,
Kansas City
Kansas City, Missouri

Norma González
Research Anthropologist
University of Arizona
Tucson, Arizona

Peter M. Hall
Professor of Sociology
and Education
University of Missouri
Columbia, Missouri

Bart Landry
Associate Professor of
Sociology
University of Maryland
College Park, Maryland

Reid Luhman
Professor of Sociology
Eastern Kentucky
University
Richmond, Kentucky

Hugh Mehan
Professor of Sociology
and Coordinator, Teacher
Education Program
University of California,
San Diego
La Jolla, California

Luis Moll
Associate Professor of
Language, Reading, and
Culture
University of Arizona
Tucson, Arizona

Ralph Parish
Professor of Education
and Urban Affairs
University of Missouri,
Kansas City
Kansas City, Missouri

Margaret Placier
Associate Professor of
Educational Leadership
and Policy Analysis
University of Missouri
Columbia, Missouri

Dianne Smith
Associate Professor of
Education and
Curriculum Theory
University of Missouri,
Kansas City
Kansas City, Missouri

Aaron Thompson
Assistant Professor of
Human Development
and Family Studies
University of Missouri
Columbia, Missouri